The Whole Grain Cookbook

Other Books by A. D. Livingston

Cast-Iron Cooking

On the Grill

Sausage

Cold-Smoking & Salt-Curing Meat, Fish, and Game

Venison Cookbook

Complete Fish & Game Cookbook

Duck and Goose Cookbook

Strictly Steak: A Cookbook

The Whole Grain

COOKBOOK

DELICIOUS RECIPES
for Wheat, Barley, Oats, Rye, Amaranth, Spelt, Corn, Millet, Quinoa, and More, with Instructions for Milling Your Own

A. D. Livingston

THE LYONS PRESS
Guilford, Connecticut
An imprint of The Globe Pequot Press

The Lyons Press is an imprint of The Globe Pequot Press.

A few of the recipes used in this book were adapted from the author's cooking columns in *Gray's Sporting Journal*. Acknowledgments to other authors and books are made in the text as appropriate.

10 9 8 7 6 5 4

Printed in the United States of America

Library of Congress Cataloging-in-Publication Data

Livingston, A. D., 1932-
    The whole grain cookbook: delicious recipes for wheat, barley, oats, rye, amaranth, spelt, corn, millet, quinoa, and more, with instructions for milling your own/A. D. Livingston.
    p.   cm.
        Includes bibliographical references and index.
        ISBN 978-1-58574-047-5
1. Cookery (Cereals). 2. Grain. I. Title.
    TX808.L58 2000
    641.6'31—dc21
                                                    00-038062
                                                    CIP

Contents

Introduction

A column that I wrote for *Gray's Sporting Journal* a few years ago drew favorable but skeptical response from surprised readers. The subject? Acorns—the staff of life for ancient Europeans as well as Native Americans. The Indian connection attracted the attention of a first-grade teacher in Blakley, Georgia, home of the famous Kolomoki Indian Mounds and State Park. She sent me a few nice large white-oak acorns along with some recipes from her students, who were studying the ways and means of the Kolomoki.

In fact, the class put together an acorn cookbook in a blue-line mimeographed edition. I obtained a copy (one of my treasures) and found that many of the recipes reflected culinary skepticism as well as imagination. For example, a recipe for acorn soup called for 2 gallons of macaroni, 1 gallon of milk, 2 cups of sugar, and 1 acorn! Obviously, the little scholar responsible for this recipe was none too fond of eating acorns in large numbers. Indeed, the sparseness of acorns and the abundance of macaroni in the ingredients list were typical of most of the recipes.

The same sort of thing has happened in modern cookbooks for "whole grain" breads and other foodstuffs. I'm looking at a recipe called Barley Loaf, for example, that calls for almost 5 cups of all-purpose white flour, some cornmeal, and only 3 tablespoons of barley flour! I won't call the recipe dishonest (and it's probably a very good bread) but the title is, it seems to me, misleading, causing me to suspect that it might well have been used to fill up an obligatory chapter about barley in a modern cookbook. In any case, the result is, essentially, a white wheat bread, not a barley bread as the name of the recipe implies.

I have tried to keep the acorn syndrome to a minimum in this book. As a consequence, any reader who is looking for airy white breads is simply in the wrong place. There are purely excellent books on the art of baking, often using special flours for breads and pastries. My emphasis is on whole grain cookery, which, in the case of bread for example, almost always yields a heavier, darker, and sometimes harder result.

Wholeheartedly I acknowledge that such breads are usually more nutritious than their white counterparts, but I must confess that my main interest in this work is in good and sometimes adventurous eating. I also lean toward the old recipes and ways, put together when our ancestors had no white flour and had to grind their own from various grains and seeds. For these reasons, I often list in the recipes such products as lard, bacon drippings, and butter. Culinarily, there is no substitute for the brute flavor of bacon drippings, but I have tried, somewhat reluctantly, to list substitutes for people who want to cut back on animal fat for one reason or another.

The goodness of true whole grain cookery comes with one drawback—the flours and meals are difficult to store for long periods of time. This is because they contain the germ of the grain, which in turn contains a natural oil that tends to turn rancid when crushed and released into the flour or meal.

Clearly, long shelf life is a highly desirable feature for large commercial millers, distributors, bakers, and retailers. It is also good for the consumer, who can buy flours and meals that haven't gone bad and can with reasonable care keep them at home for some time. In order to supply the market with what they thought consumers wanted, the large commercial millers entirely removed the germ as well as the bran from wheat and corn before milling. As a result, modern flours and meals are remarkably stable, making them very convenient for the food industry and the consumer.

But this convenience is gained at the expense of flavor and the grain's natural oil and nutrients, concentrated for the most part in the germ. Removing the bran robs the grain of much of its fiber and still more nutrients.

In recent years health-food stores and even some upscale supermarkets have started stocking whole grains as well as whole grain meals and flours. In some areas, small local mills—which often produce a purely excellent product—sell their meals and flours either directly to the consumer or through local stores, taking care to rotate the stock properly. The same stores have also started stocking the whole grains, making them easy to obtain for grinding into meal or flour at home with the aid of an inexpensive kitchen mill.

Although a kitchen grain mill is not necessary to the enjoyment of whole kernel meals and flours, it is highly desirable simply because it enables the cook to grind the grains on an as-needed basis. This pretty much solves the shelf life problem because the grains, with germ intact, keep much better than the meal or flour. Why? Because the germ is not crushed, holding in its natural oil and nutrients until the moment of milling.

The wide availability of the whole grains for flours and meals also opens the door to an ancient cookery that has never been fully realized in America and has been pretty much forgotten in modern Europe: cooking with the whole grain, which is much like cooking with rice. For that reason, many of the recipes in this book are for cooking with not just the meal or flour but the whole grain, or perhaps grits.

Grits? Yes. By definition this term applies to grains other than corn or to cookery outside the American South. Because there is some confusion in word usage, I'm setting forth below a short working guide to the terms commonly used in milling and whole grain cookery.

What's What

The diagram below shows a typical grain configuration. What is used in commercial flour and meal is, for the most part, only the endosperm. Even some commercial brown flour billed as "whole wheat" isn't really made by grinding the whole grain. I'll cover this in more detail in chapter 4, Wheat.

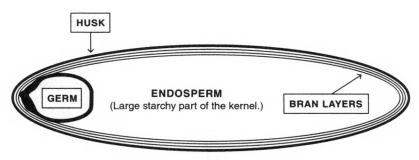

Schematic of Wheat Kernel

Although this simplified drawing applies mainly to wheat, most other grains have similar parts. The arrangement, however, may be quite different. Quinoa, for example, has a tail-like germ that curls around the endosperm.

Husks and Hulls. Many grains, including wheat, have a loose outer coating that is removed as part of the harvesting process. Without the husk, the grain can still sprout as a seed. How easily the husk comes off has influenced grain selection and development over the centuries. The old spelt, a form of wheat, probably lost out because the husk isn't easily removed. Some grains, such as barley, have a more tenacious husk, sometimes called a hull. Usually this is removed before cooking or grinding into flour.

Bran. A coating under the husk, designed to protect the germ and the endosperm, which it surrounds. The bran may be in several layers and in some grains, such as tef, may account for a significant part of the whole. Bran is an excellent source of fiber. It is usually sifted from flour, although the home miller can leave it in, producing a more rustic flour or meal.

Germ. The embryo of the grain—the part that sprouts into a new life. It is packed full of vitamins and minerals, as well as oil.

Endosperm. The largest part of the grain, made up mostly of starch and used as food for the developing embryo during the sprouting and early growing stages. Generally, it makes up by far the largest part, in volume, of the grain.

Berry (e.g., Wheat Berry, Rye Berry) The whole kernel of the grain, minus the easily removed outer husk. The berry always contains the several layers of bran, the germ, and the large endosperm, which contains most of the starch. Usually, the term "berry" is applied to wheat, rye, and wheatlike grains, not to corn or barley. But the term is not exacting. Essentially, however, a grain berry is simply a seed.

Grist. Grains and seeds suitable for grinding into meal or flour. I can only hope that the later chapters in this book will stir the appetite, perhaps atavistically, for some unexpected grist for the modern mill.

Groats. This term applies to hulled grains, especially buckwheat, but also works with barley and other grains.

Flour. The berry or groat ground down to a powder. The term usually applies to wheat flour, available in several forms (see chapter 4, Wheat). The term "whole wheat" can be misleading because such flour is not necessarily made by grinding the whole berry.

Meal. Similar to flour but not as finely ground. The term usually applies to cornmeal but is not limited to maize (corn).

Grits and Cracked Grain. Refers to a coarse meal. The term "hominy grits" is misleading, as discussed in chapter 3, Maize. The term "cracked" can also be used to describe grits and wheat products of similar texture. These can be made by grinding or by pounding. Ideally, the very fine grits and the very coarse will be separated by sifting, leaving the main product of uniform size.

Polished. Some commercial grains, such as white rice and pearl barley, have all or part of their bran ground away, mostly for appearance. With the bran goes all or part of the germ.

A few other terms that apply to specific grains are discussed in the following chapters as needed. Kasha, for example, is explained in chapter 15, Buckwheat.

Grinding Your Own

Fortunately, whole grain flours and meals are becoming more readily available these days, and increased demand should help the retailer move stock faster. But shelf life can still be a problem for wholesalers and retailers, and for mail-order outfits. More than once I have purchased whole-kernel cornmeal that had a slightly rancid smell and taste. In general, it's best to purchase such products from stores that have a high turnover. Even then the culinary purist may have a haunting question: How fresh is it? Like coffee beans and black pepper (as well as other spices, such as cumin seeds), meals and flours that are freshly ground simply have more flavor of their grain.

An exciting solution to the freshness problem is provided by the small kitchen mill, which allows you to take advantage of the whole grain's longer storage life. (Remember that the grain, essentially a seed, is actually designed for long storage and must protect the germ—or embryo—because that's what sprouts into a new plant.)

For readers interested in home milling, I've include more detail in chapter 22, Grinding Your Own. In principle, it's very easy to use the modern kitchen mills. You simply put the grain in the top, turn the crank or start the motor, and get the meal or flour out the bottom. There is a little more to it than that, but it's really easy once you accept the fact that the result is going to be different—usually coarser—than store-bought white flour.

Several small mills are currently available, either hand cranked or electrically driven, and small commercial mills are available for those chefs who need to feed a crowd or for people who perhaps want to start a small local business. Some of the mills are quite inexpensive—going for less than $100. See chapter 22 for discussions on the types of mills available, and then consult the appendix on sources.

The Practicality of Buying Grains in Bulk

Once you have a home mill, you may be inclined to purchase your grains, or at least some of them, in bulk; that is, in 25-, 50-, or 100-pound bags. Having a rather large store of grain will encourage you to cook the whole berries and, possibly, grits—as well as to make flour and meal. Of course, buying in bulk is much cheaper—if the grains are properly stored in a weevil-proof container. Also, make sure that bulk grains destined for the table have not been treated with pesticides, as may be the case with some grains intended to be used as seeds by the farmer.

Having a store of whole grains at hand also encourages their use as groats or berries. It's very easy to add a handful of wheat or rye berries to long-simmering soups and stews, or to cook a few for use in a salad, without even having a recipe. That's what I do as often as not.

⚜ More Grist for Your Mill ⚜

If this book opens some doors and encourages experimentation, part of my intention will have been fulfilled. Once you have a kitchen mill, you'll quite likely find yourself grinding beans and rice and nuts and seeds as well as the familiar wheat and corn. If you run across a recipe for rice flour, for example, simply grind some instead of looking all over town for a box that contains more than you need for the recipe in question. Need two tablespoons of lentil flour to cook *mohinga* (a national dish of Burma)? Not to worry. You can buy an inexpensive pack of dry lentils, available at any supermarket, and grind what you need.

The possibilities of using a portable mill are almost infinite, especially for foragers who enjoy wild foods, as I do, and who might want to grind some white-oak acorns or seeds of wild amaranth, cactus pear seeds, or chinkapins—which can be used instead of chestnuts to make a rustic and sweet Corsican polenta. Also, if the book encourages the use of just one acorn in the soup or gravy, that's better than no acorn at all. Maybe future versions will contain three or four. If not, perhaps this book will at least help lead the way back to whole grain macaroni.

⚜ For Beginners Only ⚜

Don't worry. You really don't have to purchase a grain mill or lug home a 100-pound sack of wheat or rye or gather a bunch of wild stuff to get started. Almost all the recipes in this book can be cooked with ingredients purchased from upscale supermarkets, health-food stores, through mail-order catalogs, or over the Internet.

Good eating.

—A. D. Livingston

PART ONE

New World Grains

The Native Americans were farming long before the Europeans arrived in the New World. In fact, they gave Europe and the rest of the world tomatoes, potatoes, chili peppers, and maize (corn) along with dozens of other vegetables, fruits, and nuts, some of which are now essential ingredients for many national dishes of foreign lands.

Maize, or corn, is of course the major grain from the New World, but the Native Americans did cultivate others on a large scale. In recent years, the modern world has discovered the culinary and nutritional advantages of amaranth and quinoa. These exciting grains are covered in some detail in the following chapters, along with a few recipes to try.

Many of the Native Americans also ate all manner of wild grass seeds and nuts and other breadstuff, some of which might be quite surprising to modern readers. These are discussed briefly in part four and may be enjoyed today by culinarily adventurous readers.

1

Amaranth

You can't keep a good seed down.

—Bert Greene

This ancient seed—now billed as a super grain for its nutritional properties—was cultivated on a large scale by the Aztecs of Mexico, before the Spanish explorers arrived. Although quite tiny—about the size of a poppy seed—and the color of mustard, amaranth was very important in the Aztec diet, partly because it contained lysine—essential stuff that is lacking in maize (corn) and most other grains. Amaranth rounded out the bread menu, nutritionally.

Because the Aztecs used the grain not only in their daily diets but also in religious ceremonies, conquistador Cortés and his men burned all the amaranth fields in the name of God and Spain and forbade the possession of even a single seed. But it survived here and there, and several species of amaranth grow wild even today both north and south of the Mexican border.

In any case, amaranth seeds are tasty when cooked and eaten as a porridge, and when mixed with wheat flour in breads and flapjacks. Cultivated commercially these days, the grain is available in either whole seeds or flour. It is also being used in packaged breadstuff and prepared cereals.

The leaves of amaranth are also edible and can be cooked like spinach or turnip greens.

⬥ Whole Seeds ⬥

Amaranth seeds can be purchased in health-food stores and by mail order. The seeds store well, especially when kept in a cool, dry place. They can be cooked and served like grits, or used in various recipes. Also, the seeds can be sprinkled into soups and stews during the last half hour of simmering, adding a nutritional punch. They have a mild but slightly peppery flavor.

Basic Amaranth

Cooked amaranth tends to form clumps and stick to the side of the pot, making it advisable to use a nonstick saucepan for cooking. Although the grains are small and may lose their identity in salads and stews, cooked amaranth goes nicely as a side dish (served like mashed potatoes), or as a cereal for breakfast, topped with a little cream and honey. There are several ways to prepare the grain, but I prefer to cook it uncovered, as follows.

1 cup amaranth
5 cups water
1 tablespoon butter or margarine
¾ teaspoon salt

Bring the water to a rolling boil. Add the salt and amaranth. Reduce the heat and cook, uncovered, for 20 minutes or more, until al dente or to the consistency of mush, depending on how you like it. Stir frequently during the last 5 minutes of cooking to prevent lumping. For a breakfast cereal, drain, stir in the butter, and serve hot. Makes about 2 cups, maybe a little more. Mushy amaranth can be put into a dish (used as a mold), refrigerated, sliced, and fried like polenta or scrapple.

Popped Amaranth

When heated, amaranth seeds swell and pop like popcorn, but they are too small (even smaller than mustard seeds) to be used as noshing fare. Instead, try the popped seeds in quick-cooking soups and stews, and in breadstuff and "rice crispy" cookies and crumbly pie crusts. The procedure is simple. Simply add about 1 tablespoon of amaranth seeds to a cast-iron skillet or stove-top Dutch oven over high heat, and cook for a few seconds, shaking the skillet constantly and stirring with a wooden spoon, until most of the seeds pop. If you listen closely, you can hear the seeds popping. Pop only 1 tablespoon of seeds at a time—or just enough to cover the bottom of the pan or pot. Be warned that amaranth scorches easily and pops unevenly. For 1 cup of popped amaranth, you'll need about 5 tablespoons of seeds.

Aztec Candy

Here's an old Aztec recipe for a candy called *alegria*, ("happiness"). Reportedly, it is still sold by street vendors in some rural areas of Mexico. It's hard to find, I understand—so why not make your own? The original might have been made with a little blood and the wild honey taken from replete ants, a sweet enjoyed by the Aztecs. I might also point out that vanilla is a Native American treat (along with chocolate).

¾ cup amaranth
¼ cup dark corn syrup or cane syrup
¼ cup wild honey
¼ cup butter or margarine
½ teaspoon vanilla extract (optional)

Heat the amaranth a little at a time, until it pops, in a large nongreased, hot cast-iron skillet, stirring with a wooden spoon and shaking the skillet as you go. Transfer the popped seeds to a bowl and cook some more until you have done the whole batch, yielding about 2 cups. Lightly grease a 9- by 13-inch cake pan with a little butter; set aside. In the skillet (now empty) mix the corn syrup, honey, butter, and vanilla. Bring to a boil, reduce to medium, and cook for about 10 minutes, stirring as you go, until the mixture thickens and turns an amber color. Remove the skillet from the heat. Stir in the popped amaranth with a wooden spoon. Put the mixture into the greased cake pan, spreading it evenly. Cut into bars and set it aside to cool. Eat when cool, or store for a day or two in a sealed container.

Amaranth Flour

Amaranth flour contains little or no gluten, making it unsuitable for risen breads except as a supplement to wheat flour or perhaps rye. It can be used more freely in flatbread and pancake recipes. Try the recipes below, and the Rye Sticks recipe on page 109.

Note that the flour doesn't store as well as the whole grain. Keep it in an airtight container in a cool place—preferably the refrigerator or freezer. The best bet is to grind your own amaranth flour as needed, although it is available commercially. Any good grain mill will work, and I have ground small amounts with mortar and pestle.

Euell Gibbons and others suggest gathering wild amaranth seeds and grinding them into a flour. For flavor, the wild seeds should be toasted a little in a skillet before grinding, and the same can be said for commercial and homegrown garden amaranth. I will mention amaranth again in the chapter on wild grist.

Amaranth Pancakes

I like to make pancakes with a combination of amaranth, barley, and some other grain or seeds. For something new, I usually vary the last ingredient. My last batch was made with flour from sweet live-oak acorns. If I am cooking bacon to serve with the pancakes, I use part of the drippings in the recipe. More health-conscious cooks may want to substitute vegetable oil.

3/4 cup amaranth flour
3/4 cup barley flour
1/2 cup acorn flour
1 1/2 cups milk
2 tablespoons bacon drippings or vegetable oil
1 tablespoon baking powder
salt to taste

Mix the dry ingredients in a large bowl. Stir in the milk and bacon drippings or oil, beating until you have a nice pancake batter. Add a little more milk if needed. Pour the pancakes onto a greased hot griddle, allowing about 1/4 cup for each one. Cook for a few minutes, then turn with a spatula and cook the other side until done. Serve hot with butter, honey, and bacon.

Amaranth Crepes with Bananas and Lemon Sauce

Here's a creation with a somewhat tropical theme, adapted here from a brochure distributed by Arrowhead Mills. Arrowhead specifies milk in the recipe, noting that soy milk or water can also be used. I would also like to suggest using coconut milk.

The Crepes and Filling

1/3 cup amaranth flour
3/4 cup milk (see note above)
3 large chicken eggs
melted butter or margarine
1 teaspoon honey
1 teaspoon vanilla
finely ground sea salt to taste

The Lemon Sauce

1/4 cup freshly squeezed lemon juice
1/4 cup honey
1 cup water

2 tablespoons arrowroot or cornstarch
1 tablespoon finely grated lemon zest

Before cooking the crepes, get the sauce ready. In a saucepan mix all the sauce ingredients except for the lemon zest. Cook over medium heat, stirring as you go, until the sauce thickens. Remove from the heat, stir in the lemon zest, and keep warm. To prepare the crepes, beat the eggs in a bowl (preferably with the aid of a blender) and add the milk, honey, and vanilla. Stir in the flour and a little sea salt. Heat a cast-iron skillet and grease it lightly. For the first crepe, add 1 tablespoon melted butter to the skillet, tipping the skillet to distribute the butter evenly. Add $1/2$ cup of the batter. When the bottom sets, turn the crepe and cook the other side. Add a little more butter and cook the rest of the batch. Fill each crepe with sliced banana, roll, and top with lemon sauce.

A. D.'s Amaranth Corn Pone

Mixing amaranth with cornmeal is a natural urge because it supplies the needed lysine. I like this bread mixed half and half, without chicken eggs or other binders, and baked in a cast-iron skillet.

1 cup amaranth flour
1 cup fine whole kernel cornmeal
bacon drippings or vegetable oil
salt to taste
water

Preheat the oven to 350°F. Mix the flour, cornmeal, and salt. Stir in enough water to make a dough. Add about 2 tablespoons of bacon drippings or vegetable oil to a 10-inch-cast iron skillet. Divide the dough into 3 parts and flatten each into a hand-sized pone roughly $1/3$ the size of the bottom of the skillet. Place the pones into the skillet and dampen the tops with bacon drippings or oil, patting lightly with your fingers to make ridges and valleys. Bake in the center of the oven until the pones are nicely browned, crisp on the edges but soft inside. Serve hot with plenty of butter.

Amaranth Crackers

These crackers can be eaten alone or topped with peanut butter or sunflower butter mixed with a little honey.

1 cup amaranth flour
3 large chicken-egg whites
1 teaspoon salt
1 cup boiling water

Preheat the oven to 350°F and grease a large baking sheet. Beat the egg whites until stiff. Mix the amaranth flour and salt in a bowl. Stir in the boiling water, mixing well. Fold in the egg whites. Drop by the teaspoonful onto the baking sheet. Bake in the center of the oven for at least 20 minutes, until nicely crisp. Cool and store in a tightly covered container.

Garden Amaranth

Those readers who are not inclined to eat wild amaranth should know that several companies now market amaranth seeds for gardeners. Some are for flowers, some for seeds, and some for greens. Amaranth greens are highly regarded as a vegetable in China and other parts of the world, and the seeds are raised for grain not only in the Americas but also in India. My old edition of *Larousse Gastronomique* says that amaranth is cultivated in France for the beauty of its flowers, and for its tender leaves in Italy.

Nutritional Highlights

In addition to the lysine that was so important to the Aztec diet, amaranth also contains plenty of calcium, iron, and phosphorus. It is packed with protein. Amaranth is, however, low in leucine, and should be mixed with other grains if it should become a regular, major part of the diet.

2

Quinoa

*The Incas were reported to live to 100 or 120 years, but then
they knew about the virtues of quinoa . . . .*

—Copeland Marks

Just as amaranth was important to the diet, culture, and religion of the Aztecs,
quinoa was the Mother Grain for the Incas of the Andes. Each year, it is said,
the Inca leader planted the first seeds with a gold spade. They considered it
a wonder food, just as today it is billed as a super grain. Reportedly, quinoa sustained the Inca armies, which sometimes had to march for days to defend their
long, narrow, far-flung Andean empire. They are said to have mixed quinoa with
fat (just as the Indians of North America mixed bear fat with dried fruits and pulverized jerky to produce pemmican) and called the food "war balls."

In any case, the Spanish conquistadors tried to destroy the grain—just as they
had done to amaranth in Mexico. But it survived here and there in the mountains, and is today making a strong comeback in Peru, Chile, and Bolivia, where
it is now called "little rice." Quinoa is also being farmed in the Rocky Mountains
of North America. Fortunately, the grain is available in modern health-food markets and in some supermarkets. The green leaves are also edible and are said to
be more nutritious than other greens, but these are difficult to market and hard
to find, at least at the time of this writing.

The plant grows best in a cool, arid environment at high altitude. Similar to millet in appearance, the stalk grows to 4 to 6 feet high, with the seed heads forming on the end.

❧ The Whole Grain ❧

There are several varieties of quinoa, producing seeds that are white, red, pale yellow, or black. The seeds are small, about the size of bird-feed millet, and oval in shape. Surprisingly, the outer germ coils around the seed. When cooked, the germ uncoils, forming a little spiral tail. The grain is soft when cooked, but the germ retains a crunch, providing an interesting combination of textures. The seeds have a nutty flavor—if they are properly processed.

Be warned, however, that quinoa seeds are coated with a bitter substance called saponin. This substance is usually removed before the grain is marketed, but it's best to rinse it thoroughly, just to be sure. If the rinse water seems soapy and forms suds, all the saponin has not been removed. Rinse the grain several times. In parts of South America that process quinoa in large volume, the saponin is used for washing clothes.

Some market quinoa can be sprouted successfully and used in salads, soups, and breads. But some won't sprout. The difference is in the processing methods used to remove the bitter saponin. Some processes nip the germ.

In any case, quinoa has a rather high oil content and will not keep indefinitely. It's best to store it in the refrigerator, preferably in glass jars.

Basic Quinoa

Quinoa is very easy to cook. It can be prepared plain, but it has more flavor if the grains are toasted lightly before cooking, as described below. One cup of dry quinoa makes about 3 cups cooked.

1 cup quinoa
2 cups water or chicken stock
2 tablespoons butter or margarine
salt to taste

Rinse the quinoa thoroughly. Bring the water or chicken stock to a boil in a pot. Add the quinoa, bring to a boil, add some salt, cover, reduce the heat to very low, and simmer for 12 to 15 minutes, until the liquid has been absorbed and the grains turn transparent. Add the butter and fluff with a fork. Serve as a cereal or in salads, or use in recipes calling for cooked quinoa.

Toasted Quinoa

Rinse and dry the quinoa grains. Heat a heavy skillet medium hot. Pour in the dry grains and cook for 2 or 3 minutes, shaking the skillet and stirring with a wooden spoon as you go, until the quinoa turns a light golden color. Be warned that quinoa is easy to scorch.

If you need precooked toasted quinoa, use a large skillet to toast it. Have 2 cups boiling water ready. Add the water to the skillet after the quinoa is nicely toasted, stir in a little salt, and boil for about 12 minutes, or until the grains look transparent.

Quinoa with Wild Rice

Here's a sort of American Indian pilaf that I like to cook, combining important grains (or seeds) from both North and South America.

1/2 cup quinoa
1/2 cup wild rice
2 1/2 cups chicken stock or water with bouillon cube
salt to taste

Rinse the wild rice and soak it in water for several hours, or overnight. Bring the chicken stock or water with bouillon cube to a boil in a pot, draining the wild rice while waiting. Add the quinoa, drained wild rice, and a little salt. Cover and simmer for 20 minutes, or until the stock or water has been absorbed. Turn off the heat and let steam, covered, for 5 minutes. Fluff with a fork and serve as you would a pilaf.

Quinoa Pudding

Cooked quinoa can be used in almost any pudding recipe that calls for cooked rice. Here's a pudding of Asian or Middle Eastern influence, where tahini is a common condiment. Canned tahini can be purchased in ethnic food markets and by mail order. Canned coconut milk is also readily available these days.

2 cups cooked quinoa
1 cup chopped dates
1 cup coconut milk
1/4 cup tahini
1 tablespoon whole wheat flour
1/2 teaspoon vanilla

$1/2$ teaspoon salt
cinnamon

Mix all the ingredients except the quinoa and cinnamon in a blender or food processor. Pour into a saucepan. Heat, stirring constantly, until the mixture thickens. Stir in the quinoa. Let set for 5 minutes. Sprinkle lightly with cinnamon and serve.

Variation: Stir in a few chopped toasted pecans or walnut pieces along with the quinoa.

Andean Soup

The Incas of old made good use of quinoa in soups and stews, with or without meat. Modern recipes calling for meat usually specify lamb, a meat brought to the Andes by the Spanish. The original called for various wild animals of the region, along with domesticated alpaca and guinea pigs, a big favorite that is still eaten in Peru. I have specified lamb, but you can also try domesticated or wild rabbit if you don't want to butcher the guinea pig.

2 pounds lamb shoulder, boned and cut into 2-inch pieces
1 cup quinoa
10 small red new potatoes (golf-ball-sized), unpeeled
1 cup diced carrot
$1/2$ cup green peas (fresh or frozen)
1 medium onion, diced
2 cloves garlic, minced
1 tablespoon cayenne pepper
1 tablespoon corn or peanut oil
$1/2$ tablespoon salt
$1/4$ teaspoon ground cumin
2 quarts water
salt to taste

Rinse the quinoa and soak it in 2 quarts of water for 1 hour. Rinse again and set aside to drain. Heat the oil in a skillet. Sauté the onion and garlic for 3 or 4 minutes. Add the cayenne and cumin. Pour in the water, add the lamb, and bring to a boil. Cover, reduce the heat, and simmer for 20 minutes. Add the quinoa and simmer for another 15 minutes. Add the potatoes, carrot, green peas, and salt. Cook for another 15 minutes, or until the potatoes are done. Add a little more salt, if needed. Feeds 6 to 8.

⚛ The Flour ⚛

Quinoa is easy to grind at home with most any sort of mill, and the flour is available commercially. Because of the grain's relatively high oil content, however, the flour has a very limited shelf life. Store it in the refrigerator or freezer in an airtight container, or, better, grind only what you need for the recipe at hand. Before grinding the grain, be sure to rinse it thoroughly to rid it of the bitter saponin. Then dry it before grinding.

On the commercial bandwagon, quinoa flour is being used in various cereals, pastas, breads, muffins, pancake mixes, and so on. It is also used in baby food.

The flour contains no gluten, however, and must be used sparingly with plenty of wheat flour to produce risen breads. In flat breads, quinoa can be used more freely, as in the recipe below, and adds a rather nutty flavor.

New World Bread

Here's a flatbread that I like to make with quinoa, corn, and amaranth. If you want to go all-American, use a duck egg or seabird egg instead of the chicken eggs, coconut milk instead of regular milk—and maybe oil rendered from armadillo fat, which was once popular as a cooking medium in parts of Central and South America. Peanut oil was also available to the Native Americans and can be used in this recipe.

1 cup quinoa flour
1 cup fine, freshly ground cornmeal
1/2 cup amaranth flour
1 cup milk
1/4 cup bacon drippings or peanut oil
1/4 cup finely chopped red bell pepper
1/4 cup finely chopped green chili pepper (seeded)
2 medium chicken eggs, whisked, or 1 large duck egg
salt to taste

Preheat the oven to 375°F and grease a 10-inch skillet. Mix the flours, cornmeal, and salt in a large bowl. Stir in the milk, egg(s), bacon drippings or oil, and peppers. Mix thoroughly until you have a smooth batter, but do not overbeat. Pour the batter into the skillet, smoothing it out with a wooden spoon. Bake in the center of the oven for about 20 minutes, or until the bread starts to pull away from the sides of the skillet. Turn off the heat and let cool a little in the skillet. Serve warm.

Nutritional Highlights

High in protein, fiber, starch, and various minerals and vitamins, quinoa is close to being the perfect food. It is very high in lysine, cystine, and amino acids that are usually lacking in other grains, making it (like amaranth) a very good grain to eat with corn and beans, both staple foods of the Americas. Quinoa is, however, rather high in oil, as compared with other grains.

3

Corn or Maize

Hush puppies can also be served by themselves,
as cocktail snacks.

—Raymond Sokolov

M any years ago Virginia Kirkus, a literary critic with much influence in the book trade, called my first novel "pure cornpone." What was a starry-eyed country boy to make of that? On the one hand, I figured that anybody named Virginia ought to know whereof she spoke, with regard to cornpone; on the other hand, I knew in my heart that the little book really wasn't all that good. I've been trying to make amends ever since, and I can only hope that this chapter will be a small step in the right direction.

There are hundreds of kinds of corn, ranging in kernel size from miniature to popcorn to a 1-inch specimen grown in the Andes. Colors of the kernels include white, yellow, red, and blue, and some are variegated. Types include dent corn (which actually has a dent in the end of the kernel), flint corn, flour, or squaw, corn (which is soft and grinds easily into meal), sweet corn (used mostly for green corn and roasting ears), and popcorn. Most of the corn grown commercially in the United States is yellow dent. White dent is also grown. I prefer the older types of corns and always in white, except possibly for making hominy. But yellow cornmeal has won out just about everywhere in our supermarkets and in most cookbooks. (Some large cookbooks don't even acknowledge the existence of white cornmeal. What a blow to American cookery.) White corn is still championed by small independent mills in parts of the South, however, and, thank God, in Rhode Island. Corn can be grown in the home garden, and anyone so inclined should get a grist mill and look into raising the old varieties used by the Indians and early settlers. Modern cornmeal from the large millers of today, by comparison, is tasteless. A few small mills still operate here and there, and these seem to be on the increase after many years of decline. I can remember when these would grind your corn on halves. That is, a farmer brought a wagon load of corn to the mill and took back half of the cornmeal.

Worldwide, the term "corn" refers to several different grains, and what Americans call corn is really maize. The name "corn" won out in this country because it was originally called "Indian corn" by the early settlers, to whom "corn" without the qualifier meant wheat or oats, depending on whether they were from England or Scotland. In time, the "Indian" qualifier was dropped and the New World's great contribution to the world's grains was called simply "corn," at least in North America.

Reluctantly, I am staying away from fresh corn in this chapter, feeling that anybody who cooks at all will know what to do with fresh roasting ears. I might add, however, that the Native Americans and early settlers made good use of the whole plant, including the corn shucks, cobs (which make good jelly), silks (which are great for thickening stews), leaves—and even the corn smut that grows from the end of some of the ears. In Mexico today this ugly fungus, called corn truffle or *cuitlacoche*, is gourmet fare, available fresh, frozen, or canned in upscale Latin markets.

For the most part, however, dried corn has been the most important form to our cookery, being used whole (hominy), cracked (grits, which are not really made from hominy), or finely milled (cornmeal), all covered at some length in the sections that follow.

Whole Kernel Hominy

Dried corn can't be simply shelled and used in soups and stews like wheat berries or other groats simply because it has a tough, hard outer coating that doesn't cook easily. The American Indians discovered that this outer coating could be removed by soaking the kernels in a solution of water and wood ashes. In the Yucatán, crushed seashells were sometimes used instead of wood ashes. Other materials such as slacked lime are sometimes used, and one of my aunts, who made hominy in batches, preferred oak ashes. In any case, the ash or lye treatment causes the inside of the corn to expand faster than the hard outer coating. This splits the husk, making it easy to remove during the rinsing process. I say "process" because the hominy must be rinsed several times to remove the lye taste. (The reason some people don't like hominy is possibly because they got hold of a batch that wasn't thoroughly rinsed.) The result is a nice fluffy kernel three or four times larger than the original. It's a truly great morsel, large enough for munching one at a time, that is misunderstood and underused in modern American cookery, north or south, east or west.

In any case, hominy is available canned or frozen, and the do-it-yourselfer can make his own. Usually, canned hominy is available in white or golden (yellow). Dried hominy is also available, sometimes under the name "pozole," usually from a source of Mexican foods or perhaps gourmet-foods outlets such as Dean & Deluca of Manhattan. Dried hominy is my choice for soups and stews that require long, slow simmering. This allows it be reconstituted without the overnight soaking. It is available in white, yellow, blue, or red, depending on the kind of corn used to make it.

Unfortunately, hominy is often and incorrectly confused with grits and is also associated with a product called *masa harina*, which, when made commercially, is really not the right stuff for making tortillas, in spite of what the cookbooks tell us. These products are discussed later under separate headings.

Hulled Corn

Here's an old recipe for hominy adapted from the 1887 edition of *Boston Cooking School Cook Book*. This work recommended using a cast-iron kettle, but other sources warn that such a kettle will turn the hominy black. The *Boston* text, however, makes use of this principle in the recipe! In any case, this recipe is similar to the one below (in which the corn is soaked overnight in a lye solution).

1 gallon dry corn
1 quart clean oak ashes
3 gallons water plus more for rinsing

Tie the oak ashes in a flannel bag. Boil the bag in 3 gallons of water for an hour, sloshing the bag a time or two. Add the corn and boil until the hulls have started to crack off, stirring from time to time with a large wooden spoon or paddle. Pour off the lye water and put the corn into a large pan of cold water, rinsing well. Rub the corn between the hands to loosen the hulls. Change the water several times, washing and rubbing the corn until it is clean and white. Keep the corn in cold water overnight, then put it into fresh water and simmer for 4 hours, or until soft, adding more water from time to time and skimming off any surface scum. Drain and serve.

Easy Old-Time Hominy

Here's an easy recipe that comes in handy for cooking up a medium-sized batch of hominy. I have used it with yellow dent hybrids. I specify spring water, but any good water will do. (I have tasted some water that was too highly chlorinated and some that tasted of sulfur, neither of which will do.) I prefer to use oak ashes, but any good hardwood ash will work. Save some from the fireplace or camp.

> **2 quarts dry dent corn**
> **2 cups oak ashes**
> **spring water**

Tie the oak ashes into a fine-mesh cloth bag and warm about a gallon of spring water. Place the corn in a nonmetallic crock or plastic container, cover with the warm water, and submerge the bag of ashes, dunking it several times. Let stand overnight, stirring and dunking the bag several times to release the lye into the solution. Wash the corn several times in cold water, rubbing the kernels vigorously to help release the outer hulls; repeat until all the hulls are removed. Put the corn into a suitable pot, cover with cold water, bring to a boil, cover tightly, and simmer for about 3 hours, or until the corn is soft, adding more water from time to time as needed. Use in recipes calling for cooked hominy, or in soups, salads, and stir-fries. I like this hominy "as is," topped with a mildly hot salsa, and often serve it with fried fish instead of french fries.

A One-Meat Pozole

Pozole, or hominy stew, is popular in Mexico and the Southwest. It often contains pig's feet and other variety meats, but I have decided to shorten this version. Anyone who wants more exotic fare should skip on to the next two recipes.

> **1$^{1}/_{2}$ pounds beef, cut into $^{1}/_{2}$-inch cubes**
> **1 can golden hominy (15-ounce size)**
> **1 can white hominy (15-ounce size)**
> **$^{1}/_{2}$ cup chopped onion**
> **3 medium to large tomatoes, chopped**
> **2 tablespoons finely chopped red bell pepper**
> **1 or 2 chopped green or red chili peppers (to taste)**
> **$^{1}/_{4}$ cup finely ground cornmeal mixed with a little water**
> **salt and pepper to taste**
> **chopped scallions (garnish)**

sliced fresh radish (garnish)
chopped tomato (garnish)
water

Put the beef into a stove-top Dutch oven. Cover with water and add the salt and chopped onion. Simmer on low heat for 1 1/2 hours, until the beef is tender, adding more water if needed. Add the hominy, tomatoes, and chili pepper. Cover and simmer for about 30 minutes, adding more water if needed. Stir in some of the cornmeal paste, cooking and stirring along until the mixture thickens and becomes bubbly. Ladle into bowls and serve hot, like chili. Garnish each bowl with chopped scallions, chopped tomatoes, or sliced radish, if desired. It's best to put the garnish in separate bowls and let everyone choose their own. Other toppings, such as black beans, will also work. Cornpone goes nicely with this, of course.

Argentine Stew

The Argentines are fond of cooking a variety of meats together in one pot. In this variation from the corn-raising state of Tucumán, freshly made hominy is used along with the meats. Canned hominy will do.

2 cups canned or precooked hominy
1/4 pound smoked sausages, cut into 1-inch pieces
1/4 pound smoked bacon
1/4 pound fresh ham, diced
1/2 smoked beef tongue, peeled and diced
1 small cabbage, chopped
1 pound small new potatoes
salt and pepper to taste
water

Put all the meats into a pot, cover with water, and simmer for about 1 1/2 hours, or until the meats are tender. Add water from time to time as needed. Add the cooked hominy, cabbage, new potatoes, salt, and pepper. Bring to a new boil, reduce the heat, cover, and simmer for about 20 minutes, until the new potatoes are done. Serve hot from a large platter.

Note: If you are using dried hominy in this recipe, add it to the meats on the first boil and increase the amount of water.

Menudo

This old recipe from Mexico and the Southwest is said to have medicinal powers that may border on the supernatural. It is especially useful as a breakfast dish, eaten the morning after an overly festive night. In any case, the recipe calls for tripe, which is the stomach lining of cud-chewing animals. Beef tripe is available in meat shops, fresh or frozen, and is really easy to prepare. The last time I made this dish, I used $1/2$ cup of red pozole, $1/2$ cup blue, $1/2$ cup white, and $1/2$ cup yellow. It was delicious. If you don't have dried hominy, freshly made or canned will work; but add it toward the end of the cooking period.

2 pounds tripe
2 pig's feet, split (optional)
2 cups dried hominy
1 large onion, diced
4 or 5 cloves garlic, minced
$1/4$ cup chopped fresh cilantro
1 tablespoon dried red pepper flakes
1 tablespoon chili powder (or to taste)
water
salt and pepper to taste

Cut the tripe into 1-inch pieces, and put it into a stove-top Dutch oven or other suitable pot along with the pig's feet. Cover with water by at least 2 inches. Add the hominy, onion, garlic, cilantro, red pepper flakes, chili powder, salt, and pepper. Bring to a boil, reduce the heat, cover tightly, and simmer for 2 hours, adding more water from time to time if needed. Serve hot in deep soup plates along with cornpone or tortillas, chopped onions or green onions in a glass of ice-cold water, roasted corn on the cob, assorted green chili peppers, and perhaps lime slices. Traditionally, chopped onions are sprinkled on the cooked menudo to taste. Cooked pinto beans can also be added. Feeds 4 to 8.

Hominy Cheese Casserole

This Tex-Mex dish goes nicely as a side dish to a barbecue pork plate, or with a regular meal. Either white or yellow hominy will do—or mixed.

3 cups cooked hominy
2 cups chopped fresh tomatoes
1 cup grated Monterey Jack cheese
rings from 1 large white or yellow onion
2 jalapeño peppers, seeded and sliced into rings

4 slices bacon
$1/4$ cup wheat flour
$1^1/2$ teaspoons chili powder
1 teaspoon sugar
salt to taste

Preheat the oven to 325°F. Fry the bacon in a skillet until it is done but not crisp. Drain the bacon. Stir the flour, chili powder, salt, and sugar into the bacon drippings, cooking a minute or so. Add the tomatoes and jalapeño peppers. Cook until the mixture thickens, stirring frequently. Grease a 2-quart casserole dish. Layer in the hominy and onion rings; top with the tomato mixture. Sprinkle with the cheese and cover with the bacon slices. Bake for 25 minutes. Serve as a side dish to a large meal.

Hominy Stuffed Poblano

The large Mexican poblano peppers, which I raise in my garden, are ideal for stuffing, but they should first be roasted and peeled. The roasting can be done over a grill or under a broiler, or you can put the peppers directly into the flame of a gas stove, which is the method I prefer. Roast until the peppers are black all around, turning carefully from time to time. Immediately wrap the hot peppers in foil. Set aside to steam for a few minutes. Carefully peel the peppers (preferably under running water), cut a slit in the side, and open the pod longways. Carefully remove the seeds and pith, leaving a nice cavity for stuffing. The measures for the ingredients don't have to be exact, but I have found that a can of canned yellow hominy makes about $1^1/2$ cups. So, I started with that measure simply to use up a whole can. Note also that I specify yellow hominy, which goes nicely with the tiny white shrimp and bits of red and green pepper in the stuffing. The small shrimp used in the recipe can be precooked cocktail shrimp, or you can cook and peel your own fresh or frozen shrimp. Note, however, that small fresh shrimp have to be boiled for only about 1 minute. Two at the most. Overcooking makes them hard to peel and too chewy. For convenience, I normally use canned hominy. If you have fresh hominy, or reconstituted dried, use two cups, fully cooked.

1 can yellow hominy ($15^1/2$-ounce size)
$1^1/2$ cups tiny precooked shrimp
4 large green poblano peppers
1 large red poblano pepper or small red bell pepper
1 or 2 green jalapeño peppers
$1/2$ cup chopped onion

1 tablespoon olive oil
salt to taste
Monterey jack cheese or sharp cheddar

Preheat the oven to 350°F. Roast and peel all the peppers, as described above. Prepare the 4 green peppers for stuffing. Dice the jalapeño and red pepper. Heat the olive oil in a large skillet. Sauté the onion for about 5 minutes. Add the diced peppers, shrimp, hominy, and salt. Simmer for about 10 minutes, stirring as you go with a wooden spoon. Stuff the 4 peppers quite full, opening them up like a boat, and sprinkle them heavily with cheese. Arrange the peppers on a baking sheet, place in the center of the oven, and bake for about 30 minutes, until the cheese starts to brown. Servings? I allow 2 peppers per person, and, I'll admit, the first time I cooked this recipe I ate the whole works.

Note: I also make this dish with flaked cooked fish (usually leftovers) instead of shrimp. I normally use black bass, but red snapper and other mild, boneless white-fleshed fish will do.

A. D.'s Easy Hominy Lunch

I normally cook this easy dish with canned golden hominy and roasted red bell peppers. Any fully cooked hominy will work, but yellow works best in the color scheme. Also use large red poblano peppers if you have them in your garden. (Most of the poblano I see in the market are in the green stage.)

2 cups fully cooked golden hominy (or a 16-ounce can)
3 strips thick sliced smoked bacon
1 red bell pepper
1 medium onion, diced
salt to taste
black pepper to taste

Roast the pepper according to the directions in the previous recipe. Peel and cut into strips. In a cast-iron skillet, fry the bacon until crisp. Set aside to drain. Sauté the onion for 4 or 5 minutes. Add the cooked hominy to the skillet and sauté for about 10 minutes, stirring from time to time. Stir in the red pepper strips during the last minute or two, along with a little salt and black pepper. Serve with the cooked bacon and white cornpone.

Note: I also serve this dish with fried fish instead of french fries.

❦ Masa without the Harina ❦

This heading should perhaps be covered under Hominy, above, but I set it apart because an important point should be made. Almost all of our modern cookbooks tell us that tortillas are made with a flour obtained by grinding dried hominy. It's true that a suitable flatbread can be made by this process, and stuff called *masa harina* (explained as tortilla flour) is commonly sold in American markets. The commercial *masa harina* has a long shelf life, but that's about all I can say in favor of this stuff.

I really prefer to make my tortillas with extra-fine stone-ground cornmeal, which contains the germ of the grain and its oil—but this too is really a shortcut. The real *masa* doesn't have the *harina* part. (My take is that *masa* refers to the tortilla dough and the *harina* is the flour for making the *masa*.) In other words, the dough is made from fresh hominy, not from dried hominy flour. Think about it. Why make the hominy, dry it, grind it, and then add the water back to it while making the dough?

To make the real stuff in the old days (and no doubt now in rural areas where the peasants raise their own corn), the Mexican cook in charge of feeding a family would usually start the day by making *masa* with fresh hominy. That is, they would simply mash the soft hominy into a dough using a *metate* (a flat stone, often made of volcanic rock) and a *metlatpilli* (a sort of stone rolling pin). Conscientious cooks worked the dough for long hours—the longer the better. Then they patted out the tortillas by hand, which is something of an art.

❦ Easy-Masa Tortillas ❦

The modern cook can make an acceptable *masa* easily by using canned hominy, preferably white. Simply open a can or two, rinse it thoroughly, and work it with a mortar and pestle—or even with a rolling pin on a suitable surface. (The same *masa* can be used for making tamales as well as tortillas, although the Mexican peasants often make a different dough by adding a little oil or, better, bone marrow to the dough.) To make tortillas from the masa, simply pull off a small piece of dough and pat it out by hand, if you can, or put it into a tortilla press, which are sold in culinary gift shops and by mail order. If you don't have a tortilla press and can't do the job by hand, try putting the dough onto wax paper, cover with wax paper, and press down with the bottom of a flat plate. By whatever method you use, the tortilla dough should be about $1/8$-inch thick. Cook this for a couple of minutes on a flat griddle or cooking stone (*comal*). Each tortilla should be cooked until lightly brown — but it should still be supple. These are usually kept soft in an earthen container, rolled at the table, and eaten as bread with a Mexican meal. But they can also be used to make hard taco shells, enchiladas, and so on.

I'm not going any deeper into Mexican cookery here. I like this food too much (Mexican seafood is probably the world's best, dating all the way back to the Aztecs) and if I started making and eating tamales here I might not be able to work my way out of this already lengthy chapter. I do, however, include a tamale recipe under the cornmeal heading.

Grits

Let's get this straight. The facts are not reported correctly in most cookbooks—not even in cookbooks about grain in general or corn in particular. Grits are not made from hominy. They may be called hominy grits in some quarters, and may even be called, simply hominy, (as in parts of coastal South Carolina). They may even be billed as hominy grits on the package. But that's not what they are.

It is possible to make grits from dried hominy but they would not taste the same and would not have the same texture—and why on earth would a commercial miller bother to go through the long hominy-making process when it's not necessary? In addition to first making the hominy, it would then have to be dried out before grinding. Grits are, in short, a product of the grist mill and are simply coarsely ground corn. (So, polenta fans might be surprised to learn that they have really been eating grits all along!) Although most authorities will disagree with what I am saying here, I am certain of my stand. Books and dictionaries that state otherwise are simply wrong.

I rest my case. At least for the time being. But it's also true that the American Indians might well have made grits from dried hominy simply because they didn't have gristmills, and the early settlers might well have followed suit, making not only grits but cornmeal and "samp," usually a very coarse grit. The Indians used a mortar and pestle, and the early colonists came up with a productive variation called the hominy block. Hence, the name "hominy grits." But the gristmill was not far behind the first wave of settlers, and Indian corn was the main grist, at least for a while. These gristmills were so common that even small towns often had several. Their mark can be seen even today on our roadmaps and street signs, as in such names as Burnt Mill Road. Always they were built on a creek, which was usually dammed up to provide waterpower. The resulting pond provided a swimming and fishing hole, and was often enjoyed by the whole community. Some of these became recreational lakes long after the mills had closed, as in McRae's Mill Pond. Most modern independent gristmills are also built on a creek, and some even have a dam for show, but they are powered for the most part by electricity or small gas engines. Their meal and grits might be labeled "water-ground style."

Before offering recipes, perhaps I should confess that I am not really a great champion of grits. I seldom eat them in a restaurant, for example, even if they come free with a breakfast menu of country ham and eggs and toast. Most people, including some of my relatives, simply don't know how to make them properly or don't take the time to do so.

Anyhow, grits of one sort or another are now widely available even in our supermarkets. These are mostly quick grits or instant grits, both of which have been partly cooked and neither of which (for the most part) are made from whole kernel corn, which gives them a long shelf life. The best ones are stone ground. These have much more flavor and a better texture, but they take longer to prepare (up to 30 or 40 minutes) and have a short shelf life. (If you are lucky enough to find some, store them in the freezer.) In any case, the recipes below are for stone-ground grits, or similar grits made from a kitchen mill. If you use commercial grits, follow the instructions on the package. If you grind your own, sift out the meal and flour for making cornpone. After grinding, some people wash the grits in water, letting the chaff float to the top.

Perfect Grits

It takes a patient cook to prepare good grits. The recipe may vary a little, depending on the kind of grits one has to work with, but the results should be the same: somewhat creamy while at the same time maintaining the grits' texture (instead of being mere mush). If the batch of grits has lumps in it, throw it all out and start over. It's probably best to follow the directions on the grits package, so long as you know what you want in the finished product. If you don't know what to aim for, there is little chance of hitting the mark. Anyhow, here's a pretty basic recipe for freshly ground grits, which is what I recommend.

1 cup stone-ground grits
5 cups water
1 teaspoon salt

Put all the ingredients into a saucepan over high heat. Stir constantly as the mixture comes to a rapid boil. Cook and stir until the grits spit back at you. Remove the grits from the stove eye, turn down the heat to very low, and put back on the stove eye. (On old wood stoves, the grits were taken off the eye and placed on the back of the stove, which was still hot.) Stir the grits constantly, watching the consistency. The idea is to cook out most of the water without causing the grits to stick or form lumps. Moreover, the grits are cooked on very low heat and for a long time, up to 30 or 40 minutes. If possible, serve the grits as soon as they are ready. If they sit too long, a sort of soft crust may form on top—and this is just as bad as lumps.

Grits are traditionally served at breakfast along with eggs and fried salt pork. If you've got really good barnyard eggs, cook them sunny-side up. Then mix the egg and grits, little by little, bite by bite, as you eat.

Fried Grits

Here's a recipe for people who think they don't like grits, or who have trouble cooking them properly.

1 cup white grits
$^1/_2$ cup white cornmeal
2 cups water
2 chicken eggs
bacon drippings or cooking oil
milk
salt and pepper to taste

Bring the water to a boil and add about 1 teaspoon of salt. Stir in the grits slowly with a wooden spoon. Simmer for 15 minutes, stirring constantly as you go. Spread the cooked grits into a buttered or greased dish or mold. Chill or refrigerate overnight. When you are ready to proceed, whisk the chicken eggs, adding a little milk, salt, and pepper. Slice the grits, dip them in the egg mixture, and dip them in cornmeal. Fry in hot bacon drippings or cooking oil about $^1/_2$-inch deep. Serve hot at breakfast or lunch.

Coo Coo for the Baby (and Old Men)

Coo coo of one sort or another is cooked all over Africa, and similar dishes followed to the New World. Recipes vary quite a bit; they are all on the mush theme and many make good use of the mucilaginous quality of okra. My recipe has been adapted from *Gullah Cooking with Maum Chrish'*, by Virginia Mixon Geraty, who says coo coo is very good to feed to young children who don't yet have teeth—and to old people who have lost teeth. It's best to use young okra, sliced into $^1/_2$-inch segments.

1 cup grits
2 handfuls sliced okra
1 tablespoon butter or margarine
salt and pepper to taste
water

In a saucepan boil the okra in 1 cup of water. In another pan, heat 4 cups of water and add the grits. Cook until the grits are done, stirring constantly to prevent lumps from forming. Drain the okra and mix it in with the cooked grits. Stir in the butter, salt, and pepper. Feed the young children first, Maum advises—and make sure they chew. If the okra causes the grits to slip down without being chewed, they will still be hungry, unhappy, and fretful.

Boggy Bayou Fried Mullet with Cheese Grits

Serving grits with fried fish has become a tradition in parts of rural Florida and I endorse the practice because it cuts back on the fried potatoes and fried hush puppies. Here's a variation from the Mullet Festival, held each year in Niceville, Florida. I will allow trout fillets instead of mullet, but I do hold out for stone-ground or home-ground grits and freshly ground cornmeal for dusting the fish.

The Fish

mullet fillets
freshly ground cornmeal
salt and pepper
peanut oil

The Cheese Grits

1 cup coarse grits
1 cup grated sharp cheddar cheese
1 quart water

For best results, the fish and the grits should be ready at the same moment. Rig for deep frying in peanut oil at 375°F. At the same time, bring 1 quart of water to a boil in a suitable pot. Add the grits and simmer, uncovered, for about 30 minutes, stirring from time to time to prevent lumping. As soon as the oil is hot, salt and pepper the fillets. Put the cornmeal and fish fillets in a bag and shake the fillets a few at a time. Fry at 375°F for a few minutes, until the fillets float and brown nicely. The fillets don't have to be turned (if you have heated enough oil), so you can stir the grits. Drain the cooked fillets on a brown bag and fry another batch, stirring the grits a time or two as you go. When all is about ready to serve, stir the cheese into the grits. Serve together on plates, along with sliced tomatoes and iced tea. If you want a real Cracker dish, add some thinly sliced swamp cabbage (billed as "heart of palm" in the gourmet section of supermarkets) along with the tomato. If you want an old-time Florida breakfast, the fish should be dried salt mullet, soaked overnight to freshen, served up with biscuit halves and sliced tomato.

Cheese Grits Casserole

Here's a dish of grits to serve as a side dish to a regular meal instead of strictly for breakfast.

1 cup regular grits
3 cups water
1 cup milk
1/4 cup butter or margarine
1/4 cup grated cheddar cheese
4 chicken eggs, whisked
salt to taste

Preheat the oven to 350°F. Bring the water to a boil in a small saucepan, adding a little salt. Stir in the grits, mixing well, and cook on medium heat until the grits thicken, stirring constantly. Add the butter, eggs, milk, and cheese. Stir and pour into a casserole dish. Bake for 30 minutes. Makes 6 servings as a sidedish.

Argentine Grits

In *South American Cook Book*, authors Cora, Rose, and Bob Brown said that these grits are traditionally stirred with a fig-wood paddle. I find that a large wooden spoon will do. They also listed "coarsely milled corn" in the ingredients—and put "hominy grits" in parenthesis. So, perhaps even in South America hominy grits aren't really made from hominy.

1 pound coarse stone-ground grits
1 quart water
2 teaspoons salt

Boil the water, add the salt, and sprinkle the grits in slowly, stirring with a wooden spoon. Reduce the heat to very low and simmer until done—about 1 hour for freshly ground, coarse grits—stirring from time to time. Pour the cooked grits into a mold and chill. Serve with milk and sugar, with dried figs or a soft white cheese on the side.

⁂ Cornmeal ⁂

Commercial cornmeal, being robbed of its germ before grinding and being heated to a high degree in fast roller mills, has a long shelf life but very little flavor. Usually it is dry, hard, and rather gritty, and most corn bread made with it will be hard, dry, and rather gritty. I have at hand one Yankee cookbook that characterizes corn bread as on the dry side; apparently the authors and editors of the book have never encountered the right stuff. I might have been stretching my point a bit when I once wrote that this stuff is not suitable for human consumption, unless perhaps it is cooked down and softened into a mush such as polenta or scrapple. I'll have to add that my dog, Nosher, doesn't like commercial cornmeal either, wanting her hushpuppies to be soft and moist—and heavy with flavor—on the inside and crunchy on the outside.

Whole kernel cornmeal, in comparison to the packaged stuff, is soft and moist, makes good breads, and doesn't need baking powder and white wheat flour and other stuff added to it. The big drawback is that it doesn't have a long shelf life. For best results, it should be stored in the refrigerator or freezer. I can purchase excellent cornmeal in local supermarkets, either in fine, medium, or coarse grinds. Sometimes I can even find extra-fine, but I really prefer the fine or medium for most purposes. I almost always prefer white cornmeal, but yellow is acceptable. Blue cornmeal is available in some areas, and by mail order, but it's not for me, possibly because I may be more Cherokee than Zuñi.

In any case, the person who owns a grain mill has the best of it, and can grind cornmeal as needed. This keeps the flavor and oil and nutrients in the kernel, where it all stores quite nicely. Some electric mills won't handle corn because of its large kernel. In this case, it's best to crack the kernels, perhaps with a hand mill set on a coarse grind. For grinding purposes, I prefer a soft white corn—if I can find it. Gardeners should look into raising their own, starting perhaps with some of the old heritage grains available from some seed companies and heritage organizations.

Corn for grinding can be purchased in bulk at feed and seed stores. If you go this route, make sure that the corn hasn't been treated with chemicals. In any case, I normally sift my home-ground cornmeal to get out the husk. But I know a banker who wants the husks left in—and I can't argue with his unusual cornpone. Suit yourself. Grind away. Experiment.

Gray's Rhode Island Johnnycakes

Mark Twain wasn't entirely accurate in his assessment of Yankee corn bread. Some of it, I say, is not all bad. A few small mills in Rhode Island have, for a long time, turned out whole cornmeal that is ground just right. (And—surprise—it's white cornmeal, which is virtually unheard of in most of Yankee country and most cookbooks.) The recipes below, for example, came from such a mill, Gray's of Adamsville, which has been going nonstop for over a hundred years. According to their information sheet and price list, the area still grows what they call Narragansett Indian Flint Corn. I don't know quite what that is, but the results are very good. This recipe, however, can be cooked with any good meal from whole grain corn that has been freshly ground to a suitable texture.

Thick Johnnycakes

2 cups whole kernel cornmeal
2 cups water
1/4 cup milk
1 teaspoon salt

Bring the water to a boil. In a bowl of suitable size, mix the meal, water, and salt. Let the mixture set for 5 minutes. Then stir in the milk. Grease the griddle (or skillet) and heat it. Dip the batter onto a greased griddle or skillet with a large spoon, helping it spread to about 2 1/2 inches in diameter. Cook until browned, flip over with a spatula, and cook the other side until browned. In order to see under the cake, you'll have to lift the edge with the spatula. After cooling a few, looking won't be necessary. In any case, cooking thin corn bread is quite like cooking flapjacks.

Thin Johnnycakes

2 cups whole kernel cornmeal
1 1/2 cups milk
3/4 cup cold water
1/2 teaspoon salt

Mix the meal, salt, and water. Slowly stir in the milk. Cook exactly like thick Johnnycakes, except spread the batter to 3 inches in diameter.

Newport Johnnycakes

Here's a thin, crisp Johnnycake from Kenyon Cornmeal Company of Usquepaugh, Rhode Island, which recommends that creamed chipped beef and chicken a la king be served over it instead of over toast.

1 cup white whole kernel cornmeal
1 3/4 cups milk
2 teaspoons sugar (optional)
1/2 teaspoon salt

Mix the ingredients in a large bowl. Cook on a well-greased griddle, just as you would cook flapjacks. Add more milk if needed to keep the mixture thin. Serve hot or cold. I like it hot, shamelessly smeared with butter.

Pueblo Blue Bread

For best results, use a cast-iron skillet for this recipe, or a heavy skillet that has an ovenproof handle. This is Pueblo fare, and was no doubt developed in the clay ovens. A modern electric or gas oven will do and requires less skill.

1½ cups blue cornmeal
1½ cups wheat flour
1½ cups milk
¼ cup chopped sweet green pepper
¼ cup chopped onion
¼ cup sugar
2 chicken eggs, lightly whisked
6 tablespoons cooking oil
6 tablespoons grated cheese
6 teaspoons baking powder
4 teaspoons chili powder
1 teaspoon salt

Preheat oven to 400°F. Sift all of the dry ingredients except the chili powder, mixing well in a large bowl. Stir in the green pepper, onion, and cheese. Melt the oil in a skillet. Stir in the chili powder. Let the skillet cool a little, then stir in the milk and chicken eggs. Stir the contents of the skillet into the dry ingredients, blending well. Turn the mixture back into the skillet, spreading evenly, and bake for 35 minutes in the center of the oven. Cut into wedges and serve hot.

A. D.'s Hush Puppies

I don't really have a recipe for hush puppies. If I've got the right meal, I simply don't need chopped onions and beer and chicken egg and baking soda and other such ingredients. The meal must be white, freshly ground, and fine (but not too fine, lest the bread pop open). Gritty yellow meal won't work, and it would need chicken egg or some such goo to hold it together. In any case, here is what I consider the real thing:

freshly ground white cornmeal, fine
boiling water
salt
bacon
peanut oil

Fry a few strips of bacon in a skillet until it they are crisp. Drain and reserve the drippings, crumble the bacon, and set aside. Dump the cornmeal into a bowl, along with a little salt, and stir in enough water to make a thin dough. Set aside. Rig for deep frying, heating 3 or 4 inches of peanut oil to 325°F. When the oil starts to move about, stir the dough again—and note that it will have stiffened considerably. Mix in the bacon bits and some of the drippings from the skillet. If needed, stir in a little more hot water. Drop by small tea-spoonfuls into the hot oil. The hush puppy should pretty much hold its shape instead of flattening out. Drop a few more spoonfuls into the oil, being careful not to overcrowd. Cook until golden brown. Drain on a brown bag. Serve hot or warm.

Variation: Vegetarians and vegans can omit the bacon and bacon drippings, but do add a little peanut oil to the batter. Also, try these cooked in a skillet with about $1/2$ inch of peanut oil, using a thinner batter so that the bread will flatten out a little and crisp up around the edges. Just don't call these patties hush puppies.

Note: I was recently watching a hunting and fishing show on which a chef mixed up a batch of store-bought yellow meal, saying that it was his favorite recipe because the hush puppies were "light." Well, I'll eat a few of these if I've got fish, but I really prefer the earthy flavor of "heavy" hush puppies made with fresh meal.

Sourmush Corn Pones

I've seen several recipes, mostly old-time, for bread made with a slightly fermented mush. Here's my favorite.

4 cups white stone-ground cornmeal
4 or 5 cups water
$1/4$ cup sorghum or unsulfured molasses
1 chicken egg, whisked
$1/2$ teaspoon salt

Boil the water, and pour 4 cups over the cornmeal. Then stir in enough water to make a stiff mush. Stir in the sorghum and salt. Cover the mush with a cheese-cloth and put it in a warm place for 12 hours, or until it ferments. Shape the mush into hand-sized pones, and cook on a greased cast-iron skillet or griddle, turning once, until lightly browned on both sides.

Ash Cakes

There are hundreds of versions of this old bread, made in a campfire or on a hearth. Here's a short one from *The Foxfire Book:* "Mix up dough for corn bread, and make sure it's thick enough to hold its shape. Clean out a corner of the fireplace, and put the 'cake' in it, and cover it up with a clean cloth. Put hot ashes over the cloth, then put hot coals on top of that. It takes about half an hour."

Also try making small corn cakes and wrapping them in fresh green corn shucks, or in dry shucks that have been soaked in water. The shucks add to the flavor.

Cross Creek Spoon Bread

"I think I never ate a poor spoon bread. Most of the good recipes are similar, the variance being largely in the number of eggs," Marjorie Kinnan Rawlings said in *Cross Creek Cookery.* I agree, but add that good cornmeal, milk, and eggs are all you need for a good spoon bread, with a pinch of salt. Again, the key is in having freshly ground, soft cornmeal.

1 cup white freshly ground cornmeal
2 cups milk
4 large chicken eggs
$1/2$ teaspoon salt

Preheat the oven to 350°F. Heat the milk (but not to boiling), then add the salt and stir until you have a mush. Separate the eggs. Beat the yolks and whites separately. Add the beaten yolks to the mush, then fold in the whites. Pour the mush into a buttered casserole dish, about $1\frac{1}{2}$-quart size, suitable for serving. Bake in the center of the oven for 40 to 50 minutes. Serve hot, spooning the bread directly from the baking dish onto plates. Mrs. Rawlings allows that a napkin may be folded around the casserole dish or baking pan if it is not "suitable for public appearance." I might add that Mrs. Rawlings's recipe includes baking powder and other ingredients.

Hoecake

The term "hoecake" might have come about, as some people believe, because the slaves cooked corn bread in the field on the blade of a hoe. I have doubts about the derivation, partly because I believe that heating a hoe in a fire would alter the temper so that it wouldn't hold an edge for very long. In any case, a piece of bread cooked on the blade of a hoe would be about the size of a human hand—very close to what most people now call a corn pone, which is an entirely different piece of bread despite having the same ingredients in it. For most modern practitioners, the "hoecake" is a thin, round piece of bread cooked on a griddle. Usually, a hoecake will be about $1/2$ inch thick and about 10 inches in diameter. It can be cooked in an oven or atop a stove. In the latter case, it must be turned over. Here's a basic recipe.

> 1 cup white cornmeal, finely ground
> $1/2$ teaspoon salt
> $1/2$ teaspoon bacon drippings or vegetable oil
> water

Bring water to boil in a pot. Add the salt to the cornmeal and sift into a glass bowl. Stir in a little of the boiling water and the bacon drippings. Add more boiling water and stir until you get a batter that spreads slowly when put onto a flat surface. Let this mixture sit for a few minutes. Grease your griddle with a little bacon drippings and heat it up, but not to the smoking point. Turn out the bread mixture and smooth it out over the griddle. Cook on low heat until the bottom starts to brown, usually about 15 minutes or so, depending on temperature, griddle, and thickness of the cake. Turn the hoecake and cook the other side until it starts to brown. Turning the hoecake without breaking it in two is a mark of accomplishment, and, I have heard, signifies when a young lady is ready for matrimony.

I like a good hoecake with a meal, especially when I've got some good pot likker from turnip greens or green field peas, or perhaps a good gravy from roast beef. In other words, corn pone is a good sopping bread. Some people like to spread butter on it while it is hot, and others like to eat it with syrup and smoked pork sausage.

Ionian Corn Bread

Here's an unusual corn bread, made with the aid of orange juice, from an unlikely place: Zakynthos, one of the Greek Ionian islands.

> 2 pounds white whole grain cornmeal
> 1 cup olive oil
> 1 cup orange juice
> 1 cup chopped walnuts
> 1 cup currants
> 2 tablespoons minced orange peel (without the white pith)

1 tablespoon aniseed
2 teaspoons baking soda
1 teaspoon ground cinnamon
1 teaspoon ground cloves
water as needed

Preheat the oven to 375°F and grease two baking pans. Mix all the ingredients in a large bowl, adding enough water to make a rather stiff dough. Divide the dough into two parts, shape into pones, and place each in a tin. Bake in the center of the oven for about 1 hour, or until cooked through.

Old Mill of Guilford Corn Bread

Established in 1753, in North Carolina, this mill now offers a pure cornmeal, both white and yellow, in what I would call a medium fine grind. It has a good flavor, and, as a quaint touch, the mill ties its bags with string instead of banding them with metal. Although the meal is not quite fine enough for most of my recipes, I allow that it is very good stuff. I cook their recipe for corn bread from time to time and find it to be unusually light.

2 cups Old Mill cornmeal
2 large chicken eggs
1 1/4 cups whole milk
1/4 cup melted shortening
1 tablespoon baking powder
1/2 teaspoon baking soda
3/4 teaspoon salt

Preheat the oven to 425°F. In a bowl, mix the meal, baking powder, baking soda, and salt. Add the chicken eggs, milk, and shortening. Beat the mixture until it is smooth, then pour it into a well-greased baking pan (I almost always use my cast-iron skillet). Bake for 20 to 25 minutes, or until nicely browned. If you are not on a diet, serve with butter and molasses or thick cane syrup.

Rocky Mountain Corn Bread

I first got hold of this recipe from *The Complete Sourdough Cookbook* by Don and Myrtle Holm. Interesting stuff—and good. Be sure to try it if you have sourdough starter at hand, or can borrow some from the good neighbors in the next wagon. Holm says it's an old-fashioned favorite from Mexico to the Arctic. He doesn't say whether it's made from yellow, white, or purple meal. I have tried it with fine ground white, and find it to be just right. I usually follow the recipe to the letter, but I really don't know where a mountain man would have got hold of cream of tartar, and early settlers would no doubt have used butter instead of margarine. But, as I said, I haven't finagled with the ingredients. Experiment at your peril. I'm satisfied with the recipe.

$^1/_2$ cup sourdough starter
1 cup all-purpose flour
$^1/_2$ cup cornmeal
2 chicken eggs, whisked lightly or stirred
2 tablespoons margarine, melted
$^1/_2$ cup sour cream or yogurt
1 tablespoon sugar
$^1/_2$ teaspoon salt
$^1/_2$ teaspoon cream of tartar
$^1/_2$ teaspoon baking powder

Preheat the oven to 375°F. Mix the melted margarine and sourdough starter. Add the cornmeal, salt, sugar, sour cream, eggs, flour, cream of tartar, and baking powder. Mix but don't stir it to death. Pour the mixture into a greased baking pan (I use a cast-iron skillet). Put the pan into the oven and bake for 15 minutes. Serve hot.

A. D.'s Jalapeño Bread

I love this bread with chili and other meat stews, and I sometimes make it with hot red pepper, such as fresh cayenne.

2 cups fine ground white cornmeal
$2^1/_2$ cups hot water
$1^1/_2$ tablespoons peanut oil
1 jalapeño
1 teaspoon salt

Preheat the oven to 400°F. Put $1^1/_2$ tablespoons of peanut oil into a 10 $^1/_2$-inch skillet, coating the bottom and sides. Mix the cornmeal, oil, and salt. Slice the jalapeño lengthwise and carefully remove the seeds and inner ribs. Cut the jalapeño halves into strips, mince them sideways, and stir into the cornmeal mixture.

Put the meal mixture into the skillet and place in the center of the oven. Cook for 30 or 40 minutes, or until the corn bread has a crispy crust on the sides and on the top. During the last 10 minutes of cooking, brush the top of the bread with oil. When the sides of the bread seem to be browning too quickly, I usually turn on the broiler heat for the last few minutes of cooking. Turn the heat off and let the bread sit in the oven for a while, which will firm it up considerably. If you like it mushy, as I sometimes do, eat it hot, right out of the oven.

Buttermilk Corn Bread

There is pretty good evidence that buttermilk makes corn bread even more healthy. Buttermilk itself is, I might add, low in fat and cholesterol. Besides, buttermilk corn bread is good stuff. In many parts of the South, buttermilk and corn bread are eaten together, often as a meal. The trick is to fill a goblet three quarters full with chunks of corn bread and then pour in ice-cold buttermilk until the goblet is full. Eat it with a spoon. The recipe below makes a good bread for eating with buttermilk, or it can be eaten as a regular bread.

$1^1/2$ cups fine white cornmeal
1 cup buttermilk
$1^1/2$ tablespoons peanut oil
1 chicken egg
1 teaspoon salt
$1/2$ teaspoon baking soda

Preheat the oven to 400°F. Sift together the cornmeal, salt, and baking soda in a bowl. Whisk the egg, add it to the buttermilk, and pour the mixture into the bowl of meal and stir well. Heat the oil in a cast-iron skillet and pour about half of it into the meal mixture, stirring it in. Leave the rest of the oil in the skillet, swirling it around so that all parts of the bottom and sides are covered. Pour the batter into the skillet and put it into the center of the preheated oven. Bake for 30 minutes, or until the bread is browned. Let it sit in the oven to cool a little, but serve while still hot, or at least warm.

Tangy Buttermilk Corn Pone

Here's a corn pone that I really love, especially when it is served up with well-cooked wild greens, such as dandelion and dock.

2 cups fine white cornmeal
2 cups buttermilk

1 teaspoon salt
1 tablespoon vegetable shortening

Preheat the oven to 370°F. Sift the salt and cornmeal into a bowl. Pour in the buttermilk, stirring as you go. You should have a medium thick batter that will hold the shape of a pone. So, you may have to hold back a little on the buttermilk, or add a little more meal. Melt 1 tablespoon vegetable shortening in a cast-iron skillet or pan, coating the bottom and sides. Divide the batter into three portions and, using your hands, shape each portion into a pone. This is done by shifting the batter from one hand to the other. When the shape is right, put it into the skillet. Make two more pones and put them into the skillet, fitting them in just so. The idea of a corn pone, of course, is to have the sides exposed to the heat, giving a little more crust than you would a similar bread that covers the entire skillet or pan. Put the skillet into the center of the preheated oven and bake for 30 minutes, or until nicely browned.

Katherine Thurber's Texas Bread

Over the years I have run across a number of recipes for corn bread made with cheese, creamed corn, jalapeño, and other ingredients. Of these, one of the best that I have tested came from *The Only Texas Cookbook*. The original, which came from Katherine Thurber, called for $1/4$ to $1/2$ cup canned jalapeño peppers. I have changed this to 2 fresh jalapeños, which are widely available these days in our supermarkets. Suit yourself.

1 cup fine cornmeal
1 small can cream-style corn (8$3/4$-ounce size)
1 cup grated longhorn cheese
$2/3$ cup buttermilk
$1/3$ cup bacon drippings or vegetable oil
2 jalapeño peppers, seeded and chopped
2 chicken eggs, beaten
$1/2$ teaspoon salt
$1/2$ teaspoon baking soda

Preheat the oven to 350°F. Sift the cornmeal, salt, and baking soda into a mixing bowl. In another bowl, beat the eggs and mix in the canned corn, buttermilk, and bacon drippings; then stir this mixture into the cornmeal. Grease a 9- by 9-inch baking pan that is at least 2 inches deep, or a 10-inch skillet with an ovenproof handle. Pour half the cornmeal batter into the baking dish.

Sprinkle on the cheese and chopped peppers. Then pour on the rest of the cornmeal mixture. Put the pan into the preheated oven and bake for 25 to 30 minutes, or until the bread browns nicely and springs back at the touch.

Variations: If you have to fry bacon in order to gain the drippings, go ahead and crumble the pieces and sprinkle them on with the cheese and peppers. Crisply fried bacon works best. Also try grated cheddar instead of longhorn.

Hoover's Biscuits with Cornmeal

I got this recipe from Hoover's Mill in Bonifay, Florida, who in turn got it from Clemson Agricultural College in South Carolina.

1 1/2 cups all-purpose flour
1/2 cup white cornmeal
1/3 cup whole milk
1 chicken egg
2 tablespoons lard or vegetable shortening
3 teaspoons baking powder
1 tablespoon sugar
1 teaspoon salt

Preheat the oven to 400°F. Mix the dry ingredients in a bowl and cut in the lard or shortening. Beat the egg and stir it into the milk, then combine the liquid with the dry ingredients. Knead slightly and shape into biscuits. Arrange the biscuits on a greased pan and bake at 400°F for 20 to 25 minutes.

The Clemson people rolled out the dough, cut it into thin rounds, folded them over like Parker House rolls, and called the result rolls. To me, the finished product resembles biscuits, not rolls, in taste and texture. Suit yourself.

Flonnie Hood's Cornmeal Dumplings

I found this recipe in *Coastal Carolina Cooking*, which credited it to Flonnie Hood of Burgaw. It's very easy to fix, so be sure to try it.

2/3 cup fine cornmeal
1/3 cup all-purpose flour
1/2 cup water or broth
1/2 teaspoon salt
1/8 teaspoon pepper

Into a bowl sift the cornmeal, flour, salt, and pepper. Mix in the water or the broth from boiled chicken, turkey, squirrel, or whatever the dumplings are going to be put into. Roll the mixture into a log about 2 inches in diameter. Cut the log into pieces about 1-inch thick. Bring the pot of broth to a boil, put the pieces into it, reduce the heat, and simmer uncovered for 20 minutes.

Baby Dumpling Variation: Roll the dough out into a longer, thinner log about 1 inch in diameter. Cut into wheels ¼ inch thick, using a sharp, thin-bladed fillet knife. Put into the pot of broth (with salt and black pepper added) for 20 minutes.

Polenta

Whole books have been devoted to this old dish, originally made in northern Italy from chestnuts, wild beechnuts, or chickpeas. These days it is made from a coarsely ground meal from corn, which Italy imported from America. Why this cornmeal mush should come back to America as sophisticated fare is a mystery to me. Even the cornmeal is billed as "polenta" in some stores and in mail-order catalogs. I suspect, however, that most of the packaged "polenta" meal is not made from the whole grain because of its limited shelf life. For greater flavor, use freshly ground cornmeal, rather coarse—making it an ideal meal for producing on the home mill. Call it polenta if you have Yankee cookbook writers or TV chefs coming for dinner. Just use yellow meal for this one, simply because many of the cookbooks define cornmeal as being made from yellow corn—and don't even acknowledge white.

2 cups yellow coarse cornmeal
8 cups water
salt to taste

Bring the water to a rapid boil. Add a little salt. Slowly pour in the cornmeal in a thin, steady stream, stirring as you go with a wooden spoon. Lower the heat. Stir constantly until the water has been absorbed and the polenta is thick and smooth. This will take 15 to 20 minutes, or maybe a little longer, depending on the heat and your meal. When it is ready, the dough will pull away from the sides of the pot. If you plan to serve the polenta right away, turn it out onto a serving platter and sprinkle with freshly grated Parmesan cheese.

The polenta can also be turned out into a mold and refrigerated. Then it can be sliced and sautéed in a skillet or toasted.

Adam's Mill Dressing

I do like a big Thanksgiving or Christmas dinner—roast turkey and ham and all the trimmings,—but if I had to choose one dish of all this, dressing with giblet gravy would be it. One of my favorite recipes comes from Adam's Mill on the little Choctawhatchee River in Alabama, near where I was born and raised. The mill burned down a few years ago, but they are now back in production.

The Bread

1½ cups fine white cornmeal
½ cup all-purpose flour
1½ cups buttermilk
2 eggs, beaten
4 tablespoons vegetable oil
2 teaspoons baking powder
½ teaspoon baking soda
1 teaspoon sugar
¾ teaspoon salt

Preheat the oven to 425°F. Sift all the dry ingredients together. In a small bowl, beat the eggs and mix in the buttermilk and vegetable oil. Mix everything together and pour into a greased baking pan or cast-iron skillet. The pan should be hot. Put the baking pan into the center of the preheated oven and bake for 25 minutes or until golden brown.

The Dressing

4 cups crumbled bread (see above)
3 cups seasoned croutons
2 cups chicken or turkey broth
⅔ cup chopped onions (or more)
¾ cup chopped celery
⅓ cup butter or margarine
3 eggs, beaten
1 teaspoon poultry seasoning
1 teaspoon salt
⅛ teaspoon pepper

Preheat the oven to 350°F. Melt the butter in a skillet and sauté the onions and celery for a few minutes over low heat. In a large bowl, toss the crumbled bread, croutons, onions, celery, poultry seasoning, salt, and pepper. Mix in the beaten eggs. Add the chicken broth and mix until the dressing is smooth. Pour into a buttered baking dish that is suitable for serving, and pour the dressing into it. Put the dish into the preheated oven and bake for 40 to 45 minutes, or until set and brown on top.

Note: Try making the dressing with turkey broth, obtained when boiling the turkey neck and other parts for use in giblet gravy. Although a recipe for giblet gravy really ought to be beyond the scope of this modest book, I feel that it would be a culinary sin to serve up corn bread dressing without a good giblet gravy to top it with. Hence, here's my recipe:

The Gravy

turkey neck and giblets
4 cups water
$1/2$ cup drippings from pan used to bake turkey
2 or 3 hard-boiled eggs
$1/4$ cup all purpose flour
salt and pepper to taste

Put the turkey neck and giblets into a pot and cover with the water. Bring to a boil, reduce heat, and simmer until tender. Meanwhile, boil the eggs and cut them into slices. Remove the giblets from the stock and pull the meat from the neck bone with a fork. Chop all the meat and giblets. In a small bowl, mix a paste of $1/4$ cup flour and cold water. Into this paste, pour some of the hot stock from the giblet pot and stir until all lumps are gone. Take $1/2$ a cup of the pan drippings from the turkey roasting pan and mix it in with the stock from the giblets. Measure out 2 cups of the stock for use in the dressing recipe (see above). Bring the rest of the stock to heat and add the flour paste. Then add the chopped giblets. Cook on low heat until the gravy thickens to the consistency that's just right for spooning over the dressing. (You may want to add a little more flour paste, but the measures above should work out just right.) Toward the end of the cooking, add the sliced eggs. Do not stir much after the eggs have been added. Serve in a gravy dish with a ladle spoon.

New England Indian Pudding

This old New England recipe is called "Indian pudding" because it uses corn-meal, which was called Indian meal in colonial times.

$1/2$ pound stone-ground cornmeal
6 cups half-and-half
1 cup molasses

¼ pound butter or margarine
6 chicken eggs
1 tablespoon ground cinnamon
1 tablespoon freshly grated ginger
1 teaspoon nutmeg
hot water

Preheat the oven to 400°F. Bring the half-and-half to a boil in a pan suitable for finishing in the oven. Stir in the butter. Then stir in the spices and cornmeal. Cook, stirring as you go, until the mixture thickens. Add the molasses. Remove the pan from the heat and stir in the eggs. Place the pan into a larger pan filled about halfway with hot water. Place the whole works into the center of the oven for 2 to 2½ hours or so, adding more water if needed.

Helen's Syrup Bread

When I was a boy, we grew corn and sugar cane on our farm. Back then, there were several water mills that ground meal for us from our own corn, pretty much as needed. Once a year, in the fall, several farms set up cane mills, in which the juice was squeezed from sugar cane in gears driven by a long pole borne by a mule that walked in a circle. The juice was boiled in cast-iron vats and thus reduced to syrup. From time to time, foam would accumulate on the surface of the juice. This would be skimmed off and put into a container. In time this stuff would ferment, and we called it cane skimmings. I suppose it was actually crude rum.

In any case, our farm, and others in the area, usually had plenty of cornmeal and cane syrup, which we stored in tin buckets. And we had "youngerns" to feed. It seems natural that these two ingredients should come together in what we called syrup bread. Syrup bread was never served with a meal. Rather, it was something to eat in between meals. I remember it as good stuff, heavy and filling. My wife also remembers syrup bread, and, after I talked about it for several days and searched through books looking for a recipe, she said that she would make some. Damned if she didn't. Here's what she used:

1¾ cups fine white cornmeal
¾ cup buttermilk
1 cup cane syrup
1 chicken egg
¼ cup brown sugar
¼ cup vegetable shortening
2 teaspoons cinnamon

2 teaspoons baking powder
1 teaspoon baking soda

Preheat the oven to 350°F. Into a bowl sift together the meal, baking soda, baking powder, and cinnamon. Whisk the egg and mix it into the buttermilk, then stir in the syrup, shortening, and sugar. Pour the liquid into the bowl of meal and stir well, until you have a well-mixed batter. Grease a cast-iron skillet (or suitable baking dish) and pour the batter into it. Put the skillet into the center of the oven and bake for 30 minutes or until it is slightly browned. If in doubt, stick a fork into the center of the bread. If the tines come out clean, the bread is done. Cut the bread into pie-shaped pieces and serve straight from the skillet. It is best when eaten hot, or warm. I like mine with lots of real butter on it, but I'll settle for margarine.

This bread isn't quite as heavy as what I remember eating as a child, but, even so, it is very filling and satisfying in every way. A bellyful of this bread will even hush the puppies.

Cherokee Blackberry Cobbler

This wonderful recipe, according to *The Art of American Indian Cooking*, goes back to the Southern Indian tribes. If this is true, I say that it was tampered with considerably after the Europeans introduced cow milk, baking powder, and lemons. Since I may be part Cherokee, I feel that I can tamper with it just a little more. I also feel that the recipe is best when cooked with a freshly ground white cornmeal, medium grind. I can't imagine a Cherokee using that gritty yellow stuff sold in our supermarkets.

The Filling

1 quart fresh blackberries
1/4 cup sugar

The Topping

1 cup white cornmeal, medium grind
1/2 cup sugar
1/2 cup buttermilk
2 tablespoons melted butter or margarine
1 teaspoon baking powder
1 teaspoon salt

The Sauce

¹/₄ cup honey
1 tablespoon melted butter or margarine
juice of 1 lemon

Preheat the oven to 375°F. Put the berries into a shallow baking dish (I use a ceramic dish about 2 inches deep and 12 by 12 inches square) and sprinkle them with the sugar. In a small bowl, mix the cornmeal, sugar, baking powder, and salt. Then stir in the buttermilk and melted butter. Using a large spoon, drop this mixture onto the berries and spread it rather roughly, leaving some of the berries exposed. Mix the sauce ingredients and dribble over the pie. Put the pie into the middle of the oven and bake for 1 hour. Cool to room temperature before serving.

Fried Green Tomatoes

I've seen a number of recipes for fried green tomatoes, and most of the variations call for dipping the tomatoes in beaten egg or milk before rolling them in flour or cornmeal. I prefer to eliminate all this stuff by using a fine or extra-fine meal that will stick to the tomatoes pretty well without help. This results in a thin coating that browns nicely and doesn't soak up much grease, and which can be cooked on a relatively high heat. Be warned that the commercial meals made from degerminated corn won't stick to the tomatoes and will produce a gritty texture. Slice the tomatoes about ¹/₂ inch thick and use about ¹/₄ inch of oil in a skillet.

sliced green tomatoes
cooking oil
extra fine cornmeal
salt
pepper

Heat the oil in a cast-iron skillet. Salt and pepper both sides of the tomatoes, then dredge them in the cornmeal. Fry until both sides are nicely browned, turning once. Serve as a vegetable with a meal. For a heavy lunch, cook up a batch of corn pone and bacon or sliced salt pork, and serve with cold sliced white onions or green onions. This is true soul food.

Mealed Chicken Fillets

I will sometimes use cornmeal instead of flour when frying chicken fillets or fingers, cut from the innermost part of the breast. Fine meal will work, but extra-fine is better. Chicken fillets—that tender strip of meat on the underside of the breast—can be cooked quicker than a pan-dressed piece of chicken, and consequently can be cooked on a higher heat. (A high heat would burn the outside of a whole chicken breast before the inside gets done, especially when cooking in a skillet.) Cooking the fillet quickly results in a moist piece with a nice outside crunch. My reason for using the cornmeal is that it doesn't burn on high heat as badly as does flour or batters containing flour. I usually purchase a large bag of chicken fillets that have been individually frozen (seemingly with a coating of water). The bag is resealable, so that I get out what I need and put the rest back into the freezer.

chicken fillets
peanut oil
extra-fine white whole-kernel cornmeal
salt
pepper

Thaw the fillets. Heat the oil in a skillet or deep fryer to at least 375°F. (If you are using a skillet, have about $1/2$ inch of oil.) Salt and pepper the fillets and shake them in a bag with a little meal. Fry a few at a time until the outside is browned, then drain on a bag. Try to turn the fillets only once. This will leave the fillet touching the bottom of the skillet, which is a little hotter than the oil, and will result in a very brown, almost burned, area on either side of the fillet. This in turn produces a sort of two-toned crunch. Be warned that using chicken egg or other ingredients in this recipe may result in a burn on either side.

Note: Also see the recipe for Boggy Bayou Fried Mullet on page 33.

Mamaliga

Cornmeal mush, in one form or another, soul food or not, isn't restricted to the American South. Indeed, it has traveled far. How far? To the heart of Balkan Europe, where mamaliga is a national dish of Romania.

2 cups yellow cornmeal
5 cups water
1 cup grated cheese

1/4 cup butter or margarine plus more for serving
1 teaspoon salt

Bring 4 cups of water to a boil. Mix the cornmeal and 1 cup cold water, making a paste. Slowly stir the paste into the boiling water in a cast-iron pot (a stove-top Dutch oven will do but a taller pot of smaller diameter works better). Cook on low heat for 30 minutes, stirring all the while with a wooden spoon. Allow no lumps. Add 1/4 cup butter and the cheese and stir. Serve immediately in individual bowls. Serve more butter for those who want to stir it in at the table.

Bidia

This recipe from the Kasai area of Zaire is one version of what is called "nsima" in Malawi and Sambia, "ugali" in Kenya and Tansania, "oshifima" in Namibia, and "mealie-meal" or "putu" among English and Zulu-speaking South Africans. It may be made with just water instead of milk and water, or with equal parts tapioca and cornmeal instead of with cornmeal alone.

1 1/4 cups white cornmeal
1 cup milk
1 cup water

Heat a cup of water to boiling in a medium-sized saucepan. Meanwhile, in a bowl or measuring cup, gradually add 3/4 cup of the cornmeal to the milk, stirring briskly to make a smooth paste. Add the mixture to the boiling water, continuing to stir constantly. Cook for 4 to 5 minutes while adding the remainder of the cornmeal. When the mixture begins to pull away from the sides of the pot and stick together, remove from heat.

Dump the bidia into a bowl. Then, with damp hands, shape it into a smooth ball, flipping it so that the rounded sides of the bowl help to smooth it. Serve immediately.

To eat bidia in the traditional manner, tear off a small chunk and make an indentation in it with your thumb. Use this hollow as a "bowl" to scoop up sauces and stews. It goes especially well with curries and highly seasoned stews. See also Coo Coo, page 32.

Turkey Scrapple

If you like scrapple for breakfast, be sure to try this recipe the next time you have leftover roast turkey, dressing, and giblet gravy. Adapted here from my *Wild*

Turkey Cookbook, this dish will keep nicely in the refrigerator for 2 to 3 weeks, and it can be frozen for even longer storage.

> **4 cups cooked turkey meat, diced**
> **4 cups stuffing or dressing**
> **1 1/2 cups white cornmeal**
> **1/2 cup giblet gravy (or more)**
> **1 chopped onion**
> **2 teaspoons celery salt seasoning**
> **turkey bones**
> **water**
> **salt to taste**
> **pepper to taste**

When you carve the turkey, be sure to save the bones from the drumsticks, thighs, and back. Cut off most of the leftover meat, chop it, and put it aside. Crack the bones or break them, put them into a large pot, add the chopped onion, cover with water, bring to a boil, reduce heat, and simmer for 30 minutes. Remove the bones from the pot and measure the liquid, then add enough water to make 12 cups total. Pull the meat from the bones and chop it. Measure the meat and add enough from the pile you put aside to make 4 cups. Add the meat and the stuffing (chopped or broken up) to the liquid in the pot. Stir in the gravy, celery salt, and pepper. Bring to heat, slowly stirring in the cornmeal. Heat and stir until the mixture is quite thick. Pour or ladle the mixture into well-greased bread pans and chill. Slice as needed and fry the pieces in a little oil until nicely browned. Although scrapple is traditionally eaten for breakfast, I like it at any time. Of course, the spices used in the dish can be varied to suit your taste or what you have on hand. I like to put some red pepper flakes in the water while boiling the turkey bones, then omit the black pepper when stirring in the gravy. Also, sage, used sparingly, goes nicely with turkey scrapple.

Atole

This old Mexican peasant hot drink, dating back to the pre-Columbian Indians, is very good, thick, filling, and warming. Make up a batch and try it on a chilly day. The measures in the list below are for a basic atole. It can be drunk as is, but I recommend the addition of chocolate or strawberries, or some other fruit. I prefer extra fine white stone-ground meal. Most of the meals on the market are too coarse and will produce a grainy drink instead of a smooth one. Commercial *masa harina* also works, but the flavor won't be as good.

1/2 cup extra fine white cornmeal
3 cups milk
3 cups water
3/4 cup sugar (or to taste)
1/2 teaspoon vanilla extract or a vanilla bean

In a saucepan, mix the water, cornmeal, and vanilla. Heat and stir until the mixture thickens. Keep hot but do not boil. In another saucepan, mix the sugar and milk. Bring the mixture to a simmer, but do not boil, and pour it into the cornmeal mixture. Bring to a simmer, stirring constantly. Serve hot in drinking cups.

Chocolate atole. Add 3 ounces of unsweetened chocolate squares in the second saucepan and use brown sugar instead of white. Heat until the chocolate melts, then combine with the first mixture and serve hot. It is delicious. I might add that chocolate is a native American treat, and it was often served with vanilla, another native product. This drink, also called *champurrado,* is traditionally served at Christmas in San Antonio.

Fruit atole. Almost any good fruit can be used in an atole, such as guava, blackberry, and others. I am especially fond of fresh strawberries in it. Pineapple, another native American fruit, is also very good. The fruit must first be crushed. I normally put the fruit in a tall, slim container and zap it with a little handheld sentry zapper. Larger food processors can be used, but the handheld unit is easier to clean.

Cinnamon atole. Cinnamon is a popular addition, used instead of vanilla. It's best to use a small piece of cinnamon stick in the water and meal mixture, then remove it before serving the drink.

Other variations: If you want a richer atole, use less water and more milk or a combination of water, milk, and cream. Ground almonds can also be added.

⇜ Popcorn ⇝

When I was a kid—only 13 years old—I made and sold popcorn in a local theater, or "picture show." Named the Joyce Theatre, it was. Back then, Saturday was the big day in small towns because all the country folks came in, mostly on mules and wagons, to buy supplies and live it up. The picture show was part of the big day, and we featured a western, a regular movie, and a serial such as *The Green Hornet,* along with cartoons. Admission was 25 cents for adults and 10 cents for children. Popcorn was cheap but a moneymaker. One Saturday I sold $53.20 worth at 5 cents per bag. That's 1,064 bags in a town and trade area of only about

2,000 people! One night, after an especially good day following a good harvest year, the owner of the picture show called me into his office to give me a nice Christmas bonus. He told me that I sold twice as much popcorn as anyone he had ever had, and he wanted to know how I did it. Pocketing the bonus check, I told him I used twice as much coconut oil as he told me to use.

So, I am clearly not sold on the trend of popping corn without the aid of oil. The trick is to use a cast-iron Dutch oven, add the oil (or clarified butter), heat it almost to the smoke point, add the corn, listen to the pops, and shake the pan from time to time, until all is silent. Then salt the popcorn to taste. Pour it into a brown grocery bag or other container and enjoy.

The late Orville Redenbacher's popcorn notwithstanding, the best popcorn does not pop quite all the way and become as fluffy as can be. Use a cheaper grade of corn—and hope it won't puff too much. Invariably, the lighter, puffier pieces will rise to the top, leaving the best at the bottom. If you are lucky, these bottom kernels will be ever so slightly burned.

In all honesty, I should add that the higher quality, and more expensive, popcorns work better if you use little or no oil. If you do use oil, stay away from coconut butter. Try olive oil. But suit yourself, or your diet, and follow the directions on the package if you purchase your popcorn in stores. Even microwaved popcorn is quite good—if you put some salt on it.

Nutritional Highlights

Dry corn is a healthy food, high in carbohydrates and various minerals, but it is not considered a "complete" food because it is lacking in lysine and tryptophan, both essential amino acids. For this reason, cultures that depended on corn—especially the Aztecs and Incas—supplemented it with such grains as amaranth and quinoa and with beans. All of the modern cornmeals sold in the United States are fortified with various additives, making commercial meal a little more healthy, in this regard, than home-ground. Personally, however, I don't think this is important to modern people who eat a variety of foods. People who eat lots of corn bread, however, should keep this in mind.

PART TWO

Grains of Gluten

The discovery of yeast as a controlled activator for risen breads led to the increased consumption of wheat in modern times. Why? When yeast, which is made up of living cells, starts to feed on a bread batter, it produces carbon dioxide bubbles. This is what makes the bread rise. The gluten in the wheat helps form tiny webs in the dough that trap and hold in the bubbles. When heated, the webs harden and the bread holds its risen form.

Some grains, such as barley and millet, have practically no gluten. Others, such as rye, have a gluten, but not as much as wheat. Some of the older gluten grains such as spelt have been rediscovered in modern times, and an entirely new form—triticale, a cross between wheat and rye—is a product of twentieth century agricultural science.

4

Wheat

Wheat is life, boy. Don't let no silly bugger tell you different.

—Five Miles from Bunkum

I do enjoy good white loaves, especially those made at home, and I consider bread making to be an art and a science. Still, I pity the people who eat only white breads made at commercial bakeries, partly because the aroma of freshly baked bread from the home oven is part of the culinary experience, and I agree with Vrest Orton, who wrote, in the introduction to his wife's *Cooking with Wholegrains*, "The white bread eater walks out of a grocery store with several loaves of white bread under his arm and in order to obtain any discernible nourishment, he must walk across the street to the drugstore and buy several bottles of vitamin pills. But even then he is missing a great deal in actual nourishment and downright eating pleasure."

In any case, any reader who is interested in baking white breads at home is simply in the wrong book. There are excellent baking books, and I especially recommend *Baking with Julia*, based on the PBS series hosted by Julia Child.

So, with a clear conscience and robust appetite, let's start off this chapter with eating the wheat berry instead of making bread with its flour. Then we'll briefly cover cracked wheat before moving somewhat cautiously into wheat flours and the baking of a few good dark breads.

⬤ Wheat Berries ⬤

These are simply the whole kernels of wheat, with the bran and germ intact. (Thanks to modern agricultural machinery, the husk is removed during the harvesting process and should not concern us here. See the illustration on page 3.)

There are several kinds of wheat berries, as well as such cousins as spelt and Kamut (covered in separate chapters). The more common of these include hard red winter wheat and summer wheat. Most of the bulk wheat sold in food outlets is the hard red winter type. All of the wheat berries have a relatively long shelf life if kept in a tightly covered container. I usually buy 10 pounds in bulk and store it in mason jars, preferably in the refrigerator, but it is much cheaper to buy the berries in 50- or 100-pound bags.

The differences in the types of wheat are (or can be) very important in making flour for breads, but there really isn't much difference when cooking the whole berry. Fortunately this permits us to get on with a few recipes using any wheat berry. We'll wrestle with flours and cracked wheats under separate headings.

I will, however, say that we Americans, including our wheat farmers, might have missed out on a great culinary treat: green wheat, as explained in the next recipe.

Fresh Wheat-Berry Pudding

Here's an old Irish country recipe—a way of using early wheat before the harvest. The ears are pulled while still turning ripe, or when newly ripe but not yet dried quite enough for harvest. After being pulled, the ears are rubbed between the hands to remove the outer husk.

If you live on a farm, or know a friendly farmer, try this one. If not, why not grow some wheat in your garden? Growing conditions vary widely from North to South.

2 ounces fresh wheat
2 cups thick milk or half-and-half
$1/2$ teaspoon salt

Heat the milk in a saucepan, stir in the salt, add the wheat, and bring to a light boil. Immediately lower the heat, cover, and simmer for 1 hour, stirring frequently. Add more liquid if needed to prevent the wheat from scorching and to maintain a porridge consistency. Serve in bowls with cream and brown sugar.

Note: An old Turkish delicacy called *frik* is a green wheat with a smoky flavor—to make it, the field of green wheat is set afire before the grain is harvested.

Cooking the Berry

After the harvest, cooked wheat berries—presoaked and boiled — can be eaten as is, but they are better when used in a salad or as an ingredient in other recipes, such as Harscho, a Russian soup-stew. Note that 1 cup of dry wheat berries will yield 2 cups of cooked wheat, maybe a little more. Cooked wheat berries, properly drained, will keep for several days in the refrigerator. If frozen, however, they become a little mushy.

1 cup wheat berries
1 quart cold water
1 to 2 teaspoons salt

Soak the berries overnight in water. Using the same water, bring to a boil, add the salt, and simmer uncovered for 30 minutes. Keep boiling, but taste the berries for softness every 5 minutes or so. Usually, they are relished al dente. Be warned that if cooked too long the berries will split and turn to mush. After they reach the desired softness, remove the pot from the heat and let the berries return to room temperature in the liquid. Drain and serve, or refrigerate for later use.

The cooked berries can be eaten as a cereal, or they can be used in quick soups and stews, pilafs, breads (such as datenut breads and muffins), and meat burgers and loafs. See the meatball recipe on page 63.

Old-Time Steamed Wheat

Eating wheat berries may seem to be a new culinary trend, but actually the practice is very old. Here's an old recipe adapted from *Stillroom Cookery*, by Grace Firth.

1 cup wheat berries
2 cups water or stock plus more for steaming
1 teaspoon salt

The night before the wheat is to be eaten, place the 2 cups of water or stock, wheatberries, and salt in an uncovered casserole dish of suitable size. In a large steaming pot, rig a rack to hold the casserole dish off the bottom. Add about an inch of water, cover the steaming pot tightly, bring to a boil, and steam the wheat for about 1 hour. (The lid should fit tightly, lest all the water boil out of the pot.) Remove the pot from the heat, still covered, and set aside overnight. The next morning, uncover the pot and check the wheat in the uncovered casserole. If it has not absorbed all the water or stock, add some water to the bottom pot, heat, and steam for another 30 minutes or so. Season the wheat with cream and a little honey. Serve for breakfast.

Mrs. Firth adds, "If the steamed wheat was to be used as a potato substitute it was flavored with minced parsley and butter. Seasoned whole grain wheat was often used in pilaf or in chicken casseroles. Chewy and satisfying, steamed wheat has a nut-like flavor. Whole grain rye was often steamed in the same manner."

Wheat Berry Caviar

Here's a dish adapted from *The Grains Cookbook*, by Bert Green, who suggested that the dish might also be called "Poor Man's Caviar." The olives turn the wheat black, like some caviar.

1 1/2 cups cooked wheat berries, chilled
1 cup small pitted black olives
1/4 cup olive oil
2 small cloves garlic
1/4 teaspoon Dijon mustard
1/4 teaspoon salt
chopped fresh chives (garnish)

Mince the garlic in a food processor. Add the olives, oil, mustard, and salt. Process until the olives are finely minced. Place the wheat berries into a serving bowl and pour the olive mixture over them, tossing to mix everything. Sprinkle with chives. Serve as an appetizer with blini or Wheat Thins.

Locro

Here's an Argentine variation of a peasant dish made in several areas of South America, adapted here from *The South American Cook Book*, by Cora, Rose, and Bob Brown.

The Locro

1 pound wheat berries
1 pound lean beef
2$\frac{1}{2}$ quarts cold water
salt and pepper to taste

The Sauce

2 medium to large tomatoes, chopped
2 medium to large onions, chopped
2 cloves garlic, minced
1 hot chili pepper, seeded and minced
1 tablespoon fresh parsley or cilantro, minced
3 tablespoons lard or vegetable shortening
1 teaspoon cumin seeds
salt, pepper, and paprika to taste

Put the wheat berries into a pot, cover with water, and cook over low heat until the grains are swollen, adding more water if needed. While waiting, cut the beef into fingers. Add the beef to the pot, sprinkle on a little salt and pepper, and cook, stirring from time to time, until the liquid becomes creamy. Prepare the sauce while waiting. Sauté the onions in the lard in a skillet for 5 minutes. Add the garlic and chili pepper. Sauté a little longer. Stir in the tomatoes and cook, stirring from time to time, until the sauce thickens. Add the parsley, and salt and paprika to taste. Crush the cumin seeds with mortar and pestle and add to the pot. Cook and stir for another minute or so. Keep hot.

When the locro is ready, put it into a serving tureen. Pour the sauce into the center and stir. Serve hot in bowls, perhaps with fried squash blossoms on the side.

Wheat-Berry Stew

I don't really have a recipe for this dish. Instead, I merely put $\frac{1}{2}$ cup or so of wheat berries into any soup or stew that will be cooked by long, slow simmering. Most Crock-Pot soups and stews are ideal. I also like to mix wheat berries with chickpeas or dried hominy in such a soup or stew. Use your imagination. Here's a suggested recipe for starters. I list frozen stew vegetables, which is a mix available at the supermarket. If you have them, use fresh vegetables instead, including perhaps some new potatoes.

2 pounds venison or lean beef, cut into 1-inch chunks
$1/2$ cup wheat berries
2 packages frozen stew vegetables (16-ounce size)
1 can tomatoes (16-ounce size) with juice
1 medium to large onion, diced
4 or more cloves garlic (diced or whole)
2 ounces dried mushrooms (preferably morels)
fresh herbs to taste (optional)
olive oil
salt and freshly ground black pepper to taste
water or stock

Heat the olive oil in a heavy stove-top Dutch oven. Brown the venison for 4 or 5 minutes, stirring once or twice with a wooden spoon. Add the rest of the ingredients, using enough water or stock to cover. Bring to a boil, reduce the heat to very low, and simmer for about 3 hours, or until the venison is tender. Stir from time to time, adding more water or stock as needed. Serve hot in bowls. This makes a wonderful hot lunch for a cold day, and, with a little crusty bread and perhaps a salad, you can even make a complete evening meal of such a hearty soup.

Meatballs with Yogurt Sauce

Several recipes from the Middle East lead to meatballs swimming in a yogurt sauce. Here's a variation that makes good use of wheat berries as a filler. For convenience, I cook it with chili powder. If you prefer, make a 2-tablespoon spice mix of freshly ground cumin, cayenne, and perhaps a little freshly ground black pepper.

2 pounds finely ground lamb
2 cups cooked wheat berries
2 cups yogurt
2 medium to large onions, chopped
2 cloves garlic, minced
2 tablespoons chili powder
$1 1/2$ tablespoons olive oil
salt to taste

Heat the olive oil in a large skillet and sauté the onion and garlic for 4 or 5 minutes, stirring with a wooden spoon. In a large bowl, mix the onions, ground lamb, wheat berries, salt, and chili powder. Shape this mixture into balls $1 1/2$ inches in diameter. Carefully place balls into the skillet. Brown the meatballs on high heat, turning carefully, and then lower the heat for about 5 minutes, or until the meat is just cooked through. Remove the skillet from the heat and place the meatballs into a serving dish. Stir the yogurt into the pan juices, then pour over the meatballs. Serve hot, along with rice pilaf and vegetables of your choice.

Cracked Wheat—Meal and Grits

The cracked wheat sold in retail outlets, billed as farina, Cream of Wheat, or something like Wheatnea, is usually a byproduct of milling hard durum wheat into pasta flour or some such mass-manufacturing operation. There are several kinds based on coarseness—from meal to grits. In any case, most commercial cracked wheat is easy to cook simply by following the directions on the package.

There is some confusion about the difference between cracked wheat and bulgur. Technically, cracked wheat is simply grits, made from the dried wheat berry. For bulgur (discussed later), the wheat berries are steamed and dried before cracking.

Anyone who has a kitchen mill with a coarse setting can easily crack their own wheat, although getting it to a uniform grit may be difficult.

Basic Cracked Wheat

This recipe works best for coarsely cracked wheat, with a texture similar to commercial corn grits.

1 cup cracked wheat (grits)
2$^1/_2$ cups water
salt to taste

Bring the water to a boil, adding the salt. Stir in the grits, cover, reduce the heat to low, and simmer for 15 minutes, or until the cracked wheat is tender. It can be rinsed and used in a salad or pilaf, or it can be cooked a little longer and used as a breakfast cereal.

Firmentry

I have adapted this recipe from a brochure from the Vermont Country Store. The ingredients list calls for maple sugar, which can be purchased from some mail-order outlets or retail shops that carry maple products. Substitute light brown sugar if you must. The recipe is best cooked in a double boiler. If you crack your own wheat, try to get it to the consistency of commercial yellow corn grits.

$1/2$ cup cracked wheat (uncooked)
3 cups milk
1 cup water plus more for steaming
$1/2$ cup raisins
$1/3$ cup maple sugar
$1/2$ teaspoon salt
$1/4$ teaspoon grated nutmeg

Bring 1 cup of water to a boil, then add it to the top part of a double boiler. Bring more water to a boil in the bottom so that it will be ready for steaming. Sprinkle the cracked wheat into the top boiler, stirring as you go until it thickens. When all the water has been absorbed, stir in the milk, maple sugar, raisins, nutmeg, and salt. Steam over low heat for 3 hours. Serve hot with thick cream, apple-cider sauce, or maple syrup.

ᴥ Wheat Flour ᴥ

The world's farmers and agricultural scientists have developed over 30,000 types of wheat. In all of these the whole berry cooks up pretty much the same, but there can be a big difference in the flour. The operative agent here is gluten—the stuff in flour that helps bread retain its structure. When a high-gluten flour is mixed with water, as explained earlier, it forms tiny webs that trap and hold the carbon dioxide produced when the bread rises. Some other grains, such as rye, also contain gluten—but not all glutens act exactly alike. Generally, hard red wheats are high in gluten of the right sort; soft white wheats, low.

In short, getting the right flour for a certain kind of bread is sometimes a big problem for serious bakers. In general, however, there are three basic types of wheat berry for making flour: hard, soft, and durum, and these make, or combine to make, several kinds of flour. Generally, most breads are made predominately from hard wheat, whereas cakes and pastries are made from soft wheat. Durum is for pasta. Here's my take, starting with the familiar:

White Flour. This is regular flour milled from what's left of the wheat berry (endosperm) after the germ and bran have been removed. It has a relatively long shelf life, but is best stored in airtight glass containers.

All-Purpose Flour. This popular flour sold at every supermarket will do just about everything pretty well and consistently, but it is not perfect for all kinds of baking. It is a commercial blend of white flours (or of hard and soft wheats) that simply can't be duplicated with the home mill. All-purpose flour stores well, but is best kept in airtight glass containers.

Bread Flour. This is a blended flour that is high in gluten, making it ideal for baking highly risen yeast breads. Bread flour is available from suppliers that cater to bakers. These days it may also be available in some upscale supermarkets.

Cake Flour. This flour is ground from soft wheat. It is not as high in gluten as regular hard red spring wheat. Its peculiar gluten produces a crumbly texture.

Pastry Flour. Similar to cake flour, finely ground.

Unbleached Flour. Most of the commercial flours have been bleached to make them whiter. Unbleached flours, preferred by some cooks, are so labeled.

Stone-Ground Whole Wheat Flour. This is flour made from the whole wheat berry, including all the germ and bran. (It may be sifted, however, which will remove some of the bran.) It is usually the product of a small mill and is actually ground between stones at a slow speed. The slow speed is more important than the "stone." High-speed milling increases the temperature of the flour or meal, which has an undesirable effect on the oil in the germ. Even so, stone-ground flour has a short shelf life and in time will smell like stale oil— which is why it is not very practical for large milling and food- distributing operations. If you buy stone-ground flour in a store, it's best to store it after opening in an airtight glass jar in the refrigerator or freezer. If you own a kitchen grain mill, it's best to grind only as much flour as you need for the recipe at hand, since the berries always store better than the flour.

Whole Berry Wheat Flour. To avoid confusion, I use this term in the recipes below. I define it as flour ground with the whole wheat berry, either with a stone mill or other burr-type mill. I consider this term necessary because some of the commercial "whole wheat" flour, discussed below, simply isn't the same thing—and because the flour doesn't necessarily have to be ground with stones.

Commercial Whole Wheat Flour. Some of the so-called whole wheat flour sold in stores is not really ground from a whole kernel. Instead, the kernels are rid of their germ and bran. Then the berries are ground into ordinary white flour. Finally, part of the bran and germ is added back to the white flour, giving it the appearance of whole wheat flour. It does have a better shelf life than stone-ground whole grain flour, but it's not the same thing. Not by a long shot.

Home-Ground Whole Wheat Flour. Excellent whole wheat flour can be ground on the home mill, using either stone or steel burr mills for the grinding process. The slow-turning hand mills are best if the flour is to be stored for any length of time. Electric mills generate some heat, but this isn't much of a problem if the flour is used right away. The best bet, always, is to grind only as much flour as you need for the day.

Graham Flour. This is a confusing old term. It generally means coarsely ground whole wheat flour that has not been sifted and therefore contains lots of bran.

Semolina or Durum Flour. This is a rather granular flour milled from the endosperm of hard durum wheat. It is a commercial product used mostly in the manufacture of pasta and couscous. (Bulgur, a great Middle Eastern staple, is also made from hard durum wheat that has been steamed, cracked, and dried; but this is not a flour. Couscous, by comparison, is actually made from semolina flour.) Semolina is not easy to find in most areas, does not store well, and should be kept in a closed glass container in the refrigerator. Generally, it is to be avoided in regular baking because it produces a tough bread. Semolina does, however, help pasta hold its shape during cooking, and that is its major use.

Farina. This is a coarse meal made from hard wheat. It is similar to the finely cracked wheat or grits used as cereal, but it can also be used in baking.

Gluten Flour. This flour is made by washing some of the starch out of regular flour. The process forms a paste that is dried and ground into a flour that has reduced starch but more gluten content. It is sometimes used in recipes to supplement regular flour.

Self-Rising Flour. This is a mix of flour and leavens. Self-rising flour is generally avoided by serious cooks, partly because the chemical additives tend to lose strength after storage. Use it only in recipes that call for it.

Enriched Flour. By federal decree, commercial flours and meals have been fortified with vitamin supplements and sometimes other additives, whether you like it or not. Read the label.

Clearly, the home miller isn't likely to produce specialized white bread flours and other commercial products at home, and certainly not on a consistent basis. (Brand-name products are usually pretty much the same from one batch to another, which takes some doing when blending the grains and flours.) The home miller must realize that each batch of wheat berries will produce a slightly different flour. Culinary sports might want to experiment with different kinds of wheat, but generally the widely available ordinary hard red wheat will produce excellent whole grain breads and will do for most of the recipes in this section, unless otherwise specified.

Be warned also that home-ground flour is usually not as powdery as commercial mixes—and it certainly won't be as white. Some cooks long accustomed to fine white blends may find the home-ground product off-putting. But I hope not, for each new batch can be an adventure.

FLAT BREADS

Singing Hinnie

This old English flatbread is usually made with plain wheat flour, currants, milk or cream, and other ingredients. There are many variations, including, rather surprisingly, the addition of rice flour. I like it with whole grain wheat flour and buttermilk. In any case, the name comes from the sizzling sound the bread makes on a hot griddle. A cast-iron griddle or a 10-inch cast-iron skillet works best.

3 cups whole grain wheat flour
1 cup buttermilk
$2/3$ cup currants
$1/4$ cup butter or margarine
$1/4$ cup lard or vegetable shortening
1 teaspoon sugar
1 teaspoon salt
1 teaspoon cream of tartar

Heat the griddle. Cut the butter and lard into the flour, mixing in the sugar, salt, and cream of tartar. Slowly stir in enough of the buttermilk to make a soft dough. Add the currants. Roll the dough out into a round to fit the griddle. Carefully place the round onto the hot griddle. Cook for a few minutes, until the bottom starts to brown. Turn carefully with the aid of a large spatula and cook the other side. Serve hot with butter.

Navajo Juniper Ash Bread

The American Indians made good culinary use of the juniper berry. They also used the ashes from freshly burned green juniper. This practice started with corn pone and grass seeds, and continued after the Spanish introduced wheat.

$1^1/2$ cups coarsely ground whole wheat flour
$1/2$ cup fresh juniper ashes
salt
vegetable oil or animal fat
water

Mix the flour, ashes, and salt. Stir in enough water to make a dough. Divide the dough into small balls, from 1 to $1^1/2$ inches in diameter. Flatten the balls, patting them with your hands, as thinly as you can. Fry each pattie in a skillet or on a griddle with a little hot oil until crisp and browned, turning with a thin spatula.

Variation: Try the same recipe with freshly ground cornmeal. Also, use a little melted bone marrow instead of oil in the skillet.

Pita Bread

Sometimes called Syrian bread or Arab bread, this flatbread is riding a wave of popularity in the United States. Its pocket, used for holding food, makes it a good choice for camp cookery and picnics. There are a number of good recipes, some calling for white flour or a mix of flours. This variation, which is quite simple, calls for whole wheat flour. If you prefer, use half all-purpose flour and half whole wheat.

3 cups whole wheat flour
1 cup warm water
1 package dry yeast
1 teaspoon salt

Mix the yeast into the water and let it work for 5 minutes. Put the flour into a large bowl and mix in the salt. Make a hole in the center and pour in the yeast water. Mix the water into the flour, stirring from the center outward, round and round. You'll need a stiff dough, so add a little more flour if needed—or a little more water if it's too stiff. Knead the dough on a floured surface for about 10 minutes, until the dough is smooth and elastic. Place the dough into a greased bowl, turning once to lightly grease all sides. Cover the dough with a clean cloth and let rise until double in size, about 30 minutes.

Toward the end of the 30-minute period, preheat the oven to 475°F and place a large cookie sheet in the center so that it will be hot. It is important to place the bread on a hot surface.

Punch the dough down and place it on a floured surface. Divide the dough into 6 equal parts and shape into balls. Quickly put the balls onto a floured surface and cover with a damp cloth. Let sit for 15 minutes. On a freshly floured surface, roll 3 of the balls (leaving the rest covered with the damp cloth) into circles about 6 inches in diameter, which will work out to be about ⅛ inch thick. These rounds should be perfectly smooth on top, without tears, punctures, or creases. Place these three rounds onto the hot cookie sheet. Bake for 5 or 6 minutes, until the bread puffs and sets. Remove the rounds with a wide spatula, leaving the cookie sheet in the oven to heat for the next batch. Stack the cooked pita rounds on a cloth and cover with another cloth while you roll and cook another batch. Keep the bread covered until cool. Then it can be stored in plastic bags. Before serving, cut each round in half crosswise. If necessary, use a thin knife to help form the pockets.

Puri

Here's a fried "crispbread" of Indian and Malayan influence from South Africa, where it is served with curries or as noshing fare. I use home-ground flour but commercial whole wheat flour also works. The same basic recipe is used in India.

4 cups whole wheat flour
2$\frac{1}{2}$ tablespoons butter or margarine
oil for deep frying
warm water

Place the flour in a large, shallow wooden bowl. Chill your fingertips with ice and dry them. Slowly rub some of the flour and a little piece of butter together, working it in a circle on the side of the bowl. When all of the butter has been worked in, slowly add enough water to form a stiff dough, stirring as you go with a wooden spoon. Knead the dough for at least 10 minutes. (The longer you knead it, the lighter it will be, within practical limits.) Place the dough onto a greased flat surface, cover with a cloth or sheet of plastic film, and let stand for an hour. When you are ready to cook, rig for deep frying at 375°F, heating about 3 inches of oil in a stove-top cast-iron Dutch oven or some such fryer. Pinch off little balls of dough and roll them out to a thickness of $\frac{1}{8}$ inch. (When rolled, the dough should be 4 or 5 inches in diameter, so adjust your pinches accordingly.) Using a thin spatula, place one of the rounds into the hot oil. When it floats, press it with the back of a large spoon, making it puff, and spoon hot oil over it. Turn the puri over and cook for another minute, or until it is golden brown. Remove the bread and drain it on a brown bag or other absorbent paper. With a little practice, you should be able to cook 2 pieces at a time. Serve hot.

Note: In India, a similar bread, called *chapati*, is cooked on a griddle instead of deep fried.

Whole Wheat Saltines

I love salty crackers with tomato soup, canned sardines, and other foods, and for this recipe I use a medium-grain sea salt. Anyone who lives in fear of salt can omit it.

1 cup whole berry wheat flour
$\frac{1}{4}$ cup fine cornmeal
$\frac{1}{2}$ cup butter or margarine
$\frac{1}{4}$ cup milk

1 teaspoon baking powder
$1/4$ teaspoon fine salt
sea salt

Preheat the oven to 375°F and butter a cookie sheet. Thoroughly mix and sift all the dry ingredients except the sea salt into a bowl. Cut in the butter, then add enough milk to make a stiff dough. On a floured surface, roll the dough, working slowly from the center out, to a thickness of $1/8$ inch. Sprinkle the dough with sea salt. Cut with a pizza wheel, knife, or cookie cutter into squares or other shapes. Prick each cracker several times with the tines of a fork. Bake in the center of the oven for 5 minutes. Turn with a spatula and bake for another 2 or 3 minutes, or until lightly browned on the bottom.

Whole Wheat Waffles with Pecans

This recipe works nicely with electric waffle irons and whole berry wheat flour. I usually use pecans in the recipe, but other nuts will work. Try English walnuts or hickory nuts if you've got them. Black walnuts may be a little too strong for some tastes.

2 cups whole berry wheat flour
$1 1/2$ cups milk
3 large chicken eggs, separated
$1/2$ cup melted butter or margarine
$3/4$ cup chopped pecans or other nuts
2 teaspoons baking powder
$1/2$ teaspoon salt

Separate the eggs and beat the whites until stiff; set aside. Preheat the waffle iron. Mix the flour, baking powder, and salt in a large bowl. In a smaller bowl, beat the egg yolks and mix in the milk and melted butter. Add to the dry ingredients, mixing well to moisten all the flour. Stir in the pecans. Fold in the beaten egg whites. Ladle or pour about $1/6$ of the mixture into the hot waffle iron, cooking until browned, 4 or 5 minutes. Cook the rest of the batch. Serve hot along with plenty of butter and a thick cane syrup or honey. Makes 6 or 7 waffles.

Pancakes from Scratch

Here's a hearty buttermilk pancake that can be made from scratch, using your own whole berry wheat flour.

71

1¼ cups whole berry wheat flour
1½ cups buttermilk
1 large chicken egg
1 tablespoon peanut oil
1 tablespoon sugar
1½ teaspoons baking soda
½ teaspoon salt

Mix the dry ingredients in a bowl. Whisk together the oil, buttermilk, and egg in a smaller bowl, pour over the dry ingredients, and stir until mixed—but don't stir too much. Heat a skillet or griddle over medium heat. Cook the pancakes, using no more than ¼ cup of batter for each one. Stack the cooked pancakes on a plate or serving platter. Serve with plenty of butter and honey or syrup.

Whole Flour Tortillas

These tortillas are easy to make, and freshly milled whole grain flour gives them an earthy flavor. I like to use the flour right out of the mill, with no sifting.

2 cups whole berry wheat flour
1 tablespoon lard or vegetable shortening
1 teaspoon baking powder
1 teaspoon salt
¾ cup warm water (110°F)

Mix the dry ingredients in a bowl and cut in the lard. Slowly mix in about ½ cup of warm water. Stir in more water, a little at a time, until the dough can be shaped into balls. Divide the dough into 12 parts, shaping each into a ball. Place each ball on a lightly floured bread board and roll into a 7-inch round. Then place each round into a hot cast-iron skillet or *cormal* and cook for about 1½ minutes on each side, until lightly browned but still supple. Stack and cover with a damp cloth until needed. For use as a bread at a Mexican meal, roll each tortilla and eat out of hand.

Note: I also make a sort of quick Mexican pizza with these. Preheat the oven broiler. Place a tortilla or two onto a flat baking sheet. Sprinkle with prepared tomato-based salsa. Sprinkle with sautéed bulk sausage and shredded cheddar cheese. Broil for a few minutes, until the cheese melts and the top browns nicely. Add diced mushrooms, pepperoni thins, and so on, as you like it.

WHOLE WHEAT LOAVES

Wyoming Ranch Bread

Here's a recipe from Mrs. Edgar T. Herring of Cheyenne, adapted from *Cooking in Wyoming* (a great regional cookbook). Mrs. Herring says the stone-ground whole wheat flour (used unsifted) can be purchased fresh from ranchers in the area.

3 cups whole berry wheat flour, unsifted, plus more for kneading
$^{1}/_{2}$ cup evaporated milk mixed with $^{1}/_{2}$ cup water
1 large chicken egg
2 tablespoons honey
1 tablespoon cooking oil
1 package dry yeast
1 teaspoon salt
$^{1}/_{3}$ cup warm water (110°F)

Beat the egg in a large bowl and stir in the honey, oil, milk-water mixture, and salt. Set the bowl aside until the ingredients reach room temperature. Preheat the oven to 315°F. Mix the yeast into the warm water. Add to the egg mixture, then stir in the flour with a wooden spoon, beating and stirring until you have a smooth dough. Cover the dough with a cloth and place the bowl in a warm place. Allow the dough to rise to almost—but not quite—double in volume. (If it rises too much, Mrs. Herring advises, the bread will be too coarse.) Spread some flour on a bread board and knead the mixture until smooth. (But not too long, Mrs. Herring advises.) Shape the dough into a loaf and place it in a loaf pan greased with 2 tablespoons of oil. Turn the loaf over to coat all sides with the oil. Cover again and let rise until not quite double in volume. Bake in the center of the oven for 40 minutes or until the bread is done. When done, it will sound hollow when tapped with the finger.

Bara Brith

This old recipe from Wales is similar to *barn brack* from Ireland. Both are speckled bread, so called because of the specks of currants and other dried fruits. This particular recipe calls for two kinds of raisins—soaked in black tea to soften them.

73

4 cups whole berry wheat flour
2 cups hot black tea
$1/2$ cup butter or margarine
$1/3$ cup dark brown sugar
6 ounces dark raisins
6 ounces golden raisins
1 tablespoon dry yeast
$1/2$ teaspoon ground nutmeg
salt to taste

In a large bowl, dissolve the sugar into the hot tea. Add the raisins and soak for 4 hours. Drain the fruit and measure out $1^1/4$ cups of the tea, adding warm water if needed to fill the measure. Warm the tea to between 110 and 115°F and put in a small bowl. Sprinkle on the yeast and set aside for 15 minutes. Combine the flour, salt, and nutmeg in a large mixing bowl. Cut in the butter and add the raisins. Make a well in the center of the flour. Pour in the yeast mixture and mix until you have a moist dough. Knead in the bowl until the dough loses its stickiness. Cover the dough with a clean cloth and leave it in a warm place for about 1 hour, until it doubles in size. Knead the dough again. Grease a loaf pan, then place the dough in the pan. Let rise for 20 minutes. While waiting, preheat the oven to 350°F. Bake the loaf for about an hour, or until a skewer inserted into the center of the loaf comes out clean. Turn the loaf out onto a wire rack and cool before slicing.

South African Bush Bread

This old recipe, adapted here from Gail Duff's *Bread*, calls for vinegar, an ingredient that shows up in several South African whole grain bush breads. The bread has a peculiar sweet-sour twang that is memorable. I'll take a slice hot with a little freshly churned butter smeared on it.

$3^1/2$ cups whole berry wheat flour
1 cup warm milk
$3/4$ cup warm water
$1/4$ cup vinegar
$1/4$ cup brown sugar
1 tablespoon dry yeast
1 tablespoon oil
1 teaspoon salt

Sprinkle the yeast into the warm water. Allow it 5 minutes to start working. Mix the flour, sugar, and salt in a large bowl. Beat in the yeast mix, milk, vinegar, and oil. Pour the batter into a loaf pan and put it in a warm place for $1^1/2$ hours, or until the batter rises to the top of the pan. Preheat the oven to 400°F. Bake in the center of the oven for 50 minutes, or until a skewer inserted into the center comes out clean.

Stone-Ground Whole Wheat Bread

If you enjoy a hearty loaf, and like to smell good bread baking, grind some wheat at home and try this recipe right away.

6 cups whole berry wheat flour
2 cups lukewarm water, divided
$1/3$ cup honey
3 tablespoons canola oil
2 packages dry yeast
$1^1/2$ teaspoons salt

Dissolve the yeast in $1/4$ cup of the warm water. Mix the honey, salt, oil, and the rest of the warm water. Combine with the yeast in a large bowl. Stir in the flour, mixing it well. Knead for 10 minutes. Place the dough into a bowl, cover, and let rise in a warm place for 1 hour, 45 minutes. Punch down. Let the dough rise again for about 45 minutes to an hour, until double in size. Punch down, shape into two loaves, and let rise until double in size. While waiting, preheat the oven to 350°F. Place the loaves in baking pans in the center of the oven and bake for 45 minutes, or until done.

Sourdough Farm Bread

Here's a dark bread recipe adapted from Don and Myrtle Holm's *The Complete Sourdough Cookbook*, where it was called North Dakota Farmer Bread. The Holms specify stone-ground wheat flour, and they advise us to use a lively sourdough starter.

6 cups whole berry wheat flour
1 cup lively sourdough starter
1 cup powdered skim milk
$1/2$ cup brown sugar

$1/4$ cup molasses
$2^1/2$ tablespoons cooking oil
2 teaspoons salt
1 package active dry yeast
2 cups warm water

Preheat the oven to 400°F. In a warm mixing bowl, dissolve the yeast in the water. Stir in the powdered milk, sugar, molasses, salt, cooking oil, and sourdough starter. Mix until well blended. Stir in the flour, making a nice dough. Knead 100 times on a floured board. Place the dough into greased bowl (warmed), cover with a cloth, set aside in a warm place, and let double in size. Divide the dough, shape into two loaves, and place in greased bread pans. Cover and let rise again. Brush the tops of the loaves with melted butter. Bake in the center of the oven for 30 to 45 minutes.

Irish Soda Bread

Here's one of the world's easiest breads, requiring no yeast. Most recipes call for white flour, or a mixture. Try it half-and-half—or go all the way with whole wheat flour, as I do.

2 cups whole berry wheat flour
1 cup buttermilk
1 chicken egg
1 tablespoon honey
1 teaspoon baking soda
1 teaspoon salt

Preheat the oven to 375°F. Mix together all the dry ingredients. Beat the egg, then stir in the buttermilk and honey. Pour the buttermilk mixture slowly into the dry ingredients, mixing with your hands as you go. Add a little more buttermilk or a little more flour if the dough is too hard or too soft. Turn the dough out onto a bread board. Knead for 5 minutes. Shape the dough into a rather flat, round loaf and put it onto a greased baking sheet. Sprinkle on a little more flour and cut a cross shape into the loaf, making the cut about $1/2$ inch deep. Put the baking sheet into the center of the oven. Bake for 25 to 35 minutes, or until the cuts have widened and the loaf is brown.

Note: Eat this bread within a few hours. If you don't, it will quite likely turn quite hard. Personally, however, I like it hard for dunking in coffee—and my dog, Nosher, is ready and willing to gnaw on a piece at any time.

Steamed Brown Breads

Brown Bread

Here's an old recipe for making bread without an oven. You will, however, need to rig a steamer of some sort. A cast-iron pot with a rack in the bottom will do. A pressure cooker can also be used (set at 15 pounds for 1 hour). For baking the loaves, use two 1-pound coffee cans or large baking powder cans. Cans with smooth sides work better. The traditional recipe calls for seedless raisins, as listed below, but chopped dates will also work and I like 'em better.

2 cups whole berry wheat flour
1 cup cornmeal
1 cup seedless raisins or chopped dates
1 cup milk
1¼ cups sorghum molasses
2 teaspoons baking powder
1 teaspoon salt
¼ teaspoon baking soda

Sift the flour, cornmeal, baking powder, baking soda, and salt. Add the raisins. Mix in the milk and molasses, stirring until you have a smooth batter. Pour half the batter into each of two well-greased cans. Put on a rack above a little water in a steamer pot. Cover the pot and steam for 3 hours, adding a little boiling water from time to time as needed.

See also Boston Brown Bread on page 106.

Sour Milk Brown Bread

This old recipe calls for steaming the bread in a mold, then drying the crust in the oven. Try it.

2 cups whole berry wheat flour
2 cups white stone-ground cornmeal
2 cups sour milk
1 cup molasses
1 teaspoon baking soda
1 teaspoon salt
water

Mix the meal, flour, soda, and salt. Add the sour milk and molasses, beating well. Add a little warm water if needed to make a dough. Grease a pail or other mold large enough to hold the dough in $2/3$ of its capacity. Place the dough into the mold and cover tightly. Rig for steaming. Place the pail or mold into or over the boiling water. Steam for 3 hours, adding more water as needed. Preheat the oven to 400°F. Remove the cover from the bread mold. Place it into the oven for 15 minutes to dry the crust.

See also Boston Brown Bread on page 106.

ROLLS AND BISCUITS

Whole Wheat Biscuits

Good white biscuits always go nicely with meat and gravy dishes, and are good for holding a slice of country ham. But for eating with butter and honey, these whole wheat creations are really hard to beat.

2 cups whole berry wheat flour
$2/3$ cup milk
$1/3$ cup vegetable oil
1 tablespoon baking powder
1 teaspoon salt

Preheat the oven to 350°F. Mix the flour, salt, and baking powder together in a large bowl. Add the milk and oil. Stirring with your hand, mix briefly but thoroughly. Roll the dough out on to a floured surface to a thickness of $1/2$ inch. Cut with biscuit cutters or cookie cutters. Place the cut biscuits into a cast-iron skillet, not quite touching, and bake in the center of the oven for 12 to 15 minutes.

Butte Creek Rolls

Here's a recipe adapted from Butte Creek Mills, where wheat is still ground by millstones powered by running water.

8 cups whole berry wheat flour
2 cups cold milk
1 pound butter or margarine
4 chicken eggs, beaten
$3/4$ cup brown sugar plus 2 tablespoons
$1/2$ cup warm water
2 tablespoons dry yeast
2 teaspoons salt

Dissolve the yeast and 2 tablespoons of brown sugar in the warm water. Set aside. Melt the butter and combine with the milk. Add the yeast mixture, eggs, salt, and the rest of the brown sugar. Slowly work in the flour—but do not knead. Refrigerate the mixture for 8 hours or overnight. Shape the mixture into 48 rolls (parker house or crescent type, or whatever you prefer). Let the rolls rise for an hour or two, until a dent remains when a roll is lightly touched. Preheat the oven to 350°F. Bake the rolls for 12 minutes, or until golden.

WHOLE WHEAT SWEETS

Miss Helen Spauling's Whole Wheat Pudding

Here's an old recipe, billed as economical and wholesome. It was submitted to the 1884 edition of *Boston Cooking School Cook Book* by Miss Helen Spauling, who adds that dates, figs, stewed prunes, or chopped apple instead of raisins make for an interesting variation.

2 cups whole berry wheat flour
1 cup milk
1 cup chopped raisins or ripe berries
$1/2$ cup molasses
$1/2$ teaspoon baking soda
$1/2$ teaspoon salt
thick cream or a pudding sauce

Mix the flour, baking soda, and salt in the top part of a double boiler. Stir in the milk, molasses, and raisins. Steam for $2^{1}/2$ hours. Serve with cream or a pudding sauce.

Festive Cookies

In the Jewish tradition, the Festival of Torah is called Shavuoth, which is also known as Feast of the Pentecost and Feast of Weeks. It also has roots in an ancient harvest festival, making use of fresh new-crop wheat and dried fruits, as in this recipe for cookies, adapted here from *The Jewish Festival Cookbook* by Fannie Engle and Gertrude Blair. I like to use walnuts or pecans in the recipe, but pine nuts or others can also be used.

2 cups freshly ground whole berry wheat flour
1 cup pitted dates

1 cup seedless raisins
$^2/_3$ cup brown sugar
$^1/_2$ cup chopped walnuts or other nuts
$^1/_2$ cup butter or margarine
$^1/_2$ cup milk
1 large chicken egg
2 teaspoons baking powder
1 teaspoon pure vanilla extract
$^1/_2$ teaspoon salt

Preheat the oven to 350°F. Take the butter, milk, and egg out of the refrigerator to warm to room temperature. Mince the nuts, dates, and raisins; set aside. Whisk the egg; set aside. Mix and sift the flour, baking powder, and salt; set aside. Whisk the butter until it is creamy. Beat the sugar into the butter a little at a time, then slowly whisk in the egg, milk, and vanilla. Stir the flour into the butter mixture. Drop the batter from a teaspoon onto a greased baking sheet, making about 3 dozen cookies. Bake in the center of the oven for 10 to 15 minutes, or until the cookies are done. Nosh away.

Note: I baked these cookies once with half palm sugar and half regular brown sugar. They were very good.

Whole Wheat Nutty Cookies

These cookies are very easy to make—and tasty. The nuts and seeds can be changed, depending on your preference and on what you have at hand. Instead of 1 cup pecans, for example, you might use $^1/_2$ cup walnuts and $^1/_2$ cup pine nuts.

$2^1/_2$ cups whole berry wheat flour
1 cup pecan pieces
1 cup sesame seeds
1 cup sunflower seeds
1 cup brown sugar
$^1/_2$ cup cane syrup
$^1/_2$ cup honey
2 large chicken eggs, well whisked
$^3/_4$ tablespoon freshly ground allspice
1 teaspoon salt
$^1/_2$ teaspoon baking soda

Mix all the ingredients in a large bowl, cover, and refrigerate for several hours or overnight. Preheat the oven to 325°F and grease a large cookie sheet. Drop teaspoonsfuls of the cookie batter onto the sheet, well spaced. Bake in the center of the oven for 10 to 12 minutes. Cook in several batches.

Gingersnaps

This old-time recipe has been adapted here from a brochure published by Kenyon Corn Meal Company, who claim that "Granny's Secret isn't secret anymore!"

2$1/2$ cups whole berry wheat flour
1 cup brown sugar, firmly packed
$3/4$ cup softened butter
$1/2$ cup molasses
white sugar (granulated)
1 chicken egg
1$1/2$ teaspoons baking soda
1 teaspoon ground ginger
$1/2$ teaspoon ground cinnamon
$1/2$ teaspoon ground cloves
$1/2$ teaspoon salt

Preheat the oven to 375°F. Mix the flour, baking soda, spices, and salt. In a large bowl, beat together the butter, egg, and brown sugar with an electric mixer until light and fluffy. Blend in the molasses. Stir in the flour mixture. Using a teaspoon, shape the mixture into balls. Roll each ball in granulated sugar and place them, 2 inches apart, on a greased cookie sheet. Bake for 8 minutes. While baking, the gingersnaps will flatten out. Remove the pan from the oven to cool.

Graham Crackers

Recipes for homemade graham crackers are hard to come by. I found this one in *Recipes from the Old Mill*, from which it has been adapted here. I find that it works nicely with home-ground or store-bought whole wheat flour. This *Old Mill* work specifies nonfat dry milk, but I confess to using regular dry milk.

3$1/2$ cups whole berry wheat flour
$3/4$ cup water
$1/2$ cup brown sugar
$1/3$ cup instant dry milk (see note above)
$1/4$ cup cooking oil
1$1/2$ teaspoons baking powder

$^{1}/_{2}$ teaspoon cinnamon (optional)
$^{1}/_{4}$ teaspoon salt

Mix all the dry ingredients in a large mixing bowl. Add the oil and water, mixing well. Chill the dough for 1 hour. When ready to proceed, preheat the oven to 375°F and lightly grease a cookie sheet or two. Dump the dough onto a floured bread board and divide into 3 equal parts. Roll each part on waxed paper until it is $^{1}/_{8}$ inch thick. Cut the sheet into 2-inch squares. Gently peel the squares off the wax paper and arrange on a cookie sheet. Prick 3 times with a 3-tined table fork. Bake in the center of the oven for 15 minutes, or until golden brown. Sprinkle with cinnamon if desired. Yields 60 graham crackers.

If you don't eat all of them while they are warm, place in an airtight plastic container for storage. I like to reheat these in a broiler, brushing them lightly with butter and sprinkling on a little extra brown sugar and cinnamon. These are great with coffee or tea.

Whole Wheat Cobbler

I cook this every spring, when the blackberries are ready in my neck of the woods. If you don't pick your own berries, use supermarket or farm market blackberries, dewberries, or similar fruit. Even canned berries will do.

2 cups blackberries
1$^{1}/_{2}$ cups whole berry wheat flour
1 cup milk
1 large chicken egg, whisked
$^{1}/_{2}$ cup honey
1$^{1}/_{2}$ tablespoons butter or margarine
1 teaspoon baking powder

Preheat the oven to 400°F. Melt the butter in an 8- by 10-inch Pyrex baking dish or a cobbler pan of suitable size. Mix in the flour, milk, honey, egg, and baking powder. Pour the mixture into the baking dish. Add the blackberries on top, evenly distributed. Bake in the center of the oven for 30 minutes.

Whole Wheat Pie Crust

These measures are for a 9- or 10-inch double crust, or for 2 single crust pies.

2 cups whole berry wheat flour
$^{1}/_{4}$ cup milk

¼ cup peanut oil
1 teaspoon salt

Bring all the ingredients to room temperature. Mix the salt and flour in a bowl. Add the oil and milk, mixing well to make a dough. Divide the dough in half. Place one half, nicely rounded, on a sheet of waxed paper. Top with another sheet of waxed paper. Roll out with a rolling pin until it is thin enough to cover the bottom and the sides of the pie pan. Roll the other half in the same manner to make a top crust.

SEMOLINA

This flour is made from hard durum wheat and is not given much coverage in most whole grain books simply because it is considered a commercial product. It is used mostly in making pasta. If you have a source of hard durum wheat and a hand grinder, experiment. Pasta is very easy to make. All you do is mix enough water with the semolina to make a thick dough. Roll out very thin and cut into strips. Cook in boiling water for a few minutes, or dry it for future use.

In any case, here are a couple of recipes to try.

Semolina Dumplings

These dumplings are cooked in boiling stock or soup. Then they are added to stews during the last few minutes of simmering; I am fond of cooking them in a pot of turnip greens. They are excellent in pot likker.

½ cup semolina
2 tablespoons lard, soft butter, or vegetable shortening
2 chicken eggs, whisked
salt to taste

In a suitable bowl, cream the butter, slowly adding in the semolina, egg, and salt. Let sit at room temperature for an hour or so. Using a teaspoon, place the dumplings into boiling soup or other liquid. Lower the heat and simmer for 15 minutes. Serve hot.

Semolina Soup with Mushrooms

Grain flour and ground seeds have been used in many cultures to thicken stews and soups, as well as gravies. Here's one from Austria. A good beef stock is recommended.

5 cups beef stock
8 ounces mushrooms, thinly sliced
2 ounces semolina
2 tablespoons butter or margarine
chopped chives
salt and pepper to taste

Brown the semolina in the butter. Add the mushrooms. Gradually stir in the stock and simmer for 30 minutes. Stir in a little salt and pepper to taste. Ladle the soup hot into bowls and sprinkle lightly with chopped chives.

OTHER WHOLE WHEAT RECIPES

Grape-Nuts from Scratch

I've always loved Grape-Nuts for breakfast, partly because they don't contain lots of air and because they stick with you until lunch. This homemade version is very good and a whole lot cheaper than the boxed cereal—and home-ground whole wheat flour, with a little barley, fits right into the scheme of things.

3 cups whole berry wheat flour
1/2 cup barley flour
2 cups buttermilk
3/4 cup brown sugar
1 teaspoon baking soda
1/2 teaspoon salt

Preheat the oven to 350°F. Mix all the ingredients in a large bowl, beating until smooth. Spread the dough on flat baking sheets or shallow pans, making it 1/4 inch thick. Bake for about 25 minutes. Remove the baking sheets and allow them to cool. Crumble and dry the cereal in the oven at 250°F, stirring from time to time. Then grind the cereal a little at a time with a 3/16-inch plate in a sausage mill. (A blender or food processor may work but tends to reduce the stuff to grits; if you want to try one instead of a more reliable sausage mill, hazard only one cup at at time.) Serve with whole milk, a little sugar or honey, and diced peaches, strawberries, blueberries, or perhaps morning-fresh wild blackberries.

Whole Wheat Egg Noodles

Traditionally, homemade noodles are often hung from the backs of straight chairs to dry. When rolled out thinly on a bread board, the dough can be cut into strips with the point of a sharp knife. Then the strips are draped over the chairs or perhaps over a portable clothes-drying rack. The dough can also be left on the board to dry, then cut.

3 or 4 cups whole berry wheat flour
3 medium chicken eggs
1 tablespoon milk
1 teaspoon salt
water

In a bowl beat together the eggs, milk, and salt. Slowly stir in enough of the flour until you have a stiff dough. Flour a bread board and turn the dough out. Knead in more flour, making a dough that can be rolled out. Roll the dough quite thin, cut into strips, and hang to dry. Cook in boiling water for a few minutes, until done to your liking.

Brown Gravy Flour

Home-ground flour that has been lightly browned makes a wonderful dark gravy. The flour can be browned as needed, or it can be stored in a jar for a few weeks. To make it, simply put a thin layer into a heavy skillet and brown on medium heat, stirring constantly. To make the gravy, mix the flour into a little cold water, making a paste, and stir it into the pan liquid. I sometimes put the flour and water into a small plastic bottle and shake it until well mixed.

Other Wheat Products

Several important kinds of pasta are made from wheat, and some of these are confused with cracked wheat. Generally, these are not products of the home mill, and are therefore not covered extensively in this book. Some other popular wheat products, such as wheat germ, are by-products of the milling process. Here is my take on what's what. See also the section above on Cracked Wheat.

Wheat Germ. Absolutely packed with nutrients—and surprisingly high in fiber—wheat germ is simply the embryo of the wheat berry. A by-product of large commercial milling operations, it is widely available these days. Packaged in sealed glass jars, it has a fairly good shelf life—until the seal is broken. After that, it should be refrigerated in tightly closed containers. The storage problem is caused by the high amount of oil in the germ, which is why it is removed from commercial flour in the first place.

Although there are recipes for using wheat germ, it is usually used as an additive to give a nutritional boost to baked breads, muffins, pancakes, piecrusts, and so on. The germ is usually available marketed in flaked form, either plain or toasted.

Wheat Bran. Although not as nutritionally packed as wheat germ, the bran, which is the several thin layers that surrounds the wheat berry, is still very healthy stuff, packed with soluble fiber. Wheat bran is made into cereal, such as All-Bran, and is sold in flaked form. Although it keeps much better than wheat germ, it still fares better under refrigeration. Use it in breads and cereals to increase their soluble fiber content.

Bulgur. This product, very important to the cuisines of some parts of the Middle East, is not simply cracked wheat. Prepared commercially, it is the wheat berry with part of the bran removed, precooked (usually steamed), dried, and cracked. It is available in fine, medium, and coarse sizes. Because it is precooked, bulgur can be eaten after merely soaking it in water. It is, however, usually cooked again before consumption. In some recipes, such as for a long-simmered soup, bulgur and cracked wheat are interchangeable. When cooking it, follow the directions on the package, or use it in Middle Eastern recipes such as tabbouleh, a salad made of bulgur, chopped scallions, fresh parsley, lemon juice, and olive oil.

Couscous. Whole books have been written about this staple of Morocco, Tunisia, and Algeria. It is essentially a commercial pasta—small and hard, which cooks into a fluffy mass—made from semolina flour. Making the pasta at home is really not very practical, and these days it is usually purchased ready-made, even in its homelands. The pasta is cooked in a two-tiered steamer called a *couscoussiere*. Always, the pasta is steamed in the top over a stew or broth, usually containing lamb or chicken. It can also be cooked over water or juice, but a meat broth really works better. The real stuff is often steamed over a meat broth colored with saffron and flavored with spices. Anyone interested in this old North African specialty—it's of Berber origin—should take a look at *The Great Book of Couscous*, by Copeland Marks.

Also note that we are seeing more and more small, hard pasta for sale, such as orzo, a rice-shaped Greek creation.

Nutritional Highlights

Wheat berries are high in protein, carbohydrates, B vitamins, and amino acids.

5

Spelt

*Farmers in and around the town of Salult grow spelt, and
the local patisserie offers pastries made with spelt flour.
They are light, buttery, and delicious.*

—Susan Herrman Loomis

An ancient grain mentioned in Exodus and Ezekiel, spelt is an ancestor of modern hybrid wheats and can be used in pretty much the same recipes, with a little adjustment. Although its exact relation to wheat has been debated, most archaeologists allow that the grain was cultivated as long as 9,000 years ago. It more or less lost out to wheat primarily because it is harder to thresh (owing to a tough outer coating), a difficulty overcome to some extent by modern mechanical devices. Actually, the tough hull, or husk, may be an advantage these days because it helps retain the nutrients after the harvest and protects the kernel from insects and pollutants. The grain also has a good shelf life.

At present, several varieties of spelt are cultivated in North America and the grain is becoming more widely available in the United States—and in Europe. It is called *farro* in Italy; *épeautre* in France; *dinkel* in Germany. In America spelt is marketed in berries, flour, and flakes, as well as in commercial breadstuff, cereal, and snacks.

⚛ Spelt Berries ⚛

In general, spelt can be used in any recipe that calls for wheat berries, and I like them especially in soups and stews. The whole berry has a chewy texture, even after long cooking, and a rich flavor.

Cooked Spelt

Spelt berries can be cooked and added to salads and stuffing as well as to soups and stews.

> 1 cup spelt berries
> 8 cups water
> salt to taste

Bring the water to a boil, add the berries, cover tightly, and simmer for $1\frac{1}{2}$ to 2 hours, or until done to your liking. Add a little salt to taste shortly before the end of the cooking period.

Note: Soaking the berries overnight, then cooking them in the soaking water will cut the cooking time in half.

Ancient Soup

This wonderful soup is a sort of chickpea puree with berries of spelt and barley. I have adapted the recipe from Raymond Sokolov's excellent work *With the Grain*. In addition to its taste, the soup has a nice texture, as Sokolov points out. The barley is soft and white; the spelt brown and a little chewy. All of the ingredients (except perhaps black pepper) were readily available to prehistoric Europeans. For perhaps a more authentic version, use some chopped wild onions or wild garlic. The recipe calls for a 15-ounce can of chickpeas. Use two cups of soaked and boiled chickpeas if you prefer.

> 1 can chickpeas (15-ounce size)
> $\frac{1}{2}$ cup spelt berries
> $\frac{1}{2}$ cup hulled barley
> 4 cups meat stock or water
> 1 large onion, chopped
> 2 cloves garlic, minced
> 1 tablespoon lard or olive oil
> salt and freshly ground black pepper to taste

Heat the lard or olive oil in a suitable pot. Sauté the onion and garlic until translucent. Add the chickpeas, the liquid from the can, and the meat broth. Bring to a boil, cover, and simmer for a few minutes. Pour the mixture through a strainer, separating the liquid from the solid. Zap the solid in a food processor until you have a puree with no chickpea or onion lumps. Put the puree and the liquid back into the original pot. Add the spelt berries and barley, bring to a boil, cover tightly, and simmer very slowly for 45 minutes or longer. Stir from time to time, and add some salt and pepper to taste. Serve hot in soup bowls, perhaps with a crusty flatbread or perhaps fried chickpea polenta (see chapter 16).

Apician Pudding

Spelt may have sustained the Roman legions, and our oldest extant cookbook, *Cookery and Dining in Imperial Rome* (usually attributed to an ancient culinary sport named Apicus) lists the grain as an ingredient in several recipes. The editor and translator of my edition of the book (Joseph Dommers Vehling) pointed out that the recipe below, one of the few desserts in the ancient work, makes a very good pudding, perfectly acceptable today with a little sweetening and some grated lemon zest for flavor. I suspect that instead of grated lemon Apicus would have used sumac, a spice popular in Imperial Rome and still in use in the Middle East. It can be purchased in spice outlets—and edible sumac berries can be gathered in very large quantities almost anywhere in North America. The early settlers used it as a substitute for lemon, and the Indians made a refreshing drink of it. The crushed berries can be used, but remember that the flavor comes from the tiny hairs on the berries. Hence, it is a mistake to wash the berries before using them; it's best to make an infusion by immersing the berries in water. Anyhow, Apicus didn't specify the amounts to use, so I'll dispense with the ingredients list.

Boil some spelt berries, pine nuts, and peeled almonds in a little water until very tender and mushy. Add some raisins, wine, and sumac, simmering a little longer. Serve in a round dish, sprinkled with chopped nuts and minced dried fruit.

Meatballs with Spelt Berries

Don't mistake the berries in this recipe as mere filler. They add a certain crunch and texture unknown to regular meatballs, or to those made with soft fillers. I specify beef in the ingredients list, but also try lamb shoulder or lean pork.

1 pound ground beef
1 cup cooked spelt berries (see recipe on p. 88)

1 cup plain yogurt
1 cup finely chopped onion
1 tablespoon chili powder
salt to taste
2 tablespoons peanut or olive oil

In a large cast-iron skillet, sauté the onion in oil until lightly browned. Put the onions in a bowl (leaving the oil in the skillet), then mix in the beef, chili powder, and salt. Stir in the spelt berries a few at a time. Shape the mixture into 16 meatballs of more or less equal size. Carefully fit the meatballs into the skillet, using the oil left from the onions. Add a little more oil if needed. Brown the meatballs on high heat, then reduce the heat and cook until done, turning each meatball from time to time. Remove the meatballs with tongs, placing them into a well-rounded serving bowl. Stir the yogurt into the skillet drippings, making a sauce. Pour the sauce over the meatballs and serve hot.

Spelt Flour

Spelt contains a gluten similar to wheat, making it suitable for risen breads. There is a little difference, however, and spelt is especially well suited for sourdoughs. In general, spelt dough should not be kneaded or beaten as long as wheat dough, and the mix should contain about 25 percent less liquid. Spelt flour is especially suited for pancakes and biscuits.

The flour should be stored in an airtight container in the refrigerator.

Spelt Loaf

I owe Arrowhead Mills (see Sources) for this recipe, and I would like to pass it on. They say to use either honey or molasses, but I'll have to add that honey is better, at least to me. I cook it with tupelo honey from the swamps near my place in the Florida panhandle.

4 or 5 cups spelt flour
1 1/2 cups warm water
2 tablespoons nonfat powdered milk
2 tablespoons honey or molasses
2 tablespoons vegetable oil
2 teaspoons active dry yeast
1 teaspoon sea salt (optional)

Dissolve the yeast in the water. Stir in the honey. Add the powdered milk, salt, oil, and half of the flour. Stir well and turn out onto a floured bread board.

Knead for 5 to 7 minutes, adding the rest of the flour as you go, until you have a smooth and elastic dough. Place the dough in an oiled bowl, turning over to coat all sides. Cover with a damp cloth and set in a warm place until the dough doubles in size. Punch it down, shape into a loaf, and place it into an oiled loaf pan. Let rise again for 30 minutes. While waiting, preheat the oven to 350°F. Bake in the center of the oven for 30 minutes, or until done.

Spelt Muffins

I like these muffins while still warm from the oven, along with a tall glass or two of cold milk.

$2^1/4$ cups spelt flour
$1^1/4$ cups milk
$1/4$ cup honey
$1/4$ cup chopped pecans
$1/4$ cup chopped almonds
$1/4$ cup chopped dates
$1/4$ cup chopped white raisins
3 chicken eggs, beaten
1 tablespoon canola oil
1 tablespoon baking powder
$1/2$ teaspoon salt

Preheat the oven to 425°F and grease some muffin tins or cups for 12 muffins. Mix the spelt flour, baking powder, and salt. Stir in the eggs, milk, oil, and honey. Into the batter stir the pecans, almonds, dates, and raisins. Fill the muffin cups about $2/3$ full. Bake in the center of the oven for 17 or 18 minutes, or until nicely browned.

Spelt Drop Biscuits

This recipe works nicely with home-ground spelt flour or commercial whole grain spelt flour.

2 cups spelt flour
1 cup buttermilk
1 tablespoon baking powder
$1/2$ tablespoon sugar
$1/4$ teaspoon finely ground sea salt

Preheat the oven to 425°F. Mix the flour, sugar, baking powder, and sea salt in a bowl. Stir in the buttermilk; blend well but do not overmix. Drop the batter in large spoonfuls onto a greased baking sheet, allowing some space between each drop; adjust the amount to make 12 or 13 biscuits. Bake in the center of the oven until browned lightly. I like these hot, topped with homemade fig preserves.

Spelt Tortillas

I eat these, rolled, with a thick chili con carne, or as bread for a Mexican meal or casserole. The same dough can be used for taco shells.

2 cups whole spelt flour
2 tablespoons lard or vegetable shortening
1 teaspoon baking powder
1 teaspoon salt
cool water

Mix the flour, baking powder, and salt. Cut in the lard and mix in enough cool water to make a stiff dough. Divide the dough into 12 balls of more or less equal size. Roll the balls out, one by one, on a floured bread board, or use a tortilla press if you've got one at hand. Roll the rounds out as thinly as possible. Heat a griddle, large skillet, or *comal* over medium heat. Cook each tortilla for about 2 minutes on each side. Serve warm.

Spelt Flakes

Sometimes available from health-food stores and by mail order, spelt flakes make a hearty breakfast cereal. It's best to follow the directions on the package, but in general stir 1 cup of spelt flakes into 2 cups of boiling water (slightly salted). Cook for 2 or 3 minutes, stirring. Serve hot in bowls. I'll take a pat or two of butter on mine.

Nutritional Highlights

Some health-food writers say that some people who are allergic or sensitive to wheat can eat spelt. This may or may not be the case, because spelt does contain gluten. Anyone who has a problem with wheat should consult a doctor before relying on spelt.

Spelt is 10 to 25 percent higher in protein than regular wheat. It is also a good source of fiber, B complex vitamins, and carbohydrates.

6

QK-77

*The humpbacked wheat berry of remarkable size
and intriguing history.*

—Anderson DuPree

It does make a good story. In 1949 a U.S. airman stationed in Portugal was given 36 large, humpbacked wheat berries. They were, he was told, gathered from a stone box in an excavated tomb near the pyramids of Saqqara. The airman sent them by mail to his father, a wheat farmer in Montana. The farmer planted them—and 32 germinated. Within a few years he had 1,500 bushels of the stuff. Because the grain was so unusual, it was billed at a county fair as "King Tut's Wheat." But it wasn't more than a novelty and was fed to cattle—which says a lot about American eating habits. Before long it was all but forgotten.

Some years later, an agricultural scientist, Bob Quinn, who had seen the large berries at the fair, started searching for some seed in the homes and barns of rural Montana. He and his father, Mack, a wheat farmer, found a pint jar full of mixed berries. From this treasure they selected only large humpbacked kernels, hoping to retain a pure strain. They planted some in a garden, gaining more seed. With commercial intent, they came up with the word "Kamut," which they believed to be the ancient Egyptian word for wheat, and coined it as a trademark. It is currently registered by a company called Kamut International, which complicates the use of the term in recipes and by the letter of the law requires the insertion of the registered trademark symbol ® after the word. Well, to hell with 'em. I'll call the stuff QK-77, as it is officially dubbed by the United States Department of Agriculture.

Also, the story may not be true. The tomb connection has been discredited, or at least questioned, on the grounds that mummified wheat does not germinate. Some scientists believed that instead, the wheat survived on some remote farm plot in Egypt or Asia Minor until recent times, isolated from other wheats. Even so, its exact taxonomic classification is under scientific debate. The consensus seems to place it as an ancient durum wheat, and some scientists believe it survived among groups of people that gathered wild wheat, long before King Tut.

All we really know for sure is that the large berry exists—and that the culinary world has indeed found a treasure. Dozens of manufacturers now use the wheat in hundreds of products. It is also sold in whole berry, as flour, pasta, and so on.

Whole QK-77 Berries

Appreciating the story, I usually bill the large berry as Ancient Egyptian wheat or perhaps King Tut wheat when I serve it to my guests in salads and pilaf. By whatever name, it is my favorite berry for noshing (unless we count the chickpea, which isn't really a grain), especially when cooked in a beef or chicken stock. I like to keep a bowl of cooked QK-77 in the refrigerator, eating a spoonful from time to time and using the rest in salads and quick soups. It's so easy, for example, to heat a can of cream of celery soup and add half a cup of precooked QK-77 berries.

The cooked berries have an interesting al dente quality and a smooth, buttery flavor. I am especially fond of putting a few cooked berries in a stir-fry, where their large size makes them an interesting mystery ingredient.

Cooked QK-77

I like QK-77 berries merely simmered in water or stock, but they can be soaked overnight to shorten the cooking time somewhat. Although some cooks prefer to add the salt after the grain has been cooked, I like to add it to the water or stock (if needed).

1 cup QK-77 berries
4 cups water or stock
salt to taste

Bring the water to a boil, add the QK-77 and salt, cover, reduce the heat, and simmer for 45 to 60 minutes, depending on the texture desired. Drain off any surplus liquid. Serve immediately as a side dish, or use in other recipes that call for wheat berries.

Yield: 1 cup dry berries makes about 2 cups, if fully cooked.

QK-77 and Bacon

This simple dish can be cooked with wheat, spelt, or rye—but the large QK-77 berries work better.

1 cup QK-77 berries
2 cups chicken stock
1 cup water
$1/2$ pound thick sliced bacon
1 large onion, diced
2 cloves garlic, minced
2 tablespoons minced fresh parsley
$1/2$ tablespoon minced fresh thyme
salt and pepper to taste

Cut the bacon crosswise into $1/4$-inch strips. (This is best accomplished by chilling or partly freezing a pack of thick sliced bacon, then cutting across the slices.) Brown the bacon in a stove-top Dutch oven or suitable pot. Drain on absorbent paper. Pour off the bacon drippings, leaving about 2 tablespoons in the skillet. Sauté the onion, garlic, and parsley for about 5 minutes. Add the QK-77 berries and cook for another 5 minutes, stirring a few times. Add the chicken stock, water, thyme, salt, and pepper. Bring to a boil, cover, reduce the heat, and simmer for 30 to 40 minutes, until the grain is tender (but still somewhat chewy) and has absorbed most of the liquid. Remove the pot from the heat and let sit for 10 to 15 minutes. Drain off any remaining liquid. Stir in the bacon pieces and serve hot as a side dish. With some bread and a large tossed salad with plenty of vine-ripened tomatoes, I can make a meal of this dish.

QK-77 Soup

I use beef and frozen vegetables for this soup, which is cooked all day in a Crock-Pot. Leftover or canned vegetables can be used, but they tend to be mushy. Along with the frozen vegetables, I use a can of tomatoes, fresh mushrooms, and other ingredients as available and if fitting.

2 pounds beef, cubed
$1/2$ pound smoked pork sausage, cut into 1/2-inch wheels
2 packages frozen soup vegetables (16-ounce size)
1 can tomatoes (16-ounce size)
fresh mushrooms
1 cup beef or chicken stock
$1/2$ cup dry red wine
$1/2$ cup QK-77 or regular wheat berries
$1/4$ cup dry chickpeas (optional)
$1/4$ cup dry pozole (optional)
2 cloves garlic, minced
1 tablespoon tapioca
1 tablespoon dried parsley
salt to taste
freshly ground black pepper to taste

Put all the ingredients into a Crock-Pot, ending with the mushrooms. It's best to fill the Crock-Pot all the way to the top, so have plenty of mushrooms on hand if needed. Cook on low heat for 8 or 9 hours. Stir every 2 hours or so, adding a little wine or stock if needed. Serve hot with plenty of crusty bread and the rest of the red wine. I like to top my bowl with a few twists of black pepper from the mill.

Leftovers can be frozen.

QK-77 Flour

QK-77 flour is marketed in health-food shops and by mail-order outfits, and more and more it is making its way into our supermarkets in cereals and breads. The large berry grinds easily in a small mill, and the resulting whole grain flour keeps better than regular whole wheat because the grain contains less moisture. In fact, the grain itself stores better than regular wheat (which might help explain how it survived in the tomb, if that was the case). Because it contains gluten, the flour can be used for making risen breads. It also makes excellent pasta, and, in fact, some scientists believe it to be an Ancient Egyptian variety of durum.

Coarse, Cracked, and Flaked QK-77

QK-77 makes good couscous and bulgur, and it is also available in a quick-cooking flaked form. Generally, the flaked form can be used as a cereal simply by cooking it in water, stirring constantly with a wooden spoon until done, or by following the directions on the package. Bulgur and couscous are discussed in chapter 4, Wheat, and are reflected in the recipe below.

Anyone with a home mill can experiment with grinding the large berries on a coarse setting, then using the grits like cracked wheat. Frankly, I prefer to use QK-77 whole, as a berry. That's where it really stands out, helped along by its history.

QK-77 and Lamb Stew

This old recipe makes a festive stew that was enjoyed along the Mediterranean coast of North Africa, but I can't really claim that the original was made with QK-77. The grain used in the recipe is kin to both couscous and bulgur, or kasha, and it can be approximated at home with coarsely milled whole berries.

1 cup coarse QK-77 meal or fine grits
1 pound ground lamb or mutton
2 cups water
1/2 cup red wine
1/2 cup diced onion
1/2 cup diced celery, including part of tops
1/2 cup raisins
2 tablespoons honey
2 tablespoons olive oil
salt to taste

Bring the water to a boil. In a skillet, heat the grain, stirring constantly with a wooden spoon, until it is browned lightly. Add the salt and boiling water, cover, lower the heat, and steam for half an hour. Put the grain into a baking dish of suitable size. Preheat the oven to 350°F. Heat the olive oil in the skillet and sauté the onion and ground lamb, stirring until browned. Add the meat to the grain, mixing well. Bake in the center of the oven for 45 minutes, adding a little water as needed to keep the stew wet. Serve hot.

Ferique with QK-77

A number of dishes in the Middle East are prepared with whole wheat berries. This Egyptian variation, adapted here from *A Book of Middle Eastern Food*, by Claudia Roden, goes back to a medieval text by one al-Baghdadi. It could well have been made with QK-77. The recipe calls for a calf's foot, a rather unusual ingredient in modern American cookery. I will allow 2 trotters (available in super-markets these days), although I don't have Ms. Roden's permission to do so.

> 1 large chicken
> 1 calf's foot (or two pig trotters)
> $^1/_2$ pound QK-77 berries
> 6 chicken eggs (shells intact)
> 3 tablespoons olive oil
> 1 to 2 teaspoons turmeric
> salt and freshly ground black pepper to taste
> 1 quart water

Put the chicken into a pot with about a quart of water to cover. Add the calf's foot (well scraped) or trotters, along with the chicken eggs and the rest of the ingredients. Bring to a boil, reduce the heat to very low, cover, and simmer for 3 to 4 hours, adding a little water from time to time if needed. Bone the chicken and calf's foot, putting the meat back into the pot. Remove the chicken eggs, peel them, and return them to the pot. (The eggs, after such long cooking, will have a creamy texture and a pale yellow color.) Cook for another 10 minutes. Add more salt or pepper if needed. Serve hot in soup bowls.

Nutritional Highlights

Studies have shown that QK-77 has a higher nutritional value than the average common wheat. It is especially high in protein, total lipids, and complex carbo-hydrates. It is truly a high energy grain. QK-77 contains gluten, but it may be less allergenic than that found in other wheats. (People who are allergic to gluten, however, should consult with their doctor before relying on QK-77.) In general, QK-77 is a superior grain—except in one regard. Owing to the large size of its berry, the grain (on a per pound basis) contains less bran and fiber than common wheats.

7

Triticale

A groat of great savor and substance.

—Waverley Root

What do you get when you cross the scientific name for wheat, Triticum, with that of rye, Secale? Triticale, of course. Efforts to develop such a hybrid grain started a century ago in Scotland and continued for many years without much success. The goal was to produce a cereal grain with the bread-making qualities and high yields of wheat and the stamina and disease resistance of rye. The researchers have achieved some success in recent years, and agricultural development continues. We can only hope, from a culinary viewpoint, that they don't breed out triticale's flavor—more pronounced than modern wheat but not as strong as rye.

Although triticale will grow in less than ideal conditions, its production to date has been mostly in areas with highly developed agriculture. Today, most of the world's production is in the United States, Canada, Europe, Argentina, and Australia. Since triticale can double as a grazing crop and a grain crop—and will produce in rather marginal agricultural lands—it may have much potential in developing countries.

In any case, a large market for triticale simply has not yet developed in North America. What's lacking is public demand and marketing structure. At present, triticale is used mostly as a minor ingredient in multigrain products for mass distribution and in the health-food market, where the grain's berries, flakes, and flour are sold.

~ Triticale Berries ~

These resemble wheat and can be used in many recipes that call for wheat berries. Triticale does, however, take longer to cook, making it unsuitable for quick soups and stews unless it is precooked, as in the next recipe. For longer simmering, the berries can simply be added to soups and stews.

Basic Triticale

Cooked triticale berries can be used in pilaf, salads, and soups, substituted freely for wheat or rye. Here is the basic recipe.

1 cup triticale berries
water
salt to taste

Place the berries in a nonmetallic container, cover with water, soak overnight at room temperature. Drain the berries and add to 1 cup of water, along with a little salt. Bring to a boil, reduce the heat, cover, and simmer for 40 minutes, or until done to your liking. Drain, cool, cover, and refrigerate until needed. Cooked berries will keep for several days in the refrigerator. Note, however, that freezing and thawing will break down the grain's texture and rob it of flavor.

A. D.'s Pot Roast with Triticale Berries

I cook this dish several times a year, sometimes using stew meat instead of a roast. It can be cooked in a regular pot or stove-top Dutch oven, but a regular Crock-Pot, with the heating elements in the sides, is ideal. The triticale berries give a good flavor to this dish, and help make an unusual gravy. I sometimes use a few strong wild onions in the recipe, chopping the green tops like chives.

beef roast, about 5 pounds
1 cup uncooked triticale berries
1 can cream of celery soup
1 medium onion, chopped
fresh mushrooms
2 or 3 jalapeños
salt to taste

Place the triticale berries in the bottom of a regular Crock-Pot. Add the meat, jalapeños, and onion. Dump in the soup and top with fresh mushrooms, filling all the way to the top. Sprinkle with a little salt. Cook on low heat for 8 or 9 hours. Serve the meat hot with vegetables, rice, and a crusty bread. (The beef will probably cook apart and will be difficult to slice; if so, serve it in chunks.) Spoon the gravy and triticale berries over the rice.

Flakes

To make flakes, triticale berries are cut into pieces, steamed, rolled, and dried. The resulting flakes can be cooked pretty much like rolled oats. To cook as a breakfast cereal, follow the directions on the package.

Flour

Triticale flour is sometimes available in health-food stores and by mail order, and, of course, anyone who has a grain mill can easily grind triticale berries at home. Triticale has more gluten than rye—but not as much as most wheats. If you want a nicely risen bread, try mixing triticale with special high-gluten wheat flour; also remember that dough containing triticale doesn't require much kneading. For heavier loaves and flatbreads, experiment.

Triticale gives us a new culinary playing field, and the rules of the game have not yet been set. Even now agricultural researchers are busy developing new varieties of triticale, looking for better bread-making qualities.

Buttermilk Waffles

I love waffles for breakfast, and this recipe hits the spot.

3/4 cup whole berry triticale flour
3/4 cup all-purpose wheat flour
1 1/2 cups buttermilk
3/4 cup melted butter or margarine
milk (if needed)
3 chicken eggs
2 tablespoons sugar
2 teaspoons baking powder

¾ teaspoon baking soda
¾ teaspoon salt

Heat the waffle irons. Mix the flours, baking powder, baking soda, sugar, and salt. Beat the eggs in a large bowl and stir in the buttermilk and butter. Stir in the flour mixture, adding a little milk if the batter seems too thick. Spoon the batter into the waffle irons. (This should make 6 waffles or more, depending on the size of your irons.) Cook until crisp and golden. Serve hot with butter and honey.

Nutritional Highlights

Triticale contains more protein than either wheat or rye, and it has a better balance of amino acids. It is especially high in lysine.

8

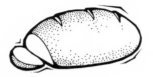

Rye

*The everyday brown bread of Northern Europe was made,
sometimes with the addition of pea flour and a little barley,
predominantly from rye.*

—Reay Tannahill

At one time during man's agricultural history, rye was considered an undesirable weed that sometimes got mixed in with the wheat crop. When the wheat crop failed, the intrusive rye sometimes saved the season. Somewhere in a cold, harsh land, maybe Siberia, farmers started sowing a little rye along with the wheat just to ensure that a grain crop of some sort would grow. The emphasis here was on protein, not a white, airy loaf of bread, and the two grains were no doubt mixed during the harvesting and milling operations. The next step was to plant rye separately, possibly so that the ratio of wheat to rye could be controlled.

Rye became popular in some northern areas for making hearty breads and brewing whiskey, and it was very, very important to some peoples because it grows where ordinary wheat won't. This was the case in early New England (before the colonists learned to grow wheat successfully in the new land) and in parts of Northern Europe. Although related to wheat, rye has less gluten. Today the grain is available commercially as berries, flour, flakes, and grits.

People who raise and grind their own grain should know that rye can contain a parasitic fungus disease called ergot. (Actually, ergot can infest other grains, but it grows best in damp, cold climates—rye country.) When baked in bread some ergot can convert to LSD—which, it has been suggested, might explain Salem's 1692 witch trials. LSD or not, ergotism can cause "fits," visions, nausea, blindness, along with other symptoms, and even death, especially in children. Fortunately, rye berries and rye flour purchased at markets these days can be assumed to be quite safe to eat, thanks in part to better harvesting and storage methods. Just remember that ergotism turns flour red.

Historically, the center of rye-bread making was in Scandinavia, Germany, Russia, and Central Europe. The best of these breads—the sourdough ryes—were far from being peasant fare. Today, most of the rye bread sold in American deli shops and supermarkets is really wheat bread with a little rye added for color and flavor, and perhaps topped with caraway or fennel seeds; and most of the recipes for pumpernickel and black breads found in our family cookbooks are, more often than not, made mostly with wheat. Anyone who wants to try the real stuff will find use in a recipe or two below, and should take a look at *The Great Scandinavian Baking Book*, by Beatrice Ojakangas, to which I stand shoulder-deep in debt. One of the most interesting of the rye breads, *rugbraud*, is still made on a large scale in Iceland. It is steamed geothermally, thanks to the hot-spring areas of that barren land. Another interesting bread (Finnish hapanleipä) was baked in rather flat, round loaves with a hole in the center, permitting it be baked in quantity and stacked on poles for storage.

Rye Berries

Somewhat surprisingly, rye berries have a mild flavor and can be used in most recipes that call for wheat berries, which they resemble in size and appearance. (The same can't be said of rye flour, however, because of the difference in gluten content and more pronounced flavor.) Try uncooked rye in soup and stew recipes that require long simmering, and try precooked berries in salads, pilafs, and stuffings.

Bulk rye berries should be stored in an airtight container, preferably in the refrigerator.

Basic Rye Berries

Rye berries cook a little quicker than wheat or triticale. Consequently, they are not usually soaked in water overnight.

    1 cup rye berries
    4 cups water
    1 teaspoon salt

Bring the water to a boil. Rinse and drain the rye berries, add them to the pot along with the salt, cover, lower the heat, and simmer for about 50 minutes, or until softened to your liking—usually al dente is best. Drain, cool, and use as needed in salads, pilafs, and other dishes. Makes about 3 cups.

Note: Toasting rye berries before cooking tends to bring out a bitter flavor.

Easy Beef and Rye Berry Stew

Many recipes call for cooking grain berries whole, then draining and adding them to the stew or soup. I prefer to cook it all together, getting the full flavor of the grain. Any suitable grain can be used, and rye is perfect. Any reasonable cut of beef can be used, but I confess to being fond of chuck steak, which contains more fat than flank or round. Suit yourself. For convenience and to minimize waste, I usually make this stew with frozen vegetable mixes. The stew mixes contain rather large chunks, as compared to the finer dice of soup mixes. Either can be used, or you can, of course, make your own mix from fresh or frozen vegetables.

    2 pounds beef, trimmed and cut into bite-sized chunks
    2 packages frozen stew vegetables (16-ounce size)
    1 can tomatoes (14$^1\!/_2$-ounce size)
    8 ounces fresh button mushrooms
    6 cups beef stock (or bouillon dissolved in water)
    $^1\!/_2$ cup rye berries, rinsed
    salt and pepper to taste

Bring the stock or water to a boil in a pot of suitable size. Add the beef and rye berries, cover, and simmer for an hour. (Check from time to time to see if more water is needed.) Add the rest of the ingredients, bring to a new boil, reduce the heat, cover, and simmer for 20 to 30 minutes. Serve hot in bowls or perhaps with a dollop of rice in a soup plate.

⪻ Rye Flour ⪼

Commercial rye flour, available in light, medium, and dark, is almost always used as a supplement to wheat flour. Rye does contain gluten, however, and all-rye flour will indeed make risen bread. But it will be heavy and flatter than most wheat breads because the gluten is not of the right sort. Also, dough made with rye flour is sticky and difficult to work. Rye bread also has a stronger flavor, which, together with its density, makes it quite filling and satisfying—unless you're expecting something light and airy.

In any case, some of the recipes below are designed to be used with home-ground whole rye either on its own or mixed with whole wheat flour as specified. Note that bread made with rye flour tends to keep longer than most other breads. Hence its use in hardtack and other "journey" breads. Rye flour (and berries) keep pretty well, but it's best to store them in the refrigerator.

Boston Brown Bread

Here's a Colonial recipe calling for graham flour (whole wheat), rye flour, and cornmeal, a common mix in those days, partly because wheat was in short supply. Bostonians ate this bread for Sunday morning breakfast, along with codfish balls and baked beans. The original calls for sour milk, but I make mine with buttermilk from the supermarket.

1 cup rye flour
1 cup whole wheat flour
1 cup stone-ground cornmeal
2 cups sour milk or buttermilk
1 cup raisins
3/4 cup molasses
1 teaspoon baking soda
1 teaspoon salt
water

Sift the flour, cornmeal, and salt. Mix the baking soda in a little water, then stir it into the molasses and sour milk. Stir the flour mixture into the liquid. Dust the raisins with flour, then fold them into the batter. Pour the mixture into two greased tin molds, until 2/3 full. Cover tightly with a lid, tying the lid down with string so that the bread will not push it off as it rises. Place the molds on a rack in a large pot of boiling water. The water should come halfway around the molds. Cover the pot and steam for 3 hours, adding more water from time to time. Remove the molds and cool down. De-mold the brown bread and slice it with a string.

Rye Mush

Here's an old recipe from Early America, sometimes used as a food for the sick or invalid, at a time when rye was more common than it is today. But it's just as nourishing now as then.

1 cup rye flour
1 teaspoon salt
4 cups water plus more for paste

Add a little water to the rye flour, making a paste. Bring 4 cups of water to a boil. Add the salt and slowly pour in the rye paste. Cook for 20 minutes, stirring as you go. Serve with either heavy cream or molasses, or both.

New York Pumpernickel

This recipe has been adapted from an old editon of *The New York Times Cook Book*, edited by Craig Claiborne. It calls for whole wheat flour mixed with rye, making it ideal for whole grain buffs, whereas many other recipes for pumpernickel and other rye breads call for the addition of white flour.

6 cups rye flour (preferably a coarse grind)
2 cups whole wheat flour (approximate measure)
2 cups mashed potatoes (cooled)
3/4 cup cornmeal (I use white only)
3 1/4 cups water
1 package yeast
2 tablespoons shortening
1 1/2 tablespoons salt
1 tablespoon sugar
1 tablespoon caraway seeds

Boil 1 1/2 cups of water in a suitable pan. In a small bowl, stir 1 1/2 cups of cold water into the cornmeal. Add the cornmeal mix to the boiling water; boil until thick, stirring as you go with a wooden spoon. Stir in the shortening, salt, sugar, and caraway seeds. Set aside until it cools to lukewarm. While waiting, add the yeast to a 1/4 cup lukewarm water. Add the potatoes and yeast water to the cornmeal mix. Stir in the rye flour and enough of the whole wheat flour to make a stiff dough. Place the dough onto a bread board, lightly floured, and knead until the dough is elastic and does not stick to the board. Place the dough in a large greased bowl, turning to grease the surface. Cover with a towel and put in a warm place until the dough doubles in volume. Preheat the oven to 375°F. Divide the dough into three equal loaves. Place the loaves in greased loaf pans, grease the tops, cover with a towel, and let rise until double in volume. Bake for about 1 hour, or until done. Let cool on a rack.

An All-Rye Bread

If the recipes above leave one with a yearning for the taste of rye, here's a recipe to try. It has been adapted here from *Cooking with Wholegrains*, by Mildred Ellen Orton. It was written with whole-grain rye flour in mind, and is perfect for home-ground rye, duly sifted.

$4^1/2$ cups rye flour
2 cups milk
1 tablespoon shortening or lard
1 package yeast ($^1/4$-ounce size) dissolved in $^1/4$ cup lukewarm water
2 teaspoons salt

Heat the milk and shortening to scalding in a saucepan. Add the salt. Let cool. When lukewarm (about 110°F) add the dissolved yeast. Sift enough rye flour to make $4^1/2$ cups. Sift again directly into the liquid, stirring in enough to make a stiff but sticky dough. Stir for 4 or 5 minutes, folding the dough into itself. Cover and place in a warm place for about 2 hours. Punch down and turn out onto a bread board sprinkled with rye flour. Knead for 10 minutes, until the dough feels springy. Shape the dough into 2 loaves on a baking sheet and set in a warm place until double in size. Preheat the oven to 300°F and place a pan of hot water beneath the rack. Place the bread pan directly over the hot water. Bake for $1^1/2$ hours.

Whole Rye Biscuits

Here's a dark, heavy breakfast biscuit that sticks with you during a hard morning's work.

2 cups whole grain rye flour (unsifted)
1 cup whole milk
3 tablespoons melted butter or margarine
1 teaspoon salt
1 teaspoon cream of tartar

$^1/_2$ teaspoon baking soda
wheat flour

Preheat the oven to 475°F and flour a bread board with a little wheat flour. Mix and sift the rye, baking soda, salt, and cream of tartar. Sift again. Stir in the melted butter or margarine and about one cup of milk, or just enough to make a biscuit dough. Beat for 1 minute. Turn the dough out onto the bread board and roll it out to a thickness of $^1/_2$ inch. Cut the dough with a biscuit cutter, placing the rounds on a cookie sheet. Bake in the center of the oven for 12 minutes, or until nicely browned. Serve hot or warm.

Rye Sticks with Amaranth

For this recipe I stand in debt to Arrowhead Mills, who published a similar version in a brochure about amaranth. These sticks are good stuff, easily made with whole kernel home-ground rye or with packaged rye flour. Arrowhead specifies nonfat dry milk, but I use whole dry milk. To follow the recipe directions, you'll need some device for spraying water. A thoroughly rinsed glass-cleaner dispenser will do.

$3^1/_4$ cups rye flour
$^1/_2$ cup amaranth flour
$1^1/_2$ cups warm water (110°F to 115°F)
1 package active dry yeast ($^1/_4$-ounce size)
1 tablespoon dry milk
1 tablespoon molasses
1 teaspoon caraway seeds
sesame seeds
$^1/_2$ teaspoon sea salt, finely ground

Preheat the oven to 425°F. In a bowl, dissolve the yeast in the warm water. Stir in the molasses, dry milk, salt, and caraway seeds. Stir in the flours, making a dough, and knead for 5 minutes. Divide the dough exactly in half; then halve each half; repeat until you have 36 pieces. Roll each piece into a 5-inch stick. Roll each stick in sesame seeds and place on a greased baking sheet; repeat for the rest of the pieces. Spray the sticks lightly with water. Bake for 18 to 20 minutes, until lightly browned. Serve warm or cold.

Rye Popovers

Whole grain rye flour makes a good popover, or you can use a combination of wheat and rye. Part of the secret is in using a popover or muffin pan in a very hot oven. The heat seals the surface of the dough, and the steam inside causes the dough to rise, popping over the top of the pan cavity.

> **1 cup whole rye flour (sifted measure)**
> **1 cup milk**
> **2 chicken eggs**
> **1 tablespoon lard or vegetable shortening**
> **salt to taste**

Preheat the oven to 500°F and grease muffin tins or popover pans. Beat the chicken eggs, then mix in the milk and shortening. Combine the salt and sifted rye flour; then beat it in with the liquid, working it for about 2 minutes. Pour some batter into each popover tin cavity, filling a little more than half. Bake for 10 minutes. Lower the heat to 350°F and bake for 20 minutes. (Do not peek; opening the oven door may cause the popovers to fall.) Remove the pan and serve the popovers hot, perhaps with butter and homemade strawberry jam.

Kalakukko

This Finnish dish is made with a rye loaf stuffed with fish and pork, or with other ingredients such as (believe it or not) diced rutabaga. There are many variations of the dough, some using yeast. I have reduced it to the basics, but I have changed the fish from fresh sardines or other small, fatty fish to fish fingers cut from boneless fillets. Sometimes I use salt pork and omit the salt from the recipe. I have also used a small-link pork sausage. Suit yourself.

> **4 cups rye flour**
> **1 pound boneless fish fillets**
> **$^1/_2$ pound pork belly or jowls**
> **$^1/_4$ cup melted lard, bacon drippings, or vegetable oil**
> **water**
> **salt and pepper to taste**

Slice the pork into thin slices, removing the rind in the process. Cut the fillets into fingers. In a large bowl, mix the rye and salt with enough water to make a dough. Knead the dough on a floured board until it is smooth. Let it rest for an hour or so. Preheat the oven to 400°F. Save out a little of the dough and roll the rest out into a 12-inch round. Layer the pork and fish fingers (like stove wood) in the center of the dough, sprinkling each layer with salt and black pepper. Bring the edges of the dough together, covering the mound. Fold over the edges and seal with pinches. Carefully place the loaf onto a baking sheet and shape the loaf as needed. Use the reserved dough to reinforce any weak spots. Set aside for 30 minutes. Place the loaf into the center of the oven for 10 minutes. Turn the heat down to 300°F and bake for about 4 hours, basting from time to time with melted lard, or until the loaf is nicely browned. Remove the pan from the oven and let it set for 10 minutes. To serve, break the crust into pieces. Serve the pieces alongside the fish and pork.

Hardtack

A favorite of seagoing folk, hardtack goes nicely in a New England fish chowder. Here's an old Swedish recipe made with a combination of rye and oats, both of which produce breadstuff with long shelf life.

3 cups freshly ground rye flour
1 cup oat flour
1 cup oatmeal
3 cups buttermilk
1/2 cup vegetable oil
1/2 cup honey
1/4 cup warm water (110°F)
1 tablespoon dry yeast granules
2 teaspoons sea salt

Mix the yeast into the water until it bubbles. Add the buttermilk, honey, oil, salt, oatmeal, and oat flour, mixing well. Work in enough rye flour to make a stiff dough. Roll the dough out cracker-thin, then cut it into squares or rounds. Place the crackers onto greased cookie sheets and set in a warm place to rise. Preheat the oven to 350°F. Prick each cracker several times with the tines of a fork, then bake in the center of the oven for 8 to 10 minutes, or until slightly browned. Cool and store in a closed container until needed. Then reheat them until crisp. Hardtack can be frozen and reheated as needed.

Sourdough Rye

Rye makes a wonderful sourdough—really sour, if that's what you yearn for. It's best to make a sourdough sponge, then proceed with the loaves. This recipe, adapted from Beatrice Trum Hunter's *The Family Whole Grain Baking Book*, calls for both sourdough and brewer's yeast, which can be obtained from bakery and brewery supply outlets.

The Sourdough Sponge

1 cup rye flour
1 cup warm water
$^{1}/_{2}$ tablespoon dry yeast granules

The Loaves

20 cups rye flour
2 cups sourdough sponge
6 cups warm water
1 cup dry milk
$^{1}/_{2}$ cup molasses
$^{1}/_{2}$ cup brewer's yeast
2 tablespoons fine sea salt

First make the sponge. Mix the yeast into the water and let it rest until it starts working, making bubbles. Stir in the rye flour. Cover with a cloth and set aside until the mixture rises and falls on its own, without being stirred or punched down. Set the mixture aside at room temperature for 2 or 3 days, until it sours and becomes a little sticky. Use immediately, or refrigerate for a few days.

To make the loaves, put the sponge into a large bowl and mix in the water and 6 cups of rye flour, alternating a little of each. Cover with a cloth and set aside in a warm place for about 3 hours. The longer it stands, the more sour the bread. (Take out 2 cups of the soured mixture and place it into a crock or glass jar, cover, and refrigerate for the next batch of sourdough; it will keep a week or so. For longer storage, feed it a little rye flour and warm fresh water.) Then stir in the rest of the rye flour and the other ingredients. Turn the dough out onto a floured surface and knead until smooth and elastic. Shape the dough into 4 loaves, placing them on greased cookie sheets. Cover and set aside in a warm place for 3 or 4 hours, during which time they will rise, but not to the conventional "double in volume" size. Preheat the oven to 350°F. Bake for $1^{1}/_{4}$ to $1^{1}/_{2}$ hours.

Finnish Black Bread

This traditional bread, according to *The Scandinavian Baking Book*, by Beatrice Ojakangas, was baked in large quantities twice a year and stored in the granary on poles. This explains the purpose of the hole in the center of the rather flat, round loaves. The shape is still popular today, although it is made throughout the year in smaller quantities. Traditionally, it's a hard loaf that is sometimes wrapped in damp towels to soften it before eating. The crust of the loaf, according to Ms. Ojakangas, was sometimes given to teething babies. My dog, Nosher, also likes to chew on it.

Be warned that this simple recipe takes 2 days to prepare, owing to a soured batter. It calls for a dark rye flour, which is difficult to find in most commercial outlets. Home-ground whole rye, duly sifted, is perfect.

7 cups dark rye flour
3 packages active dry yeast ($^1/4$ ounce size)
2 teaspoons fine sea salt
4 cups warm water (110°F)

In a plastic bowl with a tightly fitting lid, dissolve the yeast in the warm water. Add 2 cups of rye flour and beat until smooth. Sprinkle the top with 1 cup of flour, cover tightly, and place in a warm spot for 24 hours. Remove the lid, enjoy the aroma, and stir in the salt and approximately 3 cups of flour. Turn out onto a bread board (or put into a bowl if you are using an electric mixer) and knead for 30 minutes. The dough should be very sticky. Dampen your hands and shape the dough into a ball, placing it in a bowl. Sprinkle with just enough flour to make the top dry. Put in a warm place to rise for $1^1/2$ hours. Place the dough on a floured bread board and divide into 2 parts. Lightly grease 2 baking sheets and dust each with flour. Shape each loaf, one on either sheet, into a flat round about 8 inches across. Flour your finger and shape a hole in the center of each loaf, then, pulling with the finger, expand the hole until it is 2 inches in diameter. Dip your hands in water and smooth out the top and edges of each loaf. Brush the loaves with water and sprinkle generously with flour. Place the loaves in a warm place until they flatten out and the tops appear to be cracked.

Preheat the oven to 350°F and place a pan of water on the bottom rack. Place the baking sheets on a rack in the center of the oven for 1 hour, or until firm. To serve, slice the loaves very thinly. Try a slice or two, Ms. Ojakangas suggests, topped with caviar, sour cream, and minced onion, followed by Finnish vodka.

Nutritional Highlights

Rye isn't really loaded with protein, as compared with wheat. From a historical perspective, its main value is that it can be grown in cold climates and on relatively poor land, thereby providing protein and nutrients when the wheat crop fails.

People who raise and grind their own rye should perhaps read up on the fungus disease ergot, which is discussed at the beginning of this chapter.

PART THREE

Other World Grains

Barley, millet, tef, and sorghum have never been widely used as table fare in America, but they have been very important historically in some parts of the world and are still important here and there, often where wheat or corn does not grow readily. With the increasing popularity of ethnic cooking in America, these grains are becoming more widely available, making it possible to prepare authentic Ethiopian injeria and other specialties from foreign lands. These are truly great times, culinarily speaking.

Rice is well known in America as a grain, but it is not widely used in other forms. I can only hope that the chapter in this section will foster a Chinese jook or a Brazilian rice custard. And a bowl of oat gruel for breakfast does scant justice to this highly nutritious and widely available grain.

9

Oats

A grain which in England is generally given to
horses but in Scotland supports the people.

—Samuel Johnson

It's true. Historically oats have been the subject of hot debate and derision and hard feelings between cultures and subcultures. Much earlier than Samuel Johnson's day, Pliny said of the Germans, "How can one eat the same food as animals?" Even among the great oat eaters there are culinary schools. The Scots, according to foods guru Waverley Root, consider it effete to pour cream or sugar over oatmeal. Instead they put the cream in a separate bowl and dip each spoonful of oatmeal into it as they eat. The Welsh, by comparison, prefer to eat oatcakes broken into chunks and soaked in buttermilk. (Many people in the American South eat corn pone in this manner, and I am lucky enough to be counted as a devoted practitioner and something of a buttermilk lover.)

In spite of Quaker brand oatmeal boxes lining the shelves of our supermarkets, oats have never been of much importance as human food in America. Times are changing, however, thanks in part to the rise of health-food stores. Fortunately we are also discovering that oats are among the sweetest of grains, suitable for serving the people as well as our horses.

⊰ Hulled Oats ⊱

Hulled oat groats can be purchased in health-food stores, and sometimes in supermarkets. At harvest, there are both red and white oats, which must be threshed and hulled. Once hulled, the groats are rather long and of a golden tan color. Whole oats can be purchased in feed stores, or perhaps from farmers, but must be hulled before cooking. It's really best to buy hulled oats, which can be used like pearl barley in soups and stews. Cooked hulled oats can also be added to salads, pilafs, and other dishes. Also, hulled oats sprout quickly and easily, and can be used like bean sprouts in salads, stir-fries, and breads.

Oat Groats

Whole, uncut oat groats make a tasty cereal but they must be cooked longer than other forms of the grain. Whole oats are perhaps best cooked in a double boiler, although several other methods are used.

1 cup whole hulled oats
2$\frac{1}{2}$ cups hot water plus more for steaming
1 teaspoon salt

Add the hot water, oats, and salt to the top part of a double boiler. Bring some water to boil in the lower unit, insert the top, and cook on medium low heat for 1 hour. Stir and serve with butter, perhaps sprinkling each serving with a little brown sugar or palm sugar.

Other Methods: Soak the oats for 1 hour or longer in cold water. After that, bring 3 cups salted water to boil. Add the oats, bring to a new boil, reduce the heat, cover, and cook for 40 to 50 minutes, depending on how chewy you want them. This method can also be used with chicken or meat stock instead of water.

Instead of soaking the groats in water, another method is to toast them lightly in a skillet or in a broiling pan. Then cook from 40 to 50 minutes in lightly salted water. Toasted oats have a more pronounced flavor.

⊰ Steel-Cut Oats ⊱

Steel-cut oats are simply whole oats that have been cut into smaller pieces so that they can be cooked quicker, making them comparable to corn grits and cracked wheat. Unlike rolled oats or "oatmeal," they have not been steamed or cooked.

Sometimes called pinhead oats or Irish steel-cut oats or Scottish oats, these produce a very good porridge, having more flavor and a firmer texture than the oatmeal or quick oats sold in American supermarkets.

Basic Steel-Cut Oats

These cooked oats can be served as a breakfast cereal or used in other recipes.

1 cup steel-cut oats
3 cups water
salt to taste

Put the water, oats, and salt into a pot and bring to a boil. Reduce the heat, cover, and cook for 15 to 20 minutes, depending on how chewy you want them. Remove from the heat and let stand for 2 or 3 minutes. Serve warm as a cereal, or use as directed in other recipes.

Brotchan Roy

A famous old Irish recipe, Brotchan Roy is a nice broth made with steel-cut oats, leeks, milk, or stock.

$1/2$ cup steel-cut oats
6 young leeks
3 cups chicken stock or milk
2 tablespoons butter or margarine
2 tablespoons chopped fresh parsley
mace
salt and pepper
cream
chopped chives

Wash and cut the leeks into $1/2$-inch pieces, using the white and light-green parts. Melt the butter in a saucepan and soften the leeks in it. Bring the stock to a boil in a heavy pot. Sprinkle the oats on top, stirring as you go to prevent lumping. Add the leeks and butter. Simmer for 15 minutes. Add the parsley and the salt, pepper, and mace to taste. Ladle servings into warmed bowls, adding a swirl of cream and a sprinkle of chopped chives to each bowl. Serve with Irish soda bread.

Old-Time Oatmeal Pudding

Here's an old recipe, best cooked or steamed with the help of a double boiler.

The Pudding

1 1/2 cups Scotch-cut oats
1 cup hot buttermilk
1 cup raisins, or dry currants, and chopped dates
1/2 cup molasses
1/4 cup butter or margarine
1 chicken egg, whisked
1 teaspoon sea salt
1/2 teaspoon baking soda
water

The Sauce

hard cider
butter or margarine
maple sugar

Mix the oatmeal, baking soda, and salt in a pan. Cut in the butter. Add the hot buttermilk, molasses, and whisked egg, mixing well. Stir in the dates and raisins. Turn the batter out into a well-greased mold, until 2/3 full. Then place the mold into a Dutch oven partly filled with boiling water. The water should come about halfway up the mold. Cover tightly, reduce the heat, and steam for 2 hours or a little longer, adding more hot water from time to time if needed. Serve with a hot sauce made by boiling together hard cider, butter, and maple sugar to taste. The pudding can be reheated over boiling water.

Highland Haggis

Some recipes for haggis are just too long to be realistic, almost as if the authors of the recipes were trying to hide the essential ingredients. Here's a short version, closer, I think, to the original Highland recipe, adapted here from my book *Sausage.*

1 sheep stomach
1 sheep liver
1 sheep heart
1 set sheep kidneys
1 set sheep sweetbreads (if you can find them among the innards)

$^1/_2$ pound sheep fat
1 cup steel-cut oats
1 large onion, grated
water
milk
salt and pepper to taste

Clean and soak the stomach in salted water (1 box salt per gallon of water) overnight. When you are ready to proceed, simmer the heart and kidneys for $1^1/_2$ hours in a pot; cool and trim away the pipes and gristle. Cut the cooked heart and kidneys into chunks. Cut the liver and sweetbreads into chunks. Mix all the meats and fat, along with the grated onion, oats, salt, and pepper. Run the mixture through a sausage mill, using a $^1/_4$ to $^1/_2$-inch plate. Add a little water to the mixture, working it with your hands. Stuff the mixture into the stomach, leaving some room for the oats to expand. Sew up the opening with cotton twine. Place the stuffed stomach into a pot of suitable size, add enough water and milk to almost cover it, and bring to a boil. Prick the stomach here and there as soon as it begins to swell. Simmer for 3 hours. Serve the haggis plain with straight Scotch whiskey.

Highland Cocktail

Here's an old drink from the Scottish Highlands, using any good whiskey. I don't say it will cure what ails you; but it will, I guarantee, make you feel better—at least for a while. Drink it sparingly.

$1^1/_2$ cups cooked steel-cut oats
3 cups good malt whiskey
2 tablespoons honey
water

In a suitable nonmetallic container, mix enough water into the cooked oats to make a paste, cover, and let sit for an hour at room temperature. Press the paste through a fine sieve, saving the extract and discarding the rest. Mix the honey into the extract. Add the whiskey, mixing well. Place the mixture into a jar or bottle. Shake well before drinking.

Rolled Oats (Oatmeal)

Often called "oatmeal," rolled oats are readily available in our supermarkets and have been for some time. To roll oats, the mass manufacturers first hull the groats, steam them, and then pass them through rollers, therefore transforming them into flakes. In fact, "oat flakes" would be a much better popular name than "oatmeal." The thickness of the flakes varies, with the thickest being called "old-fashioned oats." (Actually, some of the rolled oats sold in health-food stores, billed as table-cut oats, may be a little thicker than regular supermarket old-fashioned.) The thicker rolled oats take the longest to cook. Thinner oats are usually billed as "quick" or "instant," covered briefly under on page 125.

The recipes below work best with old-fashioned rolled oats sold in supermarkets. Note that rolled oats are often used in dessert recipes, and in such multigrain mixes as granola and muesli, covered in chapter 21, Ezekiel Mixes.

❧ Rolled Oats for Breakfast ❧

I was brought up calling cooked oats "oatmeal," and I'm not likely to stop. Also, I usually follow the directions on the trusty Quaker Oats package from the supermarket. But I acknowledge that other rolled oats, such as those sold in some health-food stores, may have different requirements. So, follow the directions on the package.

Yet, this may not be the best way. Here's some advice from grain guru Bert Greene: "Preparing oatmeal is a very personal business. I, for one, don't agree with the standardized formula on the carton. When I whip up a batch of breakfast oatmeal for two, I always mix 1 cup of rolled oats with 2 cups of cool water (that is to say, straight from the tap). I place the mixture—without the addition of salt—over moderately low heat for about 5 minutes, stirring the thickening oats from time to time until the mixture boils. I then remove it from the heat, cover the pan, and allow the cereal to rest 2 or 3 minutes longer. The result? Perfect creamy oatmeal every time, merely waiting for butter, sugar, and cream or milk to turn it into an Olympian feed."

Well, personally, I want a little salt in the cooking water.

Irish Cranachan

This old dessert, adapted here from Ethel Minogue's *Irish Cooking*, is best served in glasses and topped with a few raspberries. While sparking a young Irish lady, I once served cranachan topped with tiny wild strawberries plucked in Appalachia.

2/3 cup rolled oats
1/3 cup slivered almonds
1 1/2 cups heavy cream

¼ cup honey
¼ cup good Irish whiskey
1 tablespoon lemon juice
raspberries

Toast the rolled oats and almonds in a shallow pan. In a bowl, whip the cream until stiff, then stir in the honey and whiskey. Fold in the oats, almonds, and lemon juice. Mound in stemmed glasses, garnishing each serving with a few raspberries, and serve immediately.

Note: The Scots enjoy a similar dish, made with malt whiskey and a little cream cheese as well as whipped cream. They also enjoy several simpler recipes, such as *stapag uachair,* which is simply steal-cut oatmeal, whipped cream, whiskey, and sugar—mixed in any proportions to taste. It is served in a glass and eaten with a spoon.

Old-Fashioned Oat Treats

These cookies are delightful, attractive, and easy. Be sure to make a batch any time you have fresh coconut to grate. It's best to use old-fashioned or perhaps steel-cut oats. Quick oats will work, but the treats won't be as chewy and toothsome.

2 cups old-fashioned oats
1 cup freshly grated coconut
⅔ cup butter or margarine
½ cup sugar
1 teaspoon freshly grated lemon zest
1 teaspoon freshly grated orange zest
1 teaspoon vanilla
½ teaspoon powdered cinnamon
½ teaspoon salt

Cream the butter and sugar together, then mix in the rest of the ingredients. Shape the mixture into a log 1 inch in diameter. Wrap the log in wax paper to hold the shape. Refrigerate for an hour or longer. Preheat the oven to 325°F, putting the rack in the center. Cut the log into ¼-inch rounds, placing these as you go onto a large ungreased cookie sheet, spacing them about 1 inch apart. Bake in the center of the oven for 15 to 20 minutes, or until light brown. Remove the cookie sheet from the oven and let cool before removing the treats.

Swedish Oat Cookies

Here's a very easy recipe from Sweden. Use ordinary oatmeal from the supermarket, but avoid the quick-cooking kind.

3 cups oatmeal
$^2/_3$ cup soft butter or shortening
$^1/_2$ cup sugar

Preheat the oven to 325°F. Mix all the ingredients and knead. Shape the dough into small balls, about 1 inch in diameter. Using a kitchen fork, flatten the balls from the top, forming flat cookies with fork marks. Place the cookies onto a buttered baking sheet or ovenproof griddle. Bake in the center of the oven for 8 to 10 minutes, or until light brown.

Oatmeal Cake

Here's an old recipe made with oats and wheat flour. All-purpose flour from the supermarket will work.

The Cake
$1^1/_3$ cups wheat flour
1 cup rolled oats
1 cup brown sugar
1 cup white sugar
$1^1/_2$ cups water
$^1/_2$ cup butter or margarine
2 large chicken eggs
1 teaspoon baking soda
1 teaspoon cinnamon
$^1/_2$ teaspoon grated nutmeg
$^1/_2$ teaspoon salt

The Topping
$^1/_2$ cup chopped pecans or other nuts
$^1/_4$ cup brown sugar
$^1/_4$ cup shredded coconut
$^1/_4$ cup heavy cream
1 teaspoon vanilla

To make the cake, bring the water to a rolling boil and pour it over the oats. Stir in the butter. Let stand for 30 minutes. Preheat the oven to 350°F. Mix the brown sugar, white sugar, eggs, wheat flour, baking soda, salt, cinnamon, and nutmeg. Stir into the oats mixture. Turn into a cast-iron skillet. Place in the center of the oven and bake for 40 minutes.

Mix all the topping ingredients. Spread over the baked cake. Broil until the topping is lightly browed. Slice and serve warm.

Applejack Oat Cake

Oats, apples, and honey always seem to go nicely together, making this cake a winner. If you must, substitute a good hard cider for the applejack.

The Filling

2 pounds cooking apples
1/3 cup chopped dates
1/4 cup brown sugar
1 tablespoon butter or margarine
1 teaspoon ground cinnamon

The Batter

3 cups rolled oats
1/2 cup butter or margarine
1/4 cup applejack
2 chicken eggs, beaten
2 tablespoons honey
1 tablespoon brown sugar
zest of 1 lemon (grated)
salt

The Topping

cream or sweetened whipped cream

For the filling, peel, core, slice, and dice the apples. Cook them in the butter in a saucepan until soft. Add the brown sugar, cinnamon, and dates. Cook for a few minutes and set aside to cool.

For the pastry, first zest the lemon with a grater, being careful to avoid the bitter white pith. Melt the butter, brown sugar, and honey in a saucepan. Mix in the oats and lemon zest, then stir in the eggs and applejack, mixing well. Divide the batter into 3 equal parts.

Preheat the oven to 375°F. In a round cake pan, spread a layer of the pastry in the bottom, distributing it evenly. Add half the filling, spreading evenly. Add another layer of pastry, the remainder of the filling, and a top layer of pastry. Bake for 30 minutes. Cut into wedges and serve warm, topping each piece with cream or, better, sweetened whipped cream.

Sopa de Avena

This oatmeal soup from Mexico is very filling and quite tasty. I like it for a light hot lunch on a cool day.

$1/2$ cup rolled oats
4 cups beef broth (or water with bouillon cubes)
$1/2$ cup heavy cream
$1/4$ cup grated cheddar cheese
2 tablespoons butter or margarine
1 chicken egg yolk, beaten
chopped fresh cilantro or parsley
salt and pepper to taste

Melt the butter in a pan. Sauté the oats slowly, stirring with a wooden spoon, for about 5 minutes. Add the beef broth, salt, and pepper. Simmer for 20 minutes. Stir in the egg yolk. Simmer for a minute or two. Stir in the cream. Sprinkle the cheese and perhaps a little chopped cilantro on top. Serve hot in bowls with hot jalapeño corn pone on the side, or with freshly made corn tortillas, rolled for dunking.

Quick and Instant Oats

These products, widely available in supermarkets these days, are processed somewhat like rolled oats. They are cut finer and rolled very thin. Some are cooked, and some contain artificial flavoring and sugar. If you are in a hurry for breakfast, use these, following the directions on the package. Otherwise, stick to rolled or steel-cut oats for more flavor and better texture.

Quick oats can also be used as meat fillers and binders for meat loaves and burgers. Here's an interesting variation.

Burger Chateaubriand, Herter Says

The cut of tenderloin known as chateaubriand was named for a French writer and gourmet named Francois Rene Vicomte de Chateaubriand, born in 1768, according to George Leonard Herter, coauthor of *Bull Cook and Authentic Historical Recipes and Practices*. But, Herter goes on, his real contribution was the use of dried grains in meats. Herter also says that this recipe is very special, and that oatmeal contains enzymes that do very strange things, especially to meats. "This hamburger Chateaubriand is the healthiest meat that exists. The liver in it builds up your blood better than any tonic ever devised." It is indeed a good recipe, and I recommend it for people who like liver and have a meat grinder at home. Herter specifies 1-minute rolled oats, but I use any precooked cereal called "quick" or "instant" oats.

1 pound freshly ground beef
1 pound freshly ground pork liver or beef liver
2 cups 1-minute rolled oats
cooking oil
salt and pepper to taste

Mix the ground beef, liver, oats, salt, and pepper. Shape the mixture into hefty burgers. Fry in hot oil until done, turning a time or two. Serve between hamburger buns, along with the condiments of your choice. I especially like thinly sliced onion with liver.

Oat Flour

Oat flour can be obtained by grinding whole groats in a grain mill, or by zapping steel-cut or rolled oats in a food processor or blender. The groats are relatively soft, however, and tend to mash flat rather than grind into tiny grits. For this reason, they are not ideal for the stone mills, tending to clog up the works. Oat flour is available in health-food stores and sometimes in supermarkets, but it should not be confused with the common term "oatmeal," which is merely steamed and rolled oats.

Hearth Cakes

These can be baked on a griddle, but for centuries they were made on a hearthstone in the European peasant cabin. These are heavy cakes, which have a very long shelf life. This version yields a lighter cake, owing to the addition of baking soda. Omit it if you want a heavier bread.

1 cup freshly ground oat flour
1/4 cup water

1 tablespoon butter or margarine, or bacon drippings
1 teaspoon baking soda
salt to taste

If you are cooking at the hearth, build a hot fire and let it burn down to coals. Rake some coals out a ways to heat the hearth. Heat the water and stir in the butter or bacon drippings. Pour this over the oat flour in a suitable bowl, stirring as you go and adding the salt and baking soda. While the dough is still warm, roll it out on a well-floured (use oat flour) board to a round about ⅛ inch thick. Cut the round into quarters. Let dry for 30 minutes, during which time you might tend the fire and rake out a few more coals to heat the hearth. Brush the ashes off the hearth and lay out the pieces. Cook until the edges begin to curl, then turn and cook the other side for a few minutes.

If you prefer, cook this bread on a cast-iron griddle over medium high heat.

Note: There are many variations of this old oat bread still cooked in Ireland, Wales, and other parts of the British Isles. Some are made only with oat flour and water, and many are made on a special cast-iron bread iron or cast-iron "breadstone." In the old days, oatcakes were cooked in quantity and dried for storage. In Wales, oatcakes were sometimes broken up with a rolling pin and mixed with buttermilk as a porridge. Anyone with a scholarly interest in this sort of old-time cookery should take a long look at *English Bread and Yeast Cookery*, by Elizabeth David, and *The Scot Kitchen*, by Miss F. Marian McNeill.

Oat Bread

This bread is very good. It can be made with whole oat groats, or with oatmeal, zapped to a flour in a food processor. I have adapted the recipe from a sheet sent to me by the Vermont Country Store, listed in the section on sources. I prefer to use chopped dates in the recipe, but substitute raisins if you must.

1 cup oat flour
½ cup soybean flour, sifted
½ cup whole wheat flour, sifted
¾ cup hot milk
½ cup chopped dates or raisins
⅓ cup molasses
¼ cup butter or margarine
1 beaten chicken egg
3 teaspoons baking power
¾ teaspoon salt

Preheat the oven to 375°F. Place the oat flour and butter in a bowl. Pour in the hot milk; stir until the butter has melted. Add the egg and molasses, mixing well. Sift the soy flour and wheat flour. Measure out ½ cup of each; mix, along with the baking powder and salt. Stir the flour into the oat batter. Add the chopped dates or raisins. Mix quickly. Turn out into an 8- by 8-inch baking pan, well buttered, and bake for 45 minutes in the center of the oven.

Oat 'n Barley Bread

This bread seems to keep forever. It is flat, heavy, and filling—and quite tasty.

2 cups oat flour
1 cup barley flour
2 tablespoons honey
1 tablespoon olive oil
1 cup warm water
1 package dry yeast (¼-ounce size)
1 teaspoon fine sea salt

Put the warm water into a bowl and sprinkle on the yeast. Let stand for a few minutes, then stir in the honey, salt, and barley flour. Stir and let stand for 15 minutes. Add the oil and oat flour to the mixture. Knead for 3 minutes, then shape into a loaf. Set aside in a warm place to rise until the loaf doubles in size. While waiting, preheat the oven to 350°F and grease a loaf pan. Bake the loaf in the center of the oven for 45 minutes, or until a wooden skewer inserted into the center comes out clean.

Irish Oat-Flour Bread

Here's a very tasty bread using oat flour steeped in buttermilk overnight! I adapted the recipe from *The Complete Book of Irish Country Cooking*, by Darina Allen, who credits it to Honor Moore of Dublin. The bread is billed as being light and pale . . . so, I cooked it with white wheat flour instead of whole wheat.

2½ cups freshly ground oat flour
2½ cups white wheat flour
2 cups buttermilk
1 teaspoon baking soda
salt to taste

Mix the oat flour and buttermilk in a suitable bowl. Place in the refrigerator or cool place overnight. Preheat the oven to 350°F and grease a loaf pan. Combine the wheat flour, salt, and baking powder. Stir into the oatmeal and buttermilk. Turn out into the loaf pan and bake in the center of the oven for 1 hour or a little longer.

Note: I have also made this in a 10-inch cast-iron skillet, placed into the oven at 350°F. It was delicious.

⇜ Oat Bran ⇝

Oat bran, the outer coating of the grain, became something of a fad a few years ago, and claims were made about its ability to reduce blood levels of LDL cholesterol. Earlier, wheat bran was touted as a digestive aid. Culinarily speaking, oat bran is more soluble than wheat bran, and produces a creamier, moister texture when cooked. Although the interest in oat bran has faded somewhat, it is still used in packaged cereal products and breadstuff, and the bran itself can be purchased in health-food stores and sometimes in supermarkets. It can be combined with wheat flour in muffins, biscuits, and so on, and gives a nutritional boost to soups and stews.

⇜ Nutritional Highlights ⇝

Whole oats are high in protein, B vitamins, calcium, iron, and other minerals. The grain also contains lots of fiber. About half the fiber is of the insoluble sort, which aids digestion. The other half is soluble, which helps the body lower cholesterol. Oats are, however, rather low in vitamins C and D. Sprouting the groats in sunlight will increase the vitamin C content, owing to the magic of chlorophyll.

10

Rice

All things are possible when leftover steamed rice is on hand.

—Victor Sodsook, *True Thai*

Whole books have been devoted to rice and its cookery, relieving me of the obligation and the temptation to cover in this short work recipes calling for purple Thai rice, Chinese black rice, Himalayan red rice, Japanese sushi rice, and so on. Obviously, we can't do justice to all these kinds of rice and to the cuisines that depend on them. But we really don't need exotic rice in order to eat well. More and more kinds of rice are becoming standard fare in America, and we can eat pretty well right out of the supermarket. Ordinary long-grain white rice, marketed everywhere in America, is really hard to beat for many uses; it is my all-round favorite rice because of its texture and appearance, although it is lacking nutritionally. Here's my quick take on what's what before we start cooking.

White Rice. This is ordinary rice that has been polished, and, in the process, has had all or part of the husk, bran, and germ removed.

Enriched White Rice. Most supermarket white rice has been enriched, meaning it has been infused with minerals and vitamins. Enriched rice should not be washed before cooking.

Converted White Rice. This product has been steamed and cooked under pressure before the milling process. This process preserves some of the nutrients from the bran and germ by forcing them deeper into the kernel. Converted rice takes longer to cook and doesn't hold its texture as well as long-grain rice.

Instant Rice. This is white rice that has been precooked and dried. It cooks quickly in very little water. It costs more than regular white rice, and is perhaps the least nutritious of any form of rice.

Brown Rice. This is unpolished whole rice. The bran is what causes it to be brown, or golden tan. The bran also adds a lot of fiber. (In fact, the bran can be purchased separately in health-food outlets.) In spite of its nutritional advantages, only about 2 percent of the rice consumed in the world is brown. This may be changing, however. Still, I'll have to admit again that I really do prefer white rice and I don't expect brown rice to become the mainstay of the cookery.

Long and Short Rice. Most of the choices and changes above are made when processing and packaging rice for market. White rice and brown rice, for example, can be produced from the same crop. The length of the rice, however, is a matter of species, and the differences are not altered by milling. A long-grain rice is about 5 times as long as it is wide. A short-grain rice, on the other hand, can be almost round. And there are species in between, some of which vary greatly. Generally, however, a long-grain rice, if properly cooked, produces grains that are fluffy and separate. The short-grain rices are in general more sticky when cooked, ideal for eating with chopsticks. There is also a medium-grain rice. We'll discuss all these in the sections below, along with recipes for each type.

Wild Rice and Rice Mixes. What we call wild rice in North America really isn't a true rice; it is discussed in chapter 20. Still, it is sold in the rice section of our supermarkets, often mixed with real rice. Other rice mixes contain beans or grains, or dry pasta, sometimes with packets of seasonings. It's usually best to cook all this stuff according to the directions on the package.

⇜ Long-Grain White Rice ⇝

This popular rice is simply polished long-grain rice. During the polishing process the husk, bran, and germ are removed or partly removed. (Brown long-grain rice, discussed below, is exactly the same grain but not as highly polished.) The result is a grain that, when properly cooked, becomes fluffy without sticking. Most of the commercial white rice has been enriched, making up for the loss of bran and germ.

There are several ways of cooking long-grain white rice. Following are my favorites. There are also infinite ways of using cooked white rice, often as a base for stir-fries and such dishes. I'm not getting into these recipes here, except to set forth a delightful recipe from Cuba called "Christians and Moors" (page 134), which has a nice color as well as flavor. Other recipes for cooked rice are set forth under the various headings throughout the chapter.

1-2-20 Rice

This is a basic rice recipe. I suspect it is used more than any other method, partly because it is so easy to remember. Although simple, it is exact and therefore not foolproof.

> 1 cup rice
> 2 cups water
> salt to taste

Bring the water to a boil, add the rice and salt, cover tightly, reduce the heat to low, and cook for exactly 20 minutes. Do not peek. More often than not, the rice will be perfect. Rarely will it be burned (in which case the crust may be the best part, if it isn't scorched to the point of smelling burnt). Sometimes it will be a little too wet, in which case leaving it on the heat a little longer may help. The method can be refined if you cook the rice in the same pot at exactly the same heat every time. Increase the measures as needed, using twice as much water as rice. Once you get over 2 cups of rice, cut back on the water. Let the rice sit for a few minutes. Fluff the rice with a fork before serving. (See also the Leftover Rice section on pages 153–157.)

Variations: Add 1 tablespoon of butter to the pot before adding the rice.

Chinese Rice

White long-grain rice is a favorite in China and is used daily. Washing it in several changes of water is almost a ritual, a procedure entirely lacking in some Western methods of rice cookery, and can be done a few hours or even a day before it is cooked. (Washing the rice will make it whiter, but, on the other hand, it will take out the nutrients added to American fortified rice.) The ingredients list depends on the number of people to be fed. Usually, the Chinese allow 1/2 cup of raw rice per person, which will make about 1 cup of cooked rice. That's about right for me.

To proceed, put the correct amount of rice into a heavy pot or heavy saucepan of suitable size. The dry rice should not fill more than half the pot. Cover the rice with cold water, then rub it between your hands. When the water turns milky, drain and cover the rice again with cold water. Repeat for 5 or 6 changes of water. After the washing is complete, cover the rice with between 3/4 and 1 inch of water, usually measured by the first joint of the index finger. (The same measure seems to work regardless of how much rice is put into the pot, provided that at least 2 cups are used. The measures will also vary depending on the diameter of the pot. Usually, however, the measure will be 1 cup of cold water per 1 cup of rice, which will yield a rather dry rice that may have some crust on the bottom. See the similar method discussed at some length in the Crusting the Rice section beginning on page 149.) After the correct amount of cold water has been added, cover the pot and place it on high heat. Bring the rice to a rolling boil, then turn the heat down at once. (Don't remove the lid. If you do, you'll lose your head of steam. When the water comes to a vigorous boil, it will cause the lid to chatter, letting out a little steam.) Cook for 5 minutes, then turn the heat down to low. Don't peek. Let the rice cook for 5 more minutes, then turn the heat down to very low. Don't peek. Cook for 10 more minutes. Remove the rice from the heat and let sit for a few minutes or longer. Fluff the rice with chopsticks or a fork before serving, scraping it off the top instead of scooping it out.

Picayune Rice

Louisiana grows some rice, along with East Texas, and does some crowing about its quality. Here's a rice recipe and philosophy from *The Picayune Creole Cookbook*, published back in 1901 by the famous New Orleans newspaper. The preamble to the recipe states that rice "will continue to become more and more a popular article of food when the people of the great North and West learn how to cook it as well as the Creole of Louisiana." In any case, here is the whole pitch.

1 cup white rice
1 quart water
1 teaspoon salt

First, pick the rice clean and wash it thoroughly in cold water, rubbing the rice between your hands. This will make the cooked rice whiter, and, when properly cooked, it should be "snowy white, perfectly dry and smooth, and every grain separate and distinct." To that end, put the quart of water and the salt into a pot and bring to a rolling boil. Add the rice. Bring to a new boil, stirring from time to time with a wooden spoon. Cover and continue to cook at a rolling boil, which will toss the grains of rice about, keeping them from clinging together. Do not under any circumstances stir the rice again. Let it boil for 20 minutes, or until the grains swell out and the mixture seems to thicken. Take the pot off the heat, remove the lid, and pour off the water. Set the pot uncovered in the oven for 10 minutes. (*The Picayune* doesn't specify the oven temperature, but I find that 300°F is about right. Putting the pot into the oven helps drive any remaining moisture from the rice without adding too much heat to the bottom of the pot.) Then pour the rice out of the pot into a serving dish.

Christians and Moors

Black beans are very popular in Cuba, where this dish is often served. Its name reflects the Spanish influence and the conflicts between the Moors and the Christians. There are many variations, but the idea is to cook the two main ingredients—white rice and black beans—separately. You want the black beans as black as possible and the rice as white as possible. To this end, you may want to wash the rice in several changes of water before cooking. Cook the rice by your favorite method, aiming for separate grains. Also use your favorite black bean recipe, or try canned black beans, well drained.

2 cups cooked long-grain rice
1 cup cooked black beans

Drain the black beans, then combine them with the rice, mixing evenly. Serve as a side dish.

Variations: I like to toss the black beans in a little olive oil before mixing with the rice, giving them a sheen. I also like some chopped onion in the dish, along with some salt and pepper. Some of the many variations on this dish in the West Indies call for minced Scotch bonnet or little but fiery bird chili peppers.

⋙ Brown Rice ⋙

Brown rice is simply the whole grain, including a natural coating of bran. Actually, it has several layers of bran, which can make up 10 percent of the whole.

In recent years, this bran has been touted as a health food, believed to help lower cholesterol. Culinarily speaking, the bran gives brown rice its color and makes it more chewy. The bran also adds a slightly nutty flavor. From a cook's viewpoint, brown rice takes longer to prepare, mostly because the bran forms a protective coating that slows the rate of liquid absorption.

Easy Brown Rice

Here's a basic recipe that will work for most of the long-grain brown rice varieties that I have tested. Note that brown rice typically yields more cooked rice than white and requires longer cooking.

1 cup long-grain brown rice
2$^{1}/_{2}$ cups water or broth
1$^{1}/_{2}$ tablespoons butter or margarine
salt to taste

Melt the butter in a heavy pot, swirling it about to coat the bottom well. Mix in the rice, water or broth, and salt. Bring to a rolling boil, stir with a wooden spatula (scraping the bottom), reduce the heat to very low, cover tightly, and simmer for 50 minutes without stirring. If you have trouble keeping the heat very low, use a flame tamer or reduce the cooking time to about 45 minutes. In any case, watch the pot closely during the last few minutes of cooking; if you don't see a little steam escaping, you may be in danger of burning the bottom. Remove the lid and test the rice. If it isn't quite ready (remembering that brown rice naturally has a firmer texture than white), immediately re-cover with the lid and leave on the stove burner (with the heat off) for 15 minutes. On the other hand, if the rice seems to be on the verge of scorching, immerse the bottom of the pan quickly into a sink half full of cold water. Fluff the rice with a fork and serve.

Brown Rice with Mushrooms

Brown rice combines nicely in this recipe with sautéed mushrooms.

$^{3}/_{4}$ cup long-grain brown rice
2 cups sliced mushrooms
2 cups chicken stock
2 tablespoons butter or margarine (divided)
$^{1}/_{2}$ cup chopped green onions with part of tops
salt to taste
black pepper to taste

Heat the chicken stock and 1 tablespoon of the butter in a saucepan. Add the rice, bring to a boil, cover, reduce the heat, and cook for 40 minutes or so. Meanwhile, heat the rest off the butter in a skillet. Sauté the mushrooms and green onions. Add the sauté to the rice pot, along with some salt and pepper, and cook for a few more minutes, until the rice is tender and the liquid has been absorbed. Serve as a side dish to broiled chicken breast or other meal.

135

⨯ Aromatic Rice ⨯

Several varieties of aromatic rice are grown here and there. Mostly they are long-grain species, but not entirely. The best, or the more pronounced, of these is the basmati rice from the Himalayan foothills. In Sanskrit, the term "basmati" means "queen of fragrance." In addition to the alluring fragrance, it has a slightly nutlike flavor. It seems to go nicely, when cooked, with a little cinnamon. Authentic basmati is usually expensive—but, ironically, it is not highly prized in the Himalayan region, where the wheat berry is king. There is also a similar rice called jasmine, and, in America, texmati, which is generally much less expensive than basmati, along with several other brand names. It's all good stuff, and some of these are available in brown as well as white. Here are some standard recipes to try.

Basic Basmati

I have cooked this rice by several methods, including basic recipes for standard long-grain rice. Here is a slightly different approach, adapted here from *The Grains Cookbook*, by Bert Greene. (I have restrained myself here, deciding not to add any salt to the recipe.) You might also try cooking this rice according to the directions given on packaged basmati rice.

1 cup basmati rice
water

Rinse the rice for several minutes, until the water runs clean. Rinse again and soak the rice in water for 30 minutes. Heat the rice in 4 quarts of water. Boil for 5 minutes. Drain and gently fluff the rice. Enjoy.

Coconut Rice

This dish is made with unsweetened coconut milk, which can be purchased in cans in ethnic-foods shops and even in some supermarkets.

1 cup long-grain jasmine or basmati rice
2 cups coconut milk (unsweetened)
1/2 cup shredded coconut (unsweetened)
1/2-inch slice peeled fresh ginger
3/4 teaspoon salt
chopped fresh cilantro (optional)

Bring the coconut milk to a boil in a suitable pot. Add the rice, ginger, and salt. Stir, bring to a new boil, reduce the heat to low, cover, and simmer for

20 minutes. While waiting, heat the shredded coconut in a skillet, toasting it lightly. Remove from the heat and set aside. When the rice has cooked for 20 minutes, fluff it with a fork (throwing out the ginger root) and place in a serving dish. Sprinkle with coconut and chopped cilantro before serving.

White Jasmine Rice

This is one of my favorite recipes for aromatic rice—partly because it is so easy, requiring no soaking and only 15 minutes on the stove.

1 cup white jasmine rice
$1^1/2$ cups water
1 tablespoon butter or margarine
$1/2$ teaspoon salt

Put all the ingredients into a pot, bring to a quick boil, and stir up the bottom with a wooden spatula. Reduce the heat, cover tightly, and simmer for 15 minutes. Remove the pot from the heat. Let stand, covered, for a few minutes. Fluff with a fork and serve.

Variation: This rice can also be cooked successfully in a larger amount of water—with an even shorter cooking time. Simply boil it vigorously in 3 or 4 quarts of water for 12 minutes. Drain, fluff, and serve.

Brown Jasmine Rice

Brown jasmine rice is simply jasmine rice that has its natural coating of bran. The bran gives the rice a brown or tan color, and a rather chewy texture. It also makes the rice take longer to cook. I like it cooked in beef or chicken stock and served as a side dish, like a pilaf, or as a bed for a stir-fry meal.

1 cup brown jasmine rice
2 cups water or chicken stock
1 tablespoon butter or margarine
$1/2$ teaspoon salt

Put all the ingredients into a pot, bring to a boil, and stir up the bottom with a spatula. Reduce the heat, cover, and simmer for 40 minutes. Remove from the heat, fluff with a fork, and serve.

⨯ Short-Grain Rice ⨯

In general, short-grain rice contains more surface starch than does long-grain. This starch causes the cooked rice to be rather sticky, making it easier to eat with chopsticks or with the fingers. What would seem at first glance to be a minor culinary detail is really a profound cultural influence. The Laotians, for example, depend on sticky rice as much as most Americans depend on a knife and fork, using little rice balls to pick up broth and small pieces of meats and vegetables.

In addition to being more glutinous, short-grain rice is also less dense than long-grain, which means it can be cooked with less water. (Actually, freshly harvested short-grain rice uses less water and has a shorter cooking time than rice that has been stored.) There are several kinds of short-grain rice, used more or less interchangeably.

Sticky Pearl Rice

This basic recipe is for rice to be served with a Japanese meal. The grain itself is very short—almost round. In fact, it is sometimes called round rice. The measures for the basic recipe call for equal amounts of rice and water. Use at least 1 cup of rice and increase as needed. For large amounts of rice, cut back on the water just a little. These measurements, however, are for new-crop or freshly harvested rice (which is preferred and which is more expensive.) As the rice ages, more water is required.

1 1/2 cups new-crop pearl white rice
1 1/2 cups cold water
salt to taste (optional)

Rinse the rice several times in cold water. Then put the measured amount of cold water into a pot. Add the rice and salt. Turn on the heat and bring to a boil. Reduce the heat to very low, cover tightly, and cook for 20 minutes. Do not peek. Remove the pot from the heat and let it sit for a few minutes.

Oriental Sweet Rice

Sometimes called glutinous short-grain rice, this variety is used in China to stuff ducks and to make jook (see page 148). This rice is also pounded into a pastry dough. Sweet rice can be cooked like sticky pearl rice (see above).

Sticky Rice with Mango

This dessert calls for coconut cream (it is similar to coconut milk but thicker), available canned, and ripe mango—a delicious combination.

2 cups raw Thai sticky rice
1 large ripe mango, peeled and sliced
1 cup coconut cream
1/4 cup sugar
salt to taste
water

Cook the rice as in the Sticky Pearl Rice recipe, above (it should be sticky but not mushy). Place the rice in a mixing bowl. Mix in the sugar, salt, and about half of the coconut cream. Mound the rice mixture on a platter and let it cool to room temperature. Top with mango slices and pour the rest of the coconut cream over the top.

Note: If you don't have coconut cream or the makings, you can use thick unsweetened whipped cream. Also, try some palm sugar instead of regular sugar. In Bali, a palm sugar syrup is used in a similar dessert, made with half white glutinous rice and half black glutinous rice, and topped with coconut cream.

Risotto alla Milanese

This creamy Italian dish is best made with arborio rice, a short-grain specialty rice from Italy, or perhaps with a short-grain Valencia from Spain. Most short-grain or medium-grain rices will work—but never use long-grain. Actually, there are hundreds of risotto recipes, all cooked pretty much the same way but with varying ingredients; in fact, whole books have been written on the subject, which has become something of a fad in recent years. I consider this recipe to be classic. It calls for bone marrow, which refers to the center of large bones from beef, caribou, and other animals, known in the far north as Eskimo butter. If your butcher can't provide the marrow bones for you, substitute more butter or margarine. Risotto is surprisingly easy to make, if you have the right ingredients and proceed with tender loving care. Constant attention to the cooking is necessary, along with good ingredients, such as homemade chicken stock and freshly grated Parmesan instead of boxed. Don't skimp on this recipe. If you are on a diet, try something else.

1 cup arborio rice
1 quart chicken stock
3 tablespoons butter or margarine
2 tablespoons bone marrow (or more butter or margarine)
1 medium to large onion, minced
1/3 cup dry white wine
Parmesan cheese, freshly grated
salt and black pepper
a pinch of saffron

Put the chicken stock into a suitable pot and bring to a boil. In a heavy saucepan, melt the bone marrow and 2 tablespoons butter. Sauté the onion for 4 or 5 minutes, until it is golden. Add the rice and stir with a wooden spoon, over medium heat, for 3 or 4 minutes, until the rice turns opaque. Add the wine and cook until it evaporates, stirring as you go. Add about half the boiling chicken stock and continue to cook over medium heat, stirring constantly. Do not cover. As the rice absorbs the stock, add a little more, and a little more, until most of the stock has been absorbed. This should take 20 minutes from the time the first stock is added. (When done just right, the rice should be creamy—but each kernel should still retain just a hint of crunch in the center.) Mix a pinch of saffron to the rest of the stock; stir into the pot. Stir in 1 tablespoon of butter, salt, and pepper. Let the risotto rest for a few minutes, then serve it up in soup bowls, topped with freshly grated Parmesan cheese.

Paella

This old Spanish dish is best prepared with a short-grain rice called Valencia, named for the region where it is grown. The dish itself gets its name from a paella pan, in which it is cooked. This thing, about 15 inches in diameter with rather shallow slanted sides, has a handle on either side. It was originally designed for cooking outside over wood or charcoal and really doesn't work too well on a stove-top simply because the heat won't cover the whole pan evenly. Modern-day cooks who use the big pan on the stove usually turn it constantly for about 10 minutes, then finish cooking the dish in the oven.

The original paella was made mostly from rabbits or chicken, with shellfish being added rather recently, culinarily speaking. These days we see all manner of stuff in a paella, including 3 or 4 different kinds of beans and even artichokes, if you can believe that. Further, the best outdoor paella pans are surprisingly thin. This permits the expert cook to produce a tasty crust on the bottom of the dish. Paella (unlike the Italian risotto) is a no-stir dish, requiring a sense of timing by the cook. Each paella pan (or large skillet) will be different, depending in part on the fire and the ingredients. If you want to try the real stuff, with crusty bottom, have at it, or perhaps look for some old-time country Spanish cookbooks for more helpful instructions, if you can find them. Most of the recipes in American cookbooks will simply yield a shellfish medley cooked in rice. Some books even specify "regular" rice. I too stand guilty. In any case, here is a reasonable paella, adapted here from my book *Sausage*.

Although shellfish tops the dish, the essential ingredients are chicken (or rab-bit), rice, and chorizo sausage. Although pimiento strips are traditionally used, they are mostly for garnish; I usually use strips of red bell pepper cooked in the dish. Part of the pleasure of this dish is in seeing the whole thing. So, serve the dish at the table right out of the skillet or paella pan, letting the diners help themselves. If you cook outdoors, let everybody eat out of the paella pan, as was the old custom.

1 pound chorizo, cut into $1/2$-inch wheels
1 fryer chicken or cottontail, cut into serving pieces
1 pound shrimp (whole)
1 pound stone-crab claws, cracked
$1/2$ pound firm fish fillets, cut into 1-inch chunks
1 dozen fresh mussels (in the shell)
2 dozen freshly shucked oysters
3 cups uncooked Valencia rice
2 cups chopped fresh tomatoes
$1 1/2$ cups chopped onion
10 cloves minced garlic
$1/2$ green bell pepper, cut into thin strips
$1/2$ red bell pepper, cut into thin strips
$3/4$ cup olive oil
salt
freshly ground black pepper
$1/2$ teaspoon Spanish (hot) paprika
$1/2$ teaspoon ground saffron
water

Wash, trim, and steam the mussels (discard any that do not open). Set the mussels aside, leaving them over the hot water. Heat the olive oil in a paella pan or large skillet on medium-high heat. Sauté the chicken or rabbit pieces, turning from time to time, until they are lightly browned. Add the chorizo slices. Cook for another 3 or 4 minutes or so, stirring with a wooden spoon. Place the chicken and chorizo on a brown paper bag. In a separate pot, bring about 7 cups of water to a boil. Sauté the onions in the remaining oil, stirring as you go, for 5 minutes. Add the tomatoes and turn the heat to high, cooking until much of the liquid has left the tomatoes. Add the red pepper, green pepper, garlic, salt, black pepper, and paprika. Cook for a few minutes until the pepper is tender. Add the rice and cook for 5 minutes, stirring constantly, until it starts to turn brown. Put the chicken and chorizo pieces back into the pan. Add 4 cups of boiling water, stirring as you go. Mix the saffron into a little boiling water, then add it to the pan and mix well.

When the liquid starts to boil nicely, add the stone-crab claws. Stir in 3 more cups of boiling water. Cook for 3 or 4 minutes, then add the shrimp and fish chunks. Cook for 3 or 4 minutes, then add the oysters. Cook for another 3 or 4 minutes, or until the oysters start to curl around the edges. (If you want to gamble on a crusty bottom, and have guests who will appreciate the texture without thinking you have burned the dish, cook for a few more minutes, watching it like a hawk and sniffing the arising vapors.) Set the pan off the heat. Fish out some of the red bell pepper strips. Garnish with steamed mussels and red pepper strips. Place the paella pan on trivets in the middle of the table. Serve immediately, spooning the paella directly onto preheated plates, along with plenty of crusty hot bread and red wine on the side.

Note that the shrimp in my recipe are not beheaded or peeled, partly because the "fat" in the head adds to the flavor. The peeling is done at the table, using the fingers. If you are serving squeamish folks, however, it will be best to behead, peel, and devein the shrimp before adding them to the pot.

Short-Grain Brown Rice

Short-grain brown rice can be cooked like regular rice, but with a longer cooking time. It is not as sticky as short-grain white rice. I often use this rice in soups and stews.

1 cup short-grain brown rice
2 cups water or broth
salt to taste

Bring the water to a boil, add the rice and salt, stir, cover, and reduce the heat to simmer. Cook for 45 minutes. Remove the pot from the heat and let sit for 10 minutes before serving.

❧ Medium-Grain Rice ❧

Yes, this rice is about halfway between long and short grains. If properly cooked and promptly served, its grains are moist and distinct. When it cools, it tends to be sticky. When cooked it can be used in various recipes, such as those for puddings, or it can be added dry to soups and stews. I do not recommend that it be served as a bed for stir-fry dishes or in pilaf.

Basic Medium-Grain Rice

Notice that this rice requires less water than long-grain. Otherwise, the cooking procedure is the same.

1 cup medium-grain white rice
1 $^1/_2$ cups water
1 tablespoon butter or margarine
salt to taste

Melt the butter in a pot. Add the water and bring to a boil. Add the rice and salt. Bring to a new boil, reduce the heat, cover tightly, and simmer for 15 minutes.

Pilaf

By whatever spelling, the word "pilaf" goes back to ancient Persia and denotes rice cooked in a meat broth, along with, perhaps, a little meat and other ingredients. It is usually served as a side dish to a large meal, and, as such, should stand on the plate instead of being mushed in a bowl.

I might add that the word "pilaf" is being used with similar dishes made from other grains or grain products, such as kasha or bulgur. We'll stick to rice—at least in this chapter.

Turkish Pilaf

The Turks, who originally came from the fringes of Mongolia and China, brought rice to Asia Minor, and on to Europe. They are masters of the pilaf, which is served daily in the Turkish home. There are many variations calling for various ingredients, but the most popular is rather plain, as follows. (I might add that some of the people in rural Turkey favor wheat berries to rice, the pilaf notwithstanding.)

12 ounces long-grain rice
1 $^1/_2$ pints chicken stock or water
2 ounces butter or margarine
1 teaspoon salt

Rinse the rice under cold water and drain. Bring the stock to a boil in a pot. Melt the butter in another pot; add the rice, stir, and fry for 3 or 4 minutes. Stir in the salt and the stock. Bring to a new boil. Boil vigorously for 3 minutes. Lower the heat, cover, and simmer for 15 minutes, or until all the liquid has been absorbed (I allow peeking). Turn off the heat, remove the lid, cover the pot with a small towel, replace the lid, and let it coast for 10 to 15 minutes. Gently fluff up the rice with a fork. Serve with meat kabobs and grilled eggplant, as a bed for stews, or as a side dish for any meat, fowl, or fish entree.

Suggestion: Try this recipe with basmati rice.

Rice Pilaf Azerbaijani

A good many recipes call for cooking the rice with a crusty bottom, and, in such places as Iran, this part is served to the elders and guests of honor, along with the sheep eyeballs. Although the ingredients for this dish of rice is quite similar to the Turkish recipe above, the cooking is a little different.

1$^{1}/_{2}$ **cups long-grain rice**
6 cups clarified butter or margarine
8 cups water or chicken broth
1$^{1}/_{2}$ **tablespoons salt**

Bring the water to a rolling boil in a large pot. Add the salt. Pour in the rice in a small stream so that the boiling is not impeded. Boil uncovered for 10 minutes, stirring the rice a time or two with a wooden spoon. Drain the rice, rinse with warm water, and drain again. Heat 2 tablespoons of butter in a saucepan with a thick bottom. Add a few tablespoons of the boiled rice, mixing and spreading over the bottom of the pot. Add the rest of the rice and sprinkle on the rest of the butter, evenly distributed. Stretch a towel or heavy cotton cloth over the pan. Cover with a lid, then tuck the sides of the cloth over the top of the lid, or tie up if necessary, to prevent it from catching fire. Place the pot over low heat and heat for 30 or 40 minutes (the cloth will absorb the moisture as it rises). Spoon the fluffy top rice onto a serving platter, forming a mound. Scrape the crusty rice from the bottom of the pot and arrange it around the mound. Serve with meats and vegetables.

Note: The Azerbaijanis and other peoples of the Caucasus have interesting variations on the pilaf. In one, a round of thin dough made of egg and flour is placed on the bottom, along with some butter, and covered with rice. The *kazmag*, as the dough is called, forms a golden-brown crust as the rice cooks. It is cut into wedges and served with the rice.

Indian Ghee Pilaf

This spiced rice can be made with any good long-grain rice, but basmati rice is best. The ghee used in the recipe is clarified butter, made by heating butter in a saucepan and then cooling it, causing the solids to either settle to the bottom or foam to the top. The top scum is skimmed off, and the clear butter is carefully poured out, leaving the bottom dredgings undisturbed. Ghee is often used in Indian cooking and is available in Indian markets. It will keep for several months without refrigeration. In India, as in many other places, the pilaf has a thousand faces, often distinguished by subtle variations of esoteric spices. Here's my simplified version.

2 cups basmati rice
3$\frac{1}{2}$ cups chicken or lamb stock
2$\frac{1}{2}$ tablespoons ghee or margarine
1 large onion, minced
3-inch stick of cinnamon
6 cardamom pods, bruised
10 whole peppercorns
4 cloves
salt to taste

Wash and drain the rice until dry. Heat the chicken stock in a pot. Heat the ghee in a skillet, then add the onion and sauté until golden. Add the spices and dry rice. Fry on medium-high heat, stirring as you go, for 5 minutes. Add the salt to the chicken stock, then add the fried rice. Bring to a boil, reduce the heat to very low, cover tightly, and cook for 15 minutes. Do not peek or stir. Remove the pot from the heat, uncover, and let cool for 5 minutes. Fluff up the rice with a fork, removing the whole spices as you go. Serve with a slotted spoon, putting the rice in the middle of the dinner plate and arranging various curries, vegetables, and sambols around it.

Note: Sometimes a chicken is simmered for about 2 hours in water to obtain a stock, perhaps using a stalk of celery and a few carrots. The meat can be boned, chopped, and added to the pilaf for the last 15 minutes of cooking. Note also that the stock can be refrigerated, causing the animal fat to rise to the top. Then the stock can be reheated before cooking the pilaf.

Chinese Pilaf

Here's a combination adapted from my *Sausage* book, used with a recipe for Chinese sausage. It can also be made with any good dried, smoked, or rather hard sausage; try chorizo for a Spanish touch or a pepperoni for an Italian.

In any case, rice and sausage go together nicely, and the Chinese (before mechanical refrigeration became common) even stored their dried sausages in the rice crock. They have an easy way of flavoring rice with sausage. Simply cook the rice as usual (or see the Chinese Crust Rice recipe on page 150), but place some links of sausage on top. Be sure to prick the sausage links so that the juice will run down into the rice during the cooking process. When done, cut the sausages into thin slices and serve them along with the rice. Many peasant families serve only the sausage and rice for a meal, but, of course, they usually add steamed vegetables and other dishes when serving guests.

Calamari Pilaf

Calamari, or squid, is a popular shellfish in the Greek islands and in most parts of the Mediterranean. For this recipe, it's best to use fresh small squid. You can also substitute baby octopus or cuttlefish, or a combination. Any of these should be cleaned and cut into circles, including the tentacles.

1 pound dressed squid
1 cup dry long-grain rice
1/2 cup olive oil
1 cup chopped tomatoes
1 cup chopped onion
4 cloves garlic, minced
1 cup chopped celery with part of tops
1/4 cup chopped green onion with part of tops
1/4 cup chopped fresh parsley
1/4 cup red wine
2 tablespoons tomato paste
salt and black pepper to taste
2 cups water

Heat the olive oil in a large skillet. Sauté the onion, garlic, and celery for 4 or 5 minutes. Stir in the squid and cook for 2 minutes. Add all the other ingredients except the rice and water. Lower the heat, cover, and simmer for 20 minutes. Bring the water to a boil in a separate pot. Stir the rice into the skillet, then add the boiling water. Bring to a new boil, cover, reduce the heat, and simmer for 25 minutes, or until the rice is done.

Korean Peasant Pilaf

Many of the Asian dishes are too spicy for American taste, but this peasant dish stands up well to pepper. It is, however, best to make it on the mild side for openers. In any case, the dish is easy to make and doesn't require lots of esoteric ingredients.

> **2 pounds pork ribs with lots of lean meat**
> **4 cups water**
> **1 cup long-grain rice**
> **1 tablespoon soy sauce**
> **salt to taste**
> **hot and mild banana peppers to taste**

Put the ribs in a pot. Add some salt and cover the ribs with water. Bring to a boil, reduce heat, cover tightly, and simmer for an hour. Remove the ribs and drain. Add the rice. Bring to boil, reduce heat, cover tightly, and cook for 20 minutes. While the rice is cooking, bone the ribs and chop the meat into $1/2$-inch cubes. Dice the peppers finely. When the rice is done, in exactly 20 minutes, stir in the soy sauce and the chopped peppers. Put the meat on top, cover, and heat on very low heat for 4 or 5 minutes.

If you don't have hot banana peppers, try a jalapeño or two. Also try a mixture of mild and hot banana peppers, if available. I like to plant some of both kinds each spring; these will produce on through the summer and into autumn. Then I dry a pod or two of each kind so that I'll have seeds to start over again the next spring.

Dirty Rice

I call this dish a pilaf, which may draw some angry words from the Cajuns. But they are responsible for what has happened to this once simple Louisiana dish. Some of the recipes call for 2 dozen ingredients or more, including wine. Basically, all you need for dirty rice is a mixture of rice and chopped chicken livers. I usually go a little further, but I won't allow more than 10 ingredients. The chicken stock can be made with water and bouillon cubes. If you don't have fresh red tabasco peppers at hand, use any hot chili pepper, red or green.

> **$1/2$ pound chicken livers**
> **1 cup long-grain rice**
> **2 cups chicken stock**

1 large onion, chopped
2 green onions, chopped with part of tops
2 fresh tabasco peppers, red
2 tablespoons peanut oil
salt and pepper to taste

Put the chicken stock into a pot and bring to a boil. Add the rice, bring to a new boil, stir with a wooden spoon, cover, and simmer for 15 minutes. In a large skillet, heat the peanut oil and sauté the (white) onion. Chop the chicken livers and add them to the onion. Sauté until the liver is cooked through. Add the green onions, chili peppers, and salt and pepper to taste. Add the rice. Cook over medium heat for a few minutes, stirring and adding more salt and pepper if needed. Serve as a side dish to a regular meal, calling it a Cajun pilaf. It may not be the perfect name for this dish—but it beats "Dirty Rice."

⚶ Jooking the Rice ⚶

This common dish, also known as *congee*, has been called both the chicken soup and the hot dog of China. Since it is a popular rice porridge, the chicken-soup connection is clear—it is even served to sickly people—but, unlike chicken soup, jook is eaten at breakfast and at other times; at noon, at dinner, or as a late-night snack, and at times in between. In addition to being cooked in the Chinese household, jook is also served from pushcarts and other fast-food outlets in China. The basic jook is kept very hot in a bubbling cauldron, and the "condiments" are added to order. These include meats, seafood, and fowl. See also Beef Jook, below, and Singing Rice on page 151.

Jook is also made in Korea, Burma, and other parts of Asia, and I understand it is a popular late-night stall food in Bangkok. It can be made with several kinds of rice, including brown and long-grain white.

Plain Jook

This is a basic recipe using water instead of stock. If you are serving meat, seafood, or fowl in the jook, consider using a meat, fish, or chicken stock when cooking the rice. Plain jook can be used as is, but it's best when eaten with a little soy sauce or at least a little salt; I consider soy sauce to be indispensable.

1 cup raw rice, preferably short-grain
3 quarts water
soy sauce (optional)

Wash the rice several times. Bring the water to a boil in a pot, add the rice, and cook somewhat vigorously over medium-high heat for 30 minutes. Reduce the heat to low, cover, and simmer for 2 hours or longer, until the rice is very soft and the grains start to disintegrate. Serve hot. (It can be cooled and reheated.) Add a little soy sauce to each serving.

Beef Jook

Precooked (or leftover) meats are often diced and served with jook, and some meats, such as beef, are cut into thin strips—ribbons—and added raw (but marinated) to the serving bowl. The raw meat—no more than 1/2 cup per serving—is added to the bowl first, then the hot jook is ladled over it. Note that the jook is much hotter than boiling water and cooks the beef. For full cooking, be certain that the beef is thinly sliced and that the jook is bubbly hot. Fresh pork, as well as turkey and chicken (which may be salmonella-infested) should be cooked separately. Be sure to try jook with smoked fish or chopped country ham. But good raw beef is really hard to beat. I use an inexpensive cut from my local butcher called chuckeye. It is easier to slice thinly when partly frozen.

Plain Jook recipe (see above)
2 cups thinly sliced beef
¹⁄₄ cup soy sauce
1 tablespoon peanut oil
¹⁄₂ tablespoon Asian sesame oil
1 teaspoon brown sugar
¹⁄₃ teaspoon white pepper
chopped green onions (optional garnish)

Prepare the jook according to the Plain Jook recipe. Mix a marinade with the soy sauce, peanut oil, sesame oil, brown sugar, and white pepper. Place the beef in a nonmetallic container, pour the marinade over it, cover, and place in the refrigerator for 1 hour. When the jook is ready—bubbly hot—place the beef in warm bowls. Pour the hot jook over it until the bowls are almost full. Let stand for 5 minutes, allowing the beef to cook through. Stir and serve, perhaps topping each bowl with chopped green onions.

Crusting the Rice

Several recipes of the Orient celebrate rice with a crusty bottom, which is sometimes served as part of the dish and sometimes served separately, or stored for future use. Crusty rice is often cooked inadvertently, so maybe this text will help elevate a miscalculation to a culinary treasure. Crusty rice, of course, can be made without elaborate recipes simply by cooking all the water out of the pot and letting the bottom brown. The trick is in browning the rice into a crust while avoiding a scorched flavor, which will ruin the whole pot of rice. It's something of a gamble, living on the culinary edge.

Rice crust is best made in a heavy pot with lots of bottom. (Of course, if for some reason you want to minimize the crust, use a tall pot with a small bottom.) A stove-top cast-iron Dutch oven is just right for most instances. In addition to the recipes below, see the Paella recipe on page 140.

Chinese Crust Rice

This method of cooking rice requires no exact measurements, making it a good choice for camp cooking. Also, the technique is designed to yield a tasty by-product: a crusty bottom, which, again, fits right in with camp cooking. The crust, considered the best part, is eaten at the table along with the rest of the rice or used in other recipes, such as Singing Rice, below. Sometimes, it is used like crackers to hold a spread of fermented bean cake.

long-grain white rice
water

Put the rice into a pot and wash it by running cold water over it, stirring it about with your hands. Drain. Repeat the process 5 or 6 times. Then add enough clean water to cover the rice by ¾ to 1 inch. (With most pots, this will be about 1¼ cups of water to each cup of rice.) If you don't have a ruler, measure, as the Chinese do, by the first joint off the index finger.

Now, let the rice sit in the water for 30 minutes. This will shorten the cooking time and promote even cooking. Place the pan over high heat, bring to a boil, and cook uncovered until the water disappears and air bubbles no longer burst out the surface. Reduce the heat to very low, cover, and simmer for 15 minutes. Do not remove the cover or peek, but watch and smell the pot carefully during the last 5 minutes of the cooking period. A little steam should escape from the top, but there should be no scorched smell. Scorching will ruin the bottom crust and disflavor the rest of the rice. If you suspect scorching, immediately remove the pot from the heat and dip the bottom into cold water. (In case the rice has burned, there are ways to save most of it except the crust, but it's really best to start over. I might add here that this rice can be cooked an hour or so before serving time.) Fluff up the rice with a fork or chopstick and transfer to a serving bowl, raking all the loose rice off the crusty bottom.

You can at this point remove the crusty bottom, but it's really best to leave the pot uncovered overnight. This will allow the crust to dry and contract; in so doing, it tends to separate from the bottom of the pot. If the crust is stuck, pry it loose with a spatula. Remove the crust either whole or in large sheets. These can be broken into smaller pieces if needed. The crust can be stored in a dry place for several days.

If properly made, the crust is a beautiful golden color and nicely crisp.

Singing Rice

Sometimes called sizzling rice, this unusual dish makes a great way to hush a noisy table as everyone, at the moment it's served, listens to the rice. It's also very tasty, adding a nice crunch to soups and stews. To obtain the rice crust, see the Chinese Crust Rice recipe on the previous page. After reading this text, you may want to cheat a little. If so, have ready some precooked fluffy rice and preheat the oven to 250°F. Grease a shallow baking pan with a good cooking oil. Spread a layer of rice across the bottom and pat it down firmly, using enough rice to make the layer $1/2$ inch thick. Brush the rice with oil, then put the pan into the hot oven. Bake until the rice is dry. Then proceed with the recipe, which can be a stir-fry, soup, or stew; it should be very hot with plenty of pan or wok gravy. I prefer a stir-fry, made with strips of fresh pork or beef and vegetables, well thinned with a good stock.

stir-fry with plenty of gravy, piping hot
rice crust
peanut oil for deep frying

Rig for deep frying at 360°F. Break the rice crust into irregular pieces about $1\,1/2$ inches across. Bring the stir-fry or soup to heat. Warm some bowls. Get ready. Fry the rice-crust pieces in peanut oil until golden brown. Drain quickly and put into serving bowls. Ladle the hot stir-fry or soup over the crust. Serve immediately, listening for the rice to sing.

Iranian Lamb with Green Beans

Here's an Iranian culinary adventure. If it has a happy ending, the rice will be cooked but not scorched; if perfect, it will bless the cook with a crusty and crunchy golden-brown bottom. Ordinary green snap beans can be used in the recipe, but in recent years I have leaned toward the yard-long Asian beans, which I raise these days in my garden. These are perfect for this dish, whereas some of the snap beans are a little large. The yard-long beans also have a better color after cooking, it seems to me. Use any good long-grain white rice. For the meat, try cubed lamb shoulder, or perhaps mutton, if you can find it.

1 pound cubed lamb
2 cups uncooked long-grain rice
$\frac{1}{2}$ pound fresh green snap beans
1 medium to large onion
2 cloves garlic
1 can tomato paste (6-ounce size)
olive oil
freshly ground cinnamon to taste (about $\frac{1}{2}$ teaspoon)
1 tablespoon salt plus more to taste
pepper to taste
water

Cut or snap the beans into 1-inch segments. Heat a little olive oil in a large skillet. Sauté the onion and garlic for 5 minutes or so. Add the lamb and green beans, stirring about until the lamb is lightly browned. Stir in the tomato paste, cinnamon, salt, and pepper. Cover the skillet and simmer on low heat.

Put 2 cups of rice into a large pot. Add enough water to cover the rice by $\frac{1}{2}$ inch, along with 1 tablespoon salt. Bring to a boil, then pour the water and rice into a colander. Without rinsing the pot, cover the bottom with olive oil, turn the heat to low, and spoon in a layer of rice. Cook until the oil bubbles up through the rice. At this point, add a layer of the lamb mixture. Follow with another layer of rice and another layer of the meat. Repeat until the pot is filled, ending with a layer of rice. Using wood spoons, form the mixture into a mound. With a long-handled spoon, make a hole through the middle of the mound down to the bottom of the pot. Make several similar holes out from the center all around. Cover the pot tightly and cook on very low heat for 30 minutes. (If your pot is thin, use a flame tamer under it to prevent scorching.)

After exactly 30 minutes, dip the pot for a few seconds in cold water. With a little luck, at this exact point the bottom will be delightfully crusty, helped along, I think, by the olive oil. Of course, the crust is reserved for the elders and guests of honor.

Note: Several old dishes of Persian origin result in a rice crust called *tah dig*. Often the crust is a part of the dish, but sometimes it is served as a side dish. Some of these dishes contain saffron and chopped dried fruits, such as apricots, golden raisins, or sour cherries.

~~ Leftover and Precooked Rice ~~

The term "cook ahead" may be more appropriate than "leftover." But start with leftovers and you may find yourself cooking ahead, as I did. Often I'll cook a large batch of white rice, then refrigerate it until needed. Usually I'll just scrape some off the top, fluffing it nicely in the process, and use without heating in stir-fries and such dishes. I'll even eat it topped with spaghetti meat sauce.

Here are a few recipes to try. Rice puddings, some of which can be made with leftovers, are covered in a separate section (see page 164).

Thai Fried Rice Dinner

Fried rice is a favorite dish in many countries. I am especially fond of the recipes from Thailand *(Cow Paht)* and Vietnam *(Com Chein)* because I love fish sauce and the stir-fry. Leftover rice can be used to prepare the dish, but long-grain rice cooked especially for this recipe is best. Use only long-grain rice, pre-cooked, fluffy, and cold. The green chili peppers should be on the hot side, but jalapeños (available in many supermarkets these days) will do. The coriander used in the recipe is the same as cilantro, but in Southeast Asia the root of the plant is also used. If you grow your own, scrape a few roots and mince them along with the leaves.

4 to 6 ounces fresh pork loin or tenderloin
3 cups cold long-grain white rice, precooked
1 chicken egg, well whisked
2 or more green chili peppers, seeded and shredded
1 medium tomato, diced
2 tablespoons Thai fish sauce
2 tablespoons chicken stock
2 cloves garlic, diced
2 tablespoons chopped green onion with tops
1 tablespoon chopped fresh coriander (cilantro)
2 tablespoons peanut oil

Cut the pork into ribbons about 4 inches long, 1 inch wide, and $\frac{1}{4}$ inch thick; it's easier to cut when partly frozen, but bring to room temperature before cooking. Heat the peanut oil in a wok or cast-iron skillet, along with the garlic and chili peppers. Add the pork. Stir-fry for 3 minutes on medium heat. Turn the heat to high. Fluff the rice and add it to the wok, along with the fish sauce and tomato. Stir in the chicken stock. Cover and cook for 1 minute. Quickly stir in the whisked egg, coriander, and onion. Serve hot.

Note: This dish is easily adapted to the flavors of many countries, and the meat quota can be chicken, turkey, beef, or emu. Using soy sauce instead of fish sauce will give it a Chinese slant. For a taste of Bali, try a little shrimp paste. The variations are almost infinite, limited only by individual cooks and available ingredients. The important thing—and the constant ingredient—is precooked rice, which should be added cold to ensure that it doesn't become soggy while cooking (on high heat).

Rice Breakfast

Although used in such packaged cereals as Rice Krispies, plain rice is not often used in America as breakfast fare like oatmeal is. I have included a recipe for cereal in the Brown Rice section beginning on page 134, and the recipe below can be used with precooked rice, preferably brown, for a quick breakfast. The basic recipe came from the USA Rice Council. I have added a little salt to the recipe.

3 cups precooked rice (preferably brown)
2 cups skim milk
1/2 cup whole milk
1/4 cup brown sugar
1/3 cup raisins
1/2 teaspoon vanilla extract
1/2 teaspoon cinnamon
salt to taste (optional)
fresh fruit
granola (optional)
vanilla-flavored yogurt

Mix the rice, skim milk, brown sugar, cinnamon, and salt in a saucepan. Cook on medium heat for 10 to 12 minutes, or until the mixture thickens. Stir in the whole milk, raisins, and vanilla. Cook for another 5 minutes, stirring as you go, until the mixture thickens to your liking. Spoon the cereal into serving bowls. Sprinkle with fresh fruit. Top each serving with about 2 tablespoons of granola and yogurt.

Use your choice of fruit. I lean toward fresh peaches or mango. The rice council recommends low-fat granola cereal and low-fat yogurt. Suit yourself. In any case, this recipe makes a good and filling breakfast for 4 to 6 people. The Rice Council calls it a Power Breakfast. I agree, although I prefer to have a log of fried country sausage with mine.

Rice Spoon Bread

This recipe makes a good way to use up leftover boiled or steamed rice—and it's good enough to warrant newly cooked rice.

1 cup boiled rice
$^1/_4$ cup white cornmeal
2 cups buttermilk
2 chicken eggs, beaten
2 tablespoons melted butter or margarine
1 teaspoon salt
$^1/_2$ teaspoon baking soda

Preheat the oven to 325°F. Mix all the ingredients, making a batter. Grease a baking dish or suitable pan. Put the batter into the pan, spreading it evenly. Bake in the center of the oven for 1 hour, or until crisp on top. Serve as a side dish, to be eaten with a spoon, with meat and vegetables.

Variations: Add a cup of diced precooked ham or chopped link sausage to the batter before baking the spoon bread.

Rice Croquettes

This old recipe makes a tasty way to use leftover rice and bread crumbs. The original calls for lard, which is hard to beat for frying but not recommended by modern health-conscious cooks. Vegetable cooking oil will work.

2 cups leftover boiled rice
3 tablespoons milk
1 tablespoon butter or margarine
2 chicken eggs, beaten (separately)
1 tablespoon minced fresh parsley
$^1/_2$ teaspoon salt
$^1/_8$ teaspoon cayenne
cooking oil or lard
bread crumbs

Heat the rice and milk in the top part of a double boiler. Stir in 1 beaten egg, butter, parsley, salt, and cayenne. Shape the mixture into croquettes. Dip each croquette in the other beaten egg, and roll in bread crumbs. Dip and roll again, then fry in hot oil until nicely browned. Drain on absorbent paper. Serve hot.

Pheasant Salad

Here's a dish for eating leftover pheasant or wild turkey, but it's really best to cook the bird especially for this recipe. Poach or steam the bird's breast until tender. Then cool and dice the meat. Both the rice and pheasant are precooked, making this one easy to prepare well ahead of serving time.

2 cups cubed pheasant breast, precooked
3 cups cooked rice
1 cup fresh bean sprouts
1 cup sliced water chestnuts
1 cup diced celery with part of tops
1 cup sliced fresh mushrooms
$1/2$ cup diced red pepper
$1/2$ cup diced green onion with tops
juice of 1 lemon
2 tablespoons Asian sesame oil
1 tablespoon soy sauce
1 tablespoon freshly grated gingerroot
$1/2$ teaspoon white pepper
$1/4$ teaspoon cayenne pepper
lettuce leaves

Mix together in a large bowl the rice, pheasant, and all the vegetables except for the lettuce. In a small bottle or jar, mix and shake the soy sauce, sesame oil, lemon juice, ginger, white pepper, and cayenne. Pour this mixture over the rice and pheasant, stirring with your hands to mix well. Serve on lettuce leaves.

Fried Rice Balls

These sweet rice balls are popular as street food in Nigeria and other parts of West Africa.

2 cups cooked rice
$1/4$ cup brown sugar
2 tablespoons grated fresh coconut
1 large chicken egg, lightly whisked
wheat flour (if needed)
water (if needed)
peanut oil

Mix the rice, coconut, sugar, and egg. If the mixture will hold together nicely, shape it into small balls about 1 inch in diameter. Add a little flour or water to bind the mixture, if needed. (The texture will depend in large measure on the kind of rice you use and how it was cooked.) Rig for deep frying at 375°F. Cook the balls in peanut oil, a few at a time, for about 5 minutes, until nicely browned. Drain on absorbent paper. Serve warm.

Rice Flour

Rice flour is often overlooked in cookbooks and culinary magazines. It is available in some stores, and the rice grain, being relatively small and not too hard, is ideal for grinding at home. Ordinary long-grain white rice will do, but brown rice can also be used. In a few of the recipes that follow, the short-grain or so-called sticky rice flour is called for.

Rice Waffles

Here's a delicious waffle, made entirely without the aid of wheat flour. The recipe is from Louisiana, where rice is an important crop and where the guinea hen is commonly eaten.

2 cups rice flour
1 cup cooked rice
3 cups milk
2 guinea eggs (or chicken eggs)
1 tablespoon butter or margarine
2 teaspoons baking powder
1 teaspoon salt

Separate the eggs. Whisk the yolks, adding the salt, baking powder, butter, and milk. Beat the whites and mix with the yolk mixture. Mash the cooked rice through a sieve; add it to the mixture. Stir in the rice flour, making a thin batter; pour the batter into a handy pitcher. Heat and thoroughly grease the waffle irons. Pour the batter onto the bottom waffle iron, covering the raised parts. Close the irons and cook for about 2 minutes, or until the waffles are lightly browned. Serve hot with butter and cane syrup or honey.

Rice Johnnycake

In modern times, recipe writers use cornmeal in johnnycake recipes, and those of scholarly bent point out that the original term, from Colonial North America, was "journey cake," meaning a bread designed to travel well in a saddlebag. I was therefore a little surprised to find a camp or hearth-side recipe called "Rice Journey, or Johnny Cake" in Mary Randolph's *The Virginia Housewife*, first published in 1824. Here's Mrs. Randolph's johnnycake, cooked on a plank:

"Boil a pint of rice quite soft, with a tea-spoonful of salt; mix with it while hot a large spoonful of butter [or margarine], and spread it on a dish to cool; when perfectly cold, add a pint of rice flour and half a pint of milk—beat them all together till well mingled. Take the middle part of the head of a barrel, make it quite clean, wet it, and put on the mixture about an inch thick, smooth with a spoon, and baste it with a little milk; set the board aslant before clean coals; when sufficiently baked, slip a thread under the cake and turn it; baste and bake that side in a similar manner, split it, and butter while hot. Small hominy [probably grits] boiled and mixed with rice flour, is better than all rice; and if baked very thin, and afterwards toasted and buttered, it is nearly as good as cassava bread."

Thai Rice Balls

This interesting recipe, adapted here from *The Food of Thailand*, is made with glutinous rice flour and coconut cream, which is available canned in Asian markets and by mail order. The dish is served in small bowls as a dessert.

3 cups glutinous rice flour
4 cups coconut cream
2 cups sugar
1 teaspoon salt
water

Put the rice flour into a bowl. Slowly add enough water to make a stiff paste. Knead the mixture and shape into small balls—each about the size of a garden pea. Bring a pot of water to a rapid boil. Add the rice balls a few at a time with a slotted spoon or strainer. Cook the balls until they float. Remove and drain. Cook the rest of the balls in the same manner. When all the rice balls are ready, bring 2 cups of the coconut milk to a boil in a large pan, stirring as you go to prevent the bottom from scorching. Add the rice balls and salt. Bring to a new boil, then immediately remove the pan from the heat. Stir in the sugar and the rest of the coconut cream. Serve warm in small bowls.

Balinese Pancakes

In Bali rice is eaten at every meal, in one guise or another. Here's an interesting rice pancake, sometimes served for breakfast, that is rolled around a filling instead of being stacked on the plate. It's an idea that deserves some thought—especially when feeding syrup to kids. The palm sugar syrup specified below is made by mixing 2 cups palm sugar with 1 cup water, boiling for 10 minutes, and chilling until ready for use. The palm sugar itself is available in Asian food markets and by mail order.

1 cup rice flour
1 cup freshly grated coconut
1 cup coconut milk
1/2 cup palm sugar syrup
4 chicken eggs
3 tablespoons sugar
3 tablespoons coconut oil
1/2 teaspoon salt

Mix the rice flour, sugar, and salt in a bowl. Stir in the coconut milk, coconut oil, and eggs, stirring out all the lumps. The batter should be on the soupy side, so add a little water or more coconut milk if needed. Heat and grease a griddle or skillet. Ladle 1/4 cup of the batter onto the griddle for each pancake. Cook for 2 minutes, then turn and cook for 1 minute. Cool the pancakes to room temperature. Mix the grated coconut into the palm sugar syrup. Place 1 tablespoon of this mixture into the center of each pancake. Fold the pancakes at the edge and roll into a cylinder shape. Serve at room temperature.

Korean Scallion Pancakes

A national dish in Korea, these pancakes are sometimes called Korean pizzas, according to *Korean Cooking*, by Hilaire Walden. They are usually made in a skillet (with a lid) and cut into squares so that they can be eaten easily with chopsticks. (I use a 10-inch cast-iron skillet for each person, with a bamboo mat.) They should be served directly from the skillet, along with a suitable dipping sauce. The measures below will make 4 pancakes. Allow at least 1 pancake for each person. The green scallions, I might add, help make an attractive pancake, not unlike an abstract painting. Maybe a Klee.

The Pancakes
1 cup rice flour
1 cup all-purpose wheat flour

6 scallions with green tops
2 medium chicken eggs, whisked
$^1\!/_4$ cup peanut oil
2 teaspoons Asian sesame oil
salt to taste
1 cup water

Dipping Sauce

$^1\!/_2$ cup soy sauce
2 tablespoons rice vinegar
2 teaspoons crushed toasted sesame seeds
1 teaspoon grated fresh ginger
$^1\!/_8$ teaspoon sugar
Korean chili powder to taste (or a pinch of cayenne and paprika)

In a suitable bowl mix the rice flour, wheat flour, and a little salt. Mix in the egg and slowly add approximately 1 cup water, until you have a smooth batter. Next, stir in the sesame oil. Set aside for 30 minutes. When you are ready to proceed, cut the scallions into quarters, lengthwise; then chop the strips into 3-inch pieces. For each pancake, place 1 tablespoon of the peanut oil into the skillet. Add $^1\!/_4$ of the scallion pieces to the skillet. Reduce the heat to medium low. Pour in $^1\!/_4$ of the batter. Cover and cook for 5 minutes. Turn with a spatula, cover, and cook for another 3 minutes. Remove the lid and cook for about 3 minutes, or until cooked through. If you are serving from the skillet, cut the pancake into 2-inch squares. (If you are serving from heated plates, slide the pancakes from the skillet and cut into squares on the plates.)

In a small bowl, mix the soy sauce and vinegar. Add the rest of the dipping sauce ingredients, stirring well, and serve hot with the pancakes.

Thai Browned White Rice Grits

Note that the product of this recipe is usually called "browned rice flour." The term should not be confused with "brown rice flour." What we have here is stuff made from toasted white rice. In the northeastern part of Thailand, where the method probably originated, sticky rice is usually used. But any good white rice will do. Being a Southern good ol' boy, I might also explain (with a hidden smile) that the term "grits" in the recipe is my own doing. But that's what they are.

1 cup white rice

Heat a dry skillet over medium heat. Add the rice to the skillet and toast for 3 minutes, or until the rice takes on a golden-brown color, shaking the skillet back and forth all the while so that all the grains are browned evenly. Remove from the heat and let the rice cool in the skillet. Grind the rice with a mortar and pestle until it is the consistency of rather fine grits (or use a hand-cranked grain mill set on a coarse grind). Place the grits into a jar, seal, and store until needed. It can be used in a meat salad, rolled in lettuce, as in the next recipe.

Note: See also Chinese Rice Grits, page 162.

Laab Mu

In the northeastern part of Thailand, rice grits are used to make a meat salad, which is rolled in a lettuce leaf and eaten out of hand. The dish is now popular throughout most of the country, especially for festive occasions. I like the dish made with freshly ground pork, but others may prefer ground chicken (called simply *laab*) or beef *(laab neua)*. The real stuff is made with the aid of fresh lemon grass, which is sometimes available in American markets. Just make sure it is fresh and tender. The real stuff also contains several fresh kaffir lime leaves, minced. I have omitted these. Some recipes call for a whole cup of Thai fish sauce, but I have reduced this measure considerably. I have also reduced the measure of fresh mint (which is a popular ingredient in Thai cookery).

1 pound lean pork loin
1½ cups chicken stock or water
½ cup fresh lemon juice
½ cup fresh mint
½ cup fresh cilantro
3 tablespoons browned rice grits (see above recipe), finely ground
2 scallions with green tops
2 stalks lemongrass
¼ cup Thai fish sauce (*nam pla*)
1 tablespoon brown sugar
½ tablespoon cayenne (or to taste)
lettuce leaves

Cut the pork into 1-inch chunks and grind it in a sausage mill. Trim the tough outer layers from the lemongrass. Chop finely across the grain. Clean the scallions and chop finely across the grain. Bring the chicken stock to a boil in the saucepan. Add the ground pork and bring to a new boil. Stir constantly with a wooden spoon 2 or 3 minutes, or until the meat is done. (The pork should be thoroughly broken up.) With a slotted spoon, place the cooked pork in a bowl, draining the saucepan. Mix the remaining ingredients, except for the lettuce leaves, into the cooked pork. Select some small cupped lettuce leaves, placing them on a serving tray. Spoon some of the meat mixture into each lettuce leaf. Serve immediately. Each diner should fold the lettuce leaf and eat out of hand.

Chinese Rice Grits

These grits, or crumbs, as they are sometimes called, are used in Chinese meat recipes, such as the one below.

1 cup long-grain white rice
1 teaspoon Szechuan peppercorns
1 star anise

Heat a skillet and turn the heat to low. Add the rice, peppercorns, and star anise. Cook until the rice is lightly toasted, about 5 minutes, stirring with a wooden spoon as you go. Remove the skillet from the heat and let the rice cool. Grind the rice in a blender or grain mill set to grind grits or coarse flour. Store in a sealed jar until needed.

Szechuan Beef with Rice Crumbs

For this recipe I am indebted to *Regional Cooking of China*, by Maggie Gin. I found the dish very easy to make—and it's very unusual to find a recipe for steamed beef. The book calls for flank or skirt steak, and I have listed these below, but I usually use a lean and well-trimmed New York strip steak. Also, the original calls for rice wine or dry sherry. I usually use dry vermouth, left over from my last martini.

1 pound flank or skirt steak
1/3 cup rice grits (see above recipe)
1 tablespoon soy sauce
1 tablespoon brown bean sauce
1 tablespoon rice wine or dry sherry (or dry vermouth)
2 teaspoons minced fresh gingerroot
1 teaspoon Asian sesame oil
1 teaspoon brown sugar
3 tablespoons water
hot water

Mix all the ingredients except the beef, rice grits, and hot water. Place the mixture into a nonmetallic container. Cut the beef into 1-inch chunks and place them into the container, stirring about to coat all sides. Marinate for 30 minutes or so. Coat each piece of marinated beef with rice grits, placing the pieces in a shallow steaming dish. Pour any leftover marinade over the pieces. Steam the beef over boiling water (covered) for 1 hour, or until the rice grits are soft. Add more water as needed. Serve with rice and steamed Chinese vegetables.

Fresh Chinese Rice Noodles

These are similar to the noodle skins that are sometimes available fresh in Chinese bakery shops. They are fully cooked—but they are not the dry noodles— and can be cut to various widths, depending on how you want them. It's easy to make these at home from freshly ground rice, as needed.

2 cups rice flour
$1/2$ teaspoon alum
salt to taste
3 tablespoons peanut oil
$2^3/4$ cups water

Place the rice flour in the center of a pastry board or other smooth surface. Sprinkle the alum and salt over the rice; mix thoroughly. Slowly, a little at a time, mix in some water and the peanut oil. Continue until you have a ball of smooth dough. Knead for 10 minutes. Place the dough into a mixing bowl. Break it apart with your fingers and slowly add the rest of the water, mixing well into a smooth batter. Let the batter sit for 30 minutes. While waiting, rig for steaming: In a wok or suitable pot with a cover, place a large pie pan on a rack over 2 inches of water. Grease several pie pans. Using a large spoon or ladle, place enough batter into a greased pie pan to cover the surface. Note that the amount of batter used and its consistency will determine the thickness of the noodle skin. Cover the pot or wok with a lid and bring the water to a boil over high heat. Lower the heat and steam for 15 minutes, or until the noodle skin sets. While the skin steams, have another pan ready. After 15 minutes, remove the first pan from the rack and replace it with another one. Repeat. When the first pan cools a little, roll the noodle skin onto a plate. Set aside until all the skins are ready. While the noodle skins are rolled, cut them into $1/2$-inch slices. Use in any recipe that calls for fresh rice noodles.

Note: If you want fried rice noodles, heat some peanut oil in a wok or skillet. Fry the noodle strips quickly a few at a time for a minute or two, until lightly brown. Do not overcook or stir too much; otherwise the noodles will be mushy and stick to the bottom of the wok.

Indonesian Crackers

These crackers are best served with curries and spicy meats. I like to use crushed peanuts, but whole ones can also be used and may be more authentic.

1 cup rice flour
1 cup coconut milk
1/2 cup chopped roasted peanuts
peanut oil
1 teaspoon ground coriander (dried cilantro corns)
1 teaspoon garlic powder
1/2 teaspoon ground cumin
1/2 teaspoon ground turmeric
1/2 teaspoon ground dried ginger (or galangal, if available)
1/2 teaspoon salt

Mix the flour into the coconut milk. Stir in all the other ingredients except the peanuts and peanut oil, mixing thoroughly. If the batter is too thick to drop nicely from a spoon, add more coconut milk. Heat about 3/4 inch of oil in a skillet. Wet a teaspoon and use it to drop some batter into the hot oil. The batter should flatten out, making a thin cookie or cracker. Fry until golden brown. Taste and adjust the seasonings (I like more salt added to the batter). Stir in the peanuts and switch to a tablespoon for dropping. Cook the cookies 3 at a time. Drain on a brown bag or paper towels. Store in an airtight container until needed.

Variation: Substitute 1/2 cup chunky peanut butter for the roasted peanuts.

Rice Puddings

Just about every family in America has a favorite recipe for rice pudding, and the same statement might well hold for most of the world. Here are a few to try.

Poor Man's Pudding

This old recipe is from New England. I have added a little cinnamon toward the end. A short-grain rice is best, producing a very creamy pudding, but try what you've got. Use rich, whole milk fresh from the cow if you've got it. Pasteurized whole milk will do, but don't expect a rich pudding from skimmed or otherwise thinned milk.

½ cup rice
½ cup sugar
1 quart milk
¼ teaspoon sea salt
cinnamon

Wash the rice well, then put into an earthenware pudding dish suitable for serving. Cover with the milk, stir in the sugar and salt, and soak for 1 hour. Preheat the oven to 300°F. Bake the pudding for an hour and a half. Increase the heat to 450°F and bake for another 30 minutes, or until the pudding browns slightly on top. Sprinkle lightly with cinnamon. Serve hot or cold.

Note: Many variations call for raisins.

Norwegian Rice and Almond Pudding

This stove-top rice pudding is best made with the aid of a double boiler instead of being finished in the oven. For the almond grits, grind blanched nuts in a food mill, using a rather coarse plate or setting.

1 cup long-grain white rice
1 quart rich milk
water
⅔ cup almond grits
2 tablespoons melted butter or margarine
2½ tablespoons sugar
1 teaspoon vanilla extract
salt to taste
freshly ground nutmeg to taste
whipped cream

Rinse the rice in hot water and drain. Place the milk in the top part of a large double boiler, over boiling water. Add the rice and salt. Cover and cook on low heat for 1 hour, or until the mixture thickens. Stir in the butter, sugar, vanilla, nutmeg, and almond grits. Serve warm topped with whipped cream.

Brazilian Rice Custard

South Americans are fond of custards and flans. Here's a good one from Brazil, tasty and attractive.

1¹/₂ cups rice flour
1 quart hot milk
1 cup sugar
¹/₂ teaspoon salt
powdered sugar
freshly ground cinnamon
water

Preheat the oven broiler. Heat the milk in the top part of a double boiler, with boiling water in the bottom. In a large bowl, sift together the rice, sugar, and salt. Stir this mixture into the hot milk. Cook for 20 minutes. Butter a custard dish. Spoon the custard into the dish with a spoon, making oval mounds. Brown in a double boiler (with boiling water in the bottom). Place the custard dish under the broiler until the top is lightly browned. Sprinkle with powdered sugar and cinnamon. Serve warm.

Brown Rice Pudding

Brown rice makes a nice, healthy pudding. Precook the rice using the Easy Brown Rice recipe on page 135. I normally use plain water instead of stock for cooking rice destined for the pudding dish.

2 cups cooked brown rice
2¹/₂ cups whole milk
³/₄ cup honey
2 large chicken eggs, whisked
¹/₂ cup raisins or chopped dates
1 teaspoon freshly crushed allspice berries

Preheat the oven to 325°F and butter a shallow baking dish suitable for serving. Mix all the ingredients in a bowl. Turn the mixture out into the baking dish, spreading evenly. Bake for 50 minutes, or until the pudding has set nicely. Serve warm, perhaps topping each serving with a dollop of whipped cream.

Brown Rice and Date Pudding

Here's a pudding of Asian or Middle East influence, where tahini is a common condiment. See the recipe on page 242, or purchase some in an Asian or health-food market. Leftover or precooked rice can be used.

2 cups cooked brown rice
1 cup chopped dates
$3/4$ cup milk
$1/4$ cup tahini
1 tablespoon whole wheat flour
$1/2$ teaspoon vanilla
$1/2$ teaspoon salt
cinnamon

Mix all the ingredients except the rice in a blender or food processor. Blend it and pour into a saucepan. Heat, stirring constantly, until the mixture thickens. Stir in the rice. Let set for 5 minutes. Sprinkle lightly with cinnamon and serve.

Variation: Stir in a few chopped toasted pecans or walnut pieces along with the rice.

Nutritional Highlights

Highly polished white rice is, for the most part, what people eat, and it is no great shakes, nutritionally. But people who depend on rice—much of the world—simply eat lots of it. In the Far East, I have read, each person eats 400 pounds of rice per year. People who depend largely on white rice have suffered from a vitamin B deficiency, resulting in beriberi, but this shouldn't be a concern in America, where people consume only about 10 pounds of rice per year. In any case, brown rice is much more healthy. It contains more fiber, calcium, vitamin E, phosphorus, and riboflavin. Enriched white rice from the supermarket, however, contains more thiamin and iron than unenriched, if it isn't all rinsed out before cooking.

11

Barley

Although, owing to its greyish crumb, barley bread may
not look immediately appetizing, those who acquire
a taste for it are likely to become addicts. I am one.

—Elizabeth David, *English Bread and Yeast Cookery*

It is an addiction which is not always easily satisfied," Ms. David goes on. "In London, barley meal is difficult to come by." It's true. Barley meal or flour is rather scarce these days—a strange circumstance, considering the importance that barley once held in parts of the Middle East and in Europe, where it was the main breadstuff until the sixteenth century. It lost out as a bread grain only after the widespread use of yeast, which required a high-gluten flour, such as that from wheat, for best results.

But Barley didn't really lose out as a grain. It simply went underground, only to gush forth in beers, ales, whiskeys, Scotch whisky, and sundry malts of the Western world. Nor did barley disappear entirely from the grocery store and supermarket. It was tucked away in small boxes in the soup section, and hidden in such breakfast cereals as Grape-Nuts. Now it's slowly coming back as breadstuff—but not, as one might expect, on the farmstead or in the peasant cabin. It's marketing stronghold is now the city health-food store and a few mail-order outlets.

An ancient grain, barley was cultivated as early as 7000 B.C. and was probably the most important crop for ancient man. It was used extensively by the ancient Hebrews, the Egyptians, the Etruscans, the Greeks, and the Romans. In modern times, most of the world's production has gone to animal feed and brewery, but there are a few cultural strongholds here and there, such as Tibet and Ecuador, Finland and Ethiopia.

Barley can be raised in home gardens and on farms just about everywhere, from the tropics to the Arctic Circle. Most of the present barley production in the United States is in the upper plains states, Idaho, and Washington. The grain is marketed in several forms, as follows, in specialty markets, in health-food stores, and in some upscale supermarkets.

⚜ Hulled and Hull-less Barley ⚜

Hulled barley is just that. The outer husk has been removed, but the berry has not been polished like the familiar pearled kind (discussed in the next section). Hulled barley has less of the bran and germ removed, and consequently contains a little more fiber, phosphorus, and potassium.

Being brownish-gray in color, hulled barley simply isn't as pretty as pearl barley and is a little gritty. (For that reason, it is not as commonly available as the pearl kind and may never be.) Hulled barley can be used in soups and stews, especially those that require long, slow simmering; it is, in fact, sometimes called pot barley or Scotch barley. It can also be used in barley beverages—which are considerable in number and variety—and in making barley flour.

In recent years, a "hull-less" or "naked" barley has been developed. It isn't really hull-less. Instead, it has a hull that is only loosely attached to the seed kernel, allowing the hull to be easily removed during harvest, as is done with wheat. Hull-less barley can be used in most of the recipes that call for hulled barley, and it may have a significant influence over the commercial use of the grain in breadstuff and cereals. The home gardener may want to experiment with this new hull-less variety, and seeds are available from some garden-supply outfits. Meanwhile, the home cook can get by nicely with ordinary hulled barley in the recipes below. Beverages and flour using hulled barley are discussed under separate headings.

Basic Hulled Barley

As a rule, hulled barley should be cooked longer than regular pearl barley, using more water. Presoaking helps.

1 cup hulled barley
water
beef broth or water
salt

Soak the barley overnight, or for at least 8 hours. In a tightly covered large pot, simmer the barley in 5 cups of water or beef stock, perhaps along with a little salt, for 1 hour, or until cooked to your liking. Add a little more liquid to the pot if needed, and stir from time to time.

⊰ Pearl Barley ⊱

This common market form is simply barley grains that have been hulled and ground down, which polishes them. Naturally, some of the germ and bran is ground away, making pearl barley a little less nutritious than hulled barley. Because it is so readily available, however, I recommend the pearl form for most recipes calling for whole barley. In supermarkets, look for it not in the grains, baking, or cereal section but in the soups section. The reason, of course, is that most of the pearl barley that is sold at consumer level goes into soups and stews. (But times are changing, slowly, and whole grains are gaining shelf space in supermarkets.) See the recipes in the Barley Soup section below. More and more, however, we are finding cooked pearl barley used in stir-fries, salads, breadstuff, and cereals. It is even used in desserts.

Basic Pearl Barley

Barley absorbs lots of liquid and expands greatly as it cooks; 1 cup of dry pearl barley will yield about $2\frac{2}{3}$ cups when cooked. This basic recipe calls for water, but beef stock can also be used.

1 cup pearl barley
4 cups water
1 teaspoon salt

Bring the water to a boil in a suitable pan. Add the barley and salt. Bring to a new boil, cover, and simmer for about 45 minutes, until all the water has been absorbed and the barley is tender. Fluff with a fork before serving or using in salads or other recipes.

Note: If you want a rather chewy barley, use 3 cups of water. If you want a softer barley, use 5 cups.

Chorizo and Barley

For this Andalucian dish I owe Bert Green, author of *Green on Grains*, who said he got it while on a tourist excursion out from Madrid. The dish has truly wonderful flavor.

1/2 to 3/4 pound chorizo sausage, cut into wheels
1 cup pearl barley
3 cups chicken stock or broth
1/2 cup sliced green olives
1 tablespoon butter or margarine
1 medium-to-large onion, chopped
1/4 teaspoon chopped fresh thyme
chopped fresh parsley
salt and freshly ground black pepper to taste

In a saucepan or skillet over medium-low heat, sauté the chorizo wheels until they are browned (if they are fatty, no grease will be required). Remove the sausages to drain. Add the butter and onion, sautéeing for a few minutes. Add the barley and thyme, tossing well. Add the chicken stock and browned chorizo. Bring to a boil, reduce the heat, and simmer for 30 to 40 minutes, or until the barley has absorbed all the liquid. The barley should be tender at this point. If it is too chewy, add a little more broth or water, cooking again until the liquid has been absorbed. If it is too wet, cook uncovered until the liquid has been absorbed. Stir in the olives, along with some salt and pepper to taste. Sprinkle with chopped parsley. Serve hot.

Barley Stuffing with Mushrooms

In recent years, we have been advised not to keep turkey stuffing overnight before using it—and to cook the bird well-done. Here's a rich stuffing that contains no ground meat or chicken egg, thereby reducing the chances of salmonella contamination.

1 1/2 cups pearl barley
1 1/2 cups sliced fresh mushrooms
4 cups chicken stock
2 cups chopped green onions with part of tops
1 cup chopped celery with green tops
1/4 cup minced fresh garlic
2 tablespoons olive oil
1 tablespoon dried tarragon

1 teaspoon powdered sage
salt and pepper to taste

Bring the stock to a boil, add the barley, cover, reduce the heat, and simmer for 45 minutes, stirring a time or two. Heat the olive oil in a large skillet. Sauté the onions, garlic, and celery for 5 minutes. Mix in the cooked barley, mushrooms, sage, tarragon, salt, and pepper. Stuff the bird loosely, truss, and bake or cook according to your turkey recipe. If you prefer dressing to stuffing, spoon the mixture into a greased baking dish and bake at 350°F for 30 minutes; serve hot in a separate dish or mounded around the bird.

Notes: This recipe can also be used to stuff or dress chicken or pheasant. To stuff fish, add a little fish sauce and a little chopped tomato. The button-type supermarket mushrooms can be used for this recipe, as well as shiitakes or oyster mushrooms. If you are into wild foods, try chanterelles or even morels, along with reduced measures of wild onion, wild garlic, or ramps.

Barley and Pecans

Because the pecan is my favorite nut (and I am fortunate enough to have 14 large trees in my yard) and barley is my favorite grain, I was indeed delighted to see them combined in the new edition of *Joy of Cooking!* I have added some salt to the recipe.

1 1/2 cups pearl barley, precooked and drained
1/4 cup pecan pieces
2 tablespoons butter or margarine
1/2 teaspoon salt

Melt the butter in a skillet. Sauté the pecans, stirring as you go, for 2 or 3 minutes. Be warned that pecans burn easily, so watch your business. Sprinkle with salt and combine with cooked barley. Serve warm. Also see the next recipe for a more elaborate treatment of barley and nuts.

Belila

According to Claudia Roden's *A Book of Middle Eastern Food*, an excellent work from which this recipe has been adapted, belila is served in the Sephardic Jewish home to celebrate the arrival of a baby's first tooth, which, of course, resembles a grain of pearl barley.

$^{1}\!/_{2}$ pound pearl barley
$^{3}\!/_{4}$ cup flaked almonds
$^{1}\!/_{3}$ cup pistachios, chopped
$^{1}\!/_{4}$ cup pine nuts
sugar to taste
$2^{1}\!/_{2}$ tablespoons orange-blossom water or rose water
water

Soak the barley in water overnight. Simmer the barley, covered, in 5 cups of water for $^{1}\!/_{4}$ hour, or until just tender. Stir in some sugar to taste. Add the nuts and orange blossom water or rose water. Stir and study, adding more water if needed. The barley and nuts should suspend perfectly in a light syrup.

Black Barley

Here's a pleasant surprise to put into your soups, stews, salads, and stir-fries. The outside of the barley is indeed black (or maybe deep purple), and naturally so. Black barley is not easy to find in most markets. It can be purchased from some mail-order catalogs, but product listings vary a little from year to year. At present, black barley is found mostly in stores that sell Ethiopian foods.

Basic Black Barley

These directions were given on an 8-ounce package of black barley. I assume that all black barley can be cooked the same way. Eight ounces, it turns out, is a little more than 1 cup. It expands considerably, depending in part on how long it is cooked.

8 ounces black barley
4 cups water
salt to taste

Bring the water to a boil, adding a little salt. Add the barley, bring to a new boil, reduce heat to low, cover, and simmer for 45 to 60 minutes, depending on whether you want it soft or al dente. Remove from the heat and let rest for 10 minutes. It may be used immediately or refrigerated for a few days.

Black Barley, Raw Bean, and Vegetable Salad

This salad can be made with regular barley, but I think the black groats go nicely with the white rice.

3/4 cup black barley, cooked
3/4 cup long-grain white basmati rice
3/4 cup shelled fresh baby lima beans or butter beans
2 cups fresh corn kernels
2 cups chopped celery with part of green tops
2 medium tomatoes, chopped
1 medium onion, finely chopped
1/2 cup feta cheese, crumbled
juice of 1 large lemon
1/4 cup extra virgin olive oil
1 tablespoon prepared mustard
1 tablespoon honey
1/2 tablespoon chopped fresh oregano
1/2 tablespoon chopped fresh basil
salt and freshly ground black pepper
lettuce leaves

In a small bowl, whisk the olive oil, lemon juice, mustard, honey, and salt and pepper to taste. Set aside. In a large wooden salad bowl suitable for serving, mix the barley, rice, corn, celery, beans, tomatoes, onion, basil, and oregano. Pour the liquid over the greens, tossing to mix well. Serve on a bed of lettuce, topped with feta cheese to taste.

Variations: Add fresh herbs of your choice. I also like a few anchovies on mine, and maybe an olive or two, and some chunks of canned octopus packed in olive oil, and . . . well, you get the idea.

Quick Barley

Several forms of quick barley have been marketed, some of which have been steamed and rolled like oats. Generally, this is supermarket fare and, unfortunately, seems to be replacing regular pearl barley in some of the smaller stores. It's right good stuff, especially for making quick soups, or perhaps for adding to canned soups, and it comes in handy for making salads and stir-fries. But it's not as versatile as pearl barley. On long simmering, quick barley becomes mushy and tends to lose its identity entirely.

Quick barley is widely available in supermarkets under brand-name packages. Look for it in the soup section.

Easy Barley

This easy barley recipe works for quick barley that has been steamed and pressed like oatmeal. The barley kernels retain their identity, look like barley, and fluff up nicely.

1 cup quick barley
2 cups water
1 teaspoon salt

Bring the water to a boil in a saucepan. Add the barley and salt. Cover, reduce the heat, and simmer for 10 to 12 minutes, until tender to your liking. Remove from the heat and let stand for 5 minutes. Use immediately or cool and refrigerate (for up to several days).

Barley Grits

Barley grits can be purchased here and there, or they can be ground at home with the mill on a coarse setting. Some of the commercial barley grits may be steamed, in which case they will probably be labeled "precooked." In any case, barley grits can be cooked and eaten as a breakfast cereal, according to the directions on the package or by the following recipe.

Barley Breakfast Grits

The seemingly natural combination of barley and honey goes nicely for breakfast.

1/2 cup barley grits
1 1/2 cups water
salt to taste
butter or margarine
honey or brown sugar

In a saucepan, bring the water to a boil, add some salt, and stir in the barley. Reduce the heat to low and cook, stirring as you go, for about 15 minutes, or until the barley is cooked to your liking. (Some forms of barley grits may require less cooking time; if so, follow the packager's instructions.) Serve hot in bowls, along with butter and a little honey or brown sugar to taste.

Barley and Lamb Stew

Here's an old Greek recipe, going back at least 2,000 years. It is unusual for a Greek dish because it is heavy on meat and sparse of vegetables. If you don't have any barley grits, coarsely grind some pearl barley. The last time I tried the recipe, I merely pounded some quick barley with a mortar and pestle to approximate grits.

2 pounds boneless lamb shoulder
1 cup barley grits
6 cups water
2 tablespoons olive oil
1 tablespoon crushed sea salt

Cut the lamb into 1-inch chunks. Put the lamb, water, and salt into a stockpot. Bring to a boil, reduce the heat, cover, and simmer for 2 hours. Drain out the liquid, measure it, and return to the pot with enough new water to make 6 cups. Stir the olive oil into the barley grits. Put the mixture into the pot with the meat and broth, stirring well. Bring to a light boil, reduce the heat, cover, and simmer for 20 to 30 minutes, or until the liquid in the pot has been mostly absorbed. Serve hot in bowls, along with a crusty sourdough bread and perhaps a good red wine.

Barley Polenta

Frederick the Great, King of Prussia, according to *Food: An Oxford Anthology*, was especially fond "of polenta, a kind of barley-cake *[sic]* ground up and roasted." The scholarly *"[sic]"* was no doubt inserted behind the "barley-cake" because the august editors allowed that real polenta is made from cornmeal, not barley. This is not necessarily the case, depending, I suppose, on your definition of the term "polenta." Remember that cornmeal, or meal made from maize, simply wasn't available to the ancient Italians, and there is good evidence that polenta was first made with chickpeas or chestnuts, or both. Even in modern times, it is made with chestnuts on the isle of Corsica, and my guess is that it has been made by the ton with sweet acorns and perhaps beech mast. So, why not make it with barley, which was available long before the Roman Empire? Maybe the King of Prussia knew his stuff.

1 cup uncooked barley grits or flaked barley
3 cups milk
3 tablespoons honey
yellow cornmeal, stone-ground (optional)
butter
salt to taste

Simmer the milk, barley, honey, and salt in a saucepan, stirring as you go, for 20 minutes. Pour the mixture into a well-greased Pyrex baking dish, about 8 by 10 inches, or a suitable pan. Cool and refrigerate overnight. Cut the polenta into squares or rectangles, roll in yellow cornmeal, and fry in butter until lightly browned. Serve with butter and honey or syrup.

Barley Flour

Barley flour is available from specialty-food shops and from mail-order sources. It is also easy to grind at home with a mill, using either hulled barley or pearl barley. Sifting is not recommended because it removes some of the nutrients. Store the flour or meal in airtight containers, preferably in the refrigerator or freezer.

Although barley flour is seldom used in modern breads, it was once very important for breadstuff in northern Europe and other regions. It is, however, a low-gluten flour, making it generally unsuitable for light risen breads. It does, however, add a certain sweetness to baked products and extends the shelf life of breads.

In addition to the recipes below, substitute a little barley flour for the wheat flour in breads, muffins, pancakes, and such. Also, use it as a thickener for soups, stews, and gravy. I even use it from time to time as a thickener for a beef stir-fry.

Wheat and Barley Round Loaf

As suggested in the introduction to this book, most of the so-called barley breads are really wheat breads with a little barley added. It is hard to find a recipe in which wheat is added to the barley, lending gluten and what was called a "lift" in Raymond Sokolov's book *With the Grain*, from which the following has been adapted. This one comes close—and with whole wheat!

2 cups barley flour
2$^{1}/_{2}$ cups whole wheat flour
2 cups warm water

1 package active dry yeast (1/4-ounce size)
2 teaspoons salt

Put the water into a large bowl, stir in the yeast, and let stand for 5 minutes. Mix in the salt and slowly work in the barley flour and whole wheat flour, stirring in first one and then the other, until you have a smooth dough. Shape the dough into a ball, turn out onto a floured bread board or suitable work surface, and knead vigorously for at least 5 minutes, until you have an elastic dough. Shape the dough into a ball and place it on a greased baking sheet. Cover with a moistened cloth and let it rise in a draft-free place for 1 hour or longer (maybe even up to 3 hours), until it doubles in bulk. Preheat the oven to 350°F. Place the loaf in the center of the oven for 50 to 60 minutes. When done, the loaf will sound hollow when tapped. Cool and slice.

Bert's Barley Flatbread

For this recipe I owe Bert Greene, author of *The Grains Cookbook*, who says it is a version of the Welsh flatbread called *haidd*. I use a little more onion than Greene might allow, and I double the garlic.

1 1/2 cups barley flour
1 1/2 cups milk
3 tablespoons olive oil
1 medium to large onion, chopped
2 cloves garlic, minced
1/4 teaspoon crushed red chili pepper
1 tablespoon sugar
1/2 teaspoon salt
water

Preheat the oven to 500°F. Using 1 tablespoon of the olive oil in a skillet, sauté the onion for 1 minute. Add the garlic and crushed red pepper. Cook for 5 minutes over medium heat, stirring as you go. Remove the skillet from the heat. Combine the barley flour, milk, sugar, salt, the rest of the olive oil, and 1/4 cup of water and mix until you have a smooth batter. Add a little more water if needed. Stir in the onion mixture. Pour the batter into a greased pizza pan or 12-inch skillet, or into a hand griddle with a ringed lip. Bake in the top third of the oven for 15 minutes. Cut into wedges with a pizza wheel. Serve hot, preferably with butter or honey, or both.

Barley Bannocks

This recipe is really primitive, used in areas of northern Europe where wheat did not thrive. It is flat and heavy, tasty and quite filling. Since it requires only a skillet and a fire for cooking, I recommend it for camp or cabin cookery. The measures will yield a round of dough just right for cooking in a 10-inch cast-iron skillet. Double the measures if you are using a large griddle and need more bread.

1¼ cups barley flour
1 cup top milk or half-and-half
1 tablespoon butter or margarine
½ teaspoon fine sea salt
1 teaspoon strong honey (buckwheat will do)

Melt the butter in a saucepan. Stir in the milk, honey, and salt. Add the barley flour, mixing well, until you have a sticky dough. Heat the skillet but do not grease it. Place the dough in the center and spread it out. Cook for about 10 minutes, or until the dough sets and browns a little on the bottom. Turn with the aid of a large spatula. Cook for 10 minutes, browning the bottom lightly. Reduce the heat and, if necessary, continue to cook until the center of the bread is done.

Berreens

This simple old recipe from the Isle of Man made use of toasted barley flour, which added flavor and made the final bread a little more moist. I found the recipe in the book *English Bread and Yeast Cookery*, by Elizabeth David. Ms. David, in turn, got the recipe from *My Grandmother's Cookery Book*, by Suzanne Woolley, who, one would surmise, got it from her grandmother. Coming out of the Middle Ages, barley grain was dried on the cabin hearth or on a stone heated over a turf fire. Then it was ground in a quern or small hand mill. But in 1647 (Ms. David goes on) the Lord Derby ordered the destruction of all hand mills, forcing the people to use the lord's mill. If you grind your own flour for this recipe, as well you should, be sure to grind it finely so that it will make a good dough. The original berreens were cooked on a griddle or flat stone, or cooked in a "pot-oven," which I assume to be what Americans call a Dutch oven. I have cooked the bread both ways and prefer a cast-iron griddle or skillet, so that I can see what it is doing and cheer it along.

freshly ground barley flour
salt
water

Mix the water into the barley, adding a little salt. Knead into a dough. Shape it into a cake, and clap it flat between the hands. Cook on a hot griddle or skillet.

Note: I might add that one of my favorite corn breads is made almost exactly the same way, using fine freshly ground cornmeal, and cooked on a griddle well-greased with bacon drippings.

Barley Flapjacks

These flapjacks are a little dark for some tastes and can be cooked with half barley flour and half wheat flour, or some such mix. But first try the whole barley recipe. Its flavor is distinctive, especially if you grind your own flour from pearl or hulled barley.

1$^1/_2$ cups barley flour
1$^1/_2$ cups milk
2 tablespoons melted butter or margarine plus more for serving
1 tablespoon sugar
2 large chicken eggs, whisked
2 teaspoons baking powder
$^1/_2$ teaspoon vanilla extract
$^1/_2$ teaspoon salt
honey, syrup, or jam

In a large bowl, mix the barley flour, baking powder, sugar, and salt. Mix in the melted butter, vanilla, eggs, and milk, stirring well to eliminate lumps. Add a little more milk if needed. Heat and grease a griddle or cast-iron skillet. Using a $^1/_4$-cup ladle, pour some batter onto the hot griddle. Cook until bubbles appear. Flip with a large spatula and cook the other side just enough to brown the surface. Cook the rest of the batch, stacking the flapjacks on a plate until you have a serving. I like to sandwich some butter between each flapjack, but this is optional. Serve hot with syrup, honey, or jam. I'll take honey, if I have a choice.

Barley Pie Crust

Here's an easy pie crust, suitable only for 1-crust pies. (It doesn't roll well, making a top crust difficult to handle.)

1 cup barley flour
$^{1}/_{4}$ cup olive oil, chilled
$^{1}/_{4}$ cup cold water

Preheat the oven to 350°F. Dump the flour into a bowl. Mix in the olive oil and about half the cold water. Add more cold water as needed to make a dough. Turn the dough out onto a pie plate and spread it with your fingers, trying for a uniform thickness. Bake in the center of the oven for 20 minutes. Use this in pie recipes that call for a precooked crust.

Barley Soups and Stews

At present, most of the whole barley sold in America for human consumption, except for that used in brewing beers and spirits, is put into soups and stews. It is ideal for this purpose, and can be used in any of its market forms. Pearl barley and sometimes quick barley is the form usually sold in supermarkets. Most of the recipes below can be made with ordinary pearl barley or perhaps hulled barley. If you proceed with quick barley, add it during the last 10 minutes or so of the suggested cooking period for the recipe.

Hulled Barley Broth

Hulled barley makes a very good broth with long, slow cooking. Pearl barley also works.

$^{1}/_{4}$ cup hulled barley
1 gallon water
4 leeks, chopped
2 carrots, chopped
2 ribs celery, chopped with part of tops
1 onion
2 cloves
salt and pepper to taste

Rinse the barley and put it into a pot with the water. Add the rest of the ingredients, bring to a boil, reduce the heat, cover, and simmer very gently for 3 hours. Strain and serve hot in bowls, or refrigerate. It can also be frozen.

Barley and Mushroom Soup

This barley soup is made with both fresh and dried mushrooms. The dried mushrooms, preferably shiitake or morels, are very flavorful, and add greatly to this soup; even the water in which they are reconstituted is used. If you gather your own wild mushrooms, as I do, it's easy to dry a few in a modern food dehydrator. The beef stock used in the recipe should be made at home from scratch, but I'll allow stock made with bouillon cubes.

1/2 cup pearl barley
8 ounces fresh mushrooms, chopped
1/4 ounce dried mushrooms
4 cups beef stock
1 cup hot water
2 tablespoons butter or margarine
1 medium onion, diced
3 cloves garlic, minced
1 small carrot, diced
1 rib celery with green tops, diced
1 tablespoon minced fresh parsley
salt and freshly ground black pepper to taste

Steep the dried mushrooms in 1 cup of hot water for 30 minutes or longer. Squeeze the liquid from the fresh mushrooms and dice them, being sure to save the liquid. Melt the butter in a soup pot or stove-top Dutch oven. Sauté the fresh mushrooms, onion, garlic, carrot, and celery until tender. Stir in the pearl barley. Cook, stirring as you go, for 5 or 6 minutes. Stir in the diced dried mushrooms and their soaking liquid. Add the stock, bring to a boil, reduce the heat, cover, and simmer for an hour. Season with salt and pepper, stirring as you go, and sprinkle with chopped fresh parsley. Serve hot in soup bowls, along with plenty of hot chewy homemade French bread. If the French bread is too tough to chew, dunk it.

Picayune Cream of Barley Soup

Here's an old New Orleans recipe for barley soup that hits the spot if served hot on a cold day, along with some chewy French bread.

1/4 cup pearl barley
2 cups hot milk
2 chicken egg yolks, whisked
1 tablespoon butter or margarine

salt and black pepper to taste
3 quarts water

Bring the water to a boil in a pot. Rinse the barley and put it in the water. Simmer for 3 hours on low heat. Strain the stock through a sieve, mashing the barley on through the sieve to break it up. Put the sieved mixture back into the pot. Add the milk, butter, and salt and black pepper to taste. Bring to a light boil. Immediately remove the pot from the heat and stir in the egg yolks. Serve in bowls with hot bread, and have a pepper mill handy for those who want another twist or two.

Duck Soup with Barley

Duck soup with lots of barley is very, very good. I also like to use a good deal of celery with the green tops. For the measures below, the exact amount of duck meat isn't critical, but two mallards are about right. If you don't have mallards, try a Long Island duckling with the fat removed.

2 wild ducks, mallard-sized
4 cups water plus more for simmering
2 cups duck broth
1/2 cup red wine
1 cup pearl barley
3 large ribs celery with tops, finely chopped
1 medium onion, chopped
3 cloves garlic, minced
1 tablespoon chopped chives
1/2 teaspoon pepper
salt to taste
3 bay leaves

Skin the ducks. Fillet out each side of the breasts and set aside. Disjoint the rest of the ducks, put the pieces into a stove-top pot, cover with water, add the bay leaves, cover, and simmer slowly for 1 hour, or until the meat is tender. While the bony pieces simmer, cut the breast pieces into chunks and put them into a Crock-Pot. Add 4 cups water, the pepper, chives, celery, onion, salt, and garlic. (It's best to scrape the stalks of celery, then cut the stalks into several strips longways before chopping, making for smaller than usual pieces.) Turn the Crock-Pot to low.

When the duck in the stove-top pot is tender, take it out and bone the meat. Chop the meat and giblets, adding them to the Crock-Pot. Add two cups of the duck broth and discard the rest, or save it for future use. Stir in the pearl barley. Add the red wine. Cover and heat on low for 6 or 7 hours. Serve in bowls and eat hot with a good bread.

Warning: Make sure that you don't add more than a cup of barley. This stuff soaks up lots of water and expands greatly. It may even push the top off the Crock-Pot. After the barley has cooked for an hour or so, remember to check the liquid in the pot. Add a little very hot water if needed.

Scotch Broth with Mutton Neck

The Scots are fond of barley and mutton cooked down into a broth, along with some turnips and other vegetables. Mutton, of course, is a euphemism for mature sheep, as opposed to lamb. Some recipes for Scotch broth recommend lamb breast, but I will allow shoulder or backbone, with plenty of bone—which helps make the broth with long simmering.

2 to 3 pounds sheep neck
1/2 cup pearl barley
1/2 cup finely diced turnip root
1/4 cup finely diced carrot
1/4 cup finely diced onion
1/4 cup finely diced celery
2 tablespoons finely diced fresh parsley
2 tablespoons butter or margarine
1 tablespoon flour
salt and pepper to taste
water

Soak the barley in water overnight, or for several hours. Trim most of the meat from the bone and dice into 1/2-inch pieces. Place the bones in a pot, pour in 2 cups of water, bring to a boil, reduce the heat, cover, and simmer until the rest of the meat can be pulled from the bone, adding more water from time to time if needed. Meanwhile, place the diced meat into another pot along with 6 cups of water. Bring to a boil, skim off any scum, and add the barley. Simmer. Using a skillet, sauté the diced carrot, turnip, onion, and celery in 1 tablespoon of the butter for 5 minutes. Add the sautéed vegetables to the diced meat pot. Bring to a boil, cover, reduce the heat, and simmer for 3 hours. Remove the bones from their pot. Pull off and dice the meat, adding it to the main pot. Strain the water left in the bone pot. In a saucepan, melt the remaining butter and stir in the flour. Slowly stir in the broth from the bone pot, then add the mixture to the main pot. Stir in the parsley, and salt and pepper to taste. Simmer for a few minutes, then serve hot in bowls.

Note that the fine dice and long cooking tend to disintegrate the vegetables, resulting in a thick broth. If you want a more chunky soup, use a larger dice and reduce the cooking times for the vegetables.

Barley and Yogurt Soup

Here's a soup from Turkey, where yogurt is an important part of the cuisine, as it is in other parts of the Middle East.

1 quart chicken stock
1 quart plain yogurt
1 cup dry pearl barley (soaked overnight in water)
3 tablespoons butter
1 large onion, finely chopped
2 tablespoons finely chopped fresh parsley
1 tablespoon finely chopped fresh mint
salt and pepper to taste

Melt the butter in a large saucepan. Sauté the onion for about 5 minutes. Add the chicken stock and barley. Bring to a boil, cover, reduce the heat, and simmer for 1 hour. Stir in the parsley and salt and pepper to taste. Beat the yogurt, add a little of the soup stock, and beat it again. Gradually add the yogurt to the soup, beating as you go, and heat almost to the boiling point. But do not boil unless you want a curled mess. Sprinkle with mint and serve in bowls.

Barley Drinks and Tonics

Barley has lent spirit and substance, throughout recorded history, to comfort foods and drink. As the poet A. E. Housman said, "Malt does more than Milton can/To justify God's ways to man." Most of the dark European beers are made from sprouted barley (malt) and so are some whiskeys and whisky (Scotch). Barley beer was brewed by the ancient Cimbri and Celts; the Gauls brewed a barley beer with the aid of a grape-juice yeast; the ancient Egyptians brewed beer on a large scale with a red barley of the Nile; and the Babylonians made several alcoholic brews from barley as early as 4000 B.C. In modern times there have been thousands of beers and ales made with the aid of this ancient grain.

Of course, the barley need not be sprouted or fermented to inspire a palpable beverage or tonic, and, indeed, a simple barley water was one of the more common medicines prescribed by Hippocrates. It has been in such use ever since, hot or cold, perhaps flavored here and there with this and that. Barley tea flavored with licorice, for example, was once quite popular in the British Isles and parts of Europe, and is still used, hot or cold, in Japan. In France, the drink known as tisane (a name that now denotes an herbal tea) was once made with barley water sweetened with sugar, and, I understand, the original orgeat was also made from barley water. These days, barley water is very popular in Korea, the source of the following recipe. Try it hot on a cold day.

Korean Poricha

In modern times, most people (even Koreans) make *poricha* from a commercially packaged product (available in some ethnic grocery shops), or at least from roasted barley. Or, using ordinary pearl barley from the supermarket or perhaps hulled barley, you can roast your own over some hot coals in a camp skillet. I have even made it with quick barley.

$^1\!/_4$ cup roasted barley
6 cups water
honey

In a pot, soak the barley in the water for at least 30 minutes. Bring to a boil, reduce the heat, cover tightly, and simmer for an hour. Strain the tea and serve it hot or cold, sweetened to taste with a little honey. This is a mild drink—but it grows on you.

Gulf City Barley Water

I found this old recipe in *Gulf City Cook Book*, published in 1878 by the Ladies of the St. Francis Street Methodist Episcopal Church, Mobile, Alabama. Here's the recipe as printed in a chapter fittingly called "Comforts for the Sick":

"Wash a tablespoonful of pearl barley through several waters till perfectly clean, and put it in a jug or pitcher. Rub several lumps of sugar on a lemon to absorb all the oil [?], and throw into the jug with the barley. Peel the lemon, leaving as little of the white pulp on the rind as possible; put this also into the jug, and pour on boiling water till the vessel is full. In half an hour it is ready for use. This is a palpable beverage."

Finding the last sentence reassuring, I made a batch and found it to be soothing and emollient even when I was not ailing.

Barley Beer

This easy recipe uses ordinary baker's yeast (not the brewer's yeast, which can be hard to find). There are several beer-supply catalogs (see Sources) that sell yeast, hops, grains, and other supplies, as well as equipment, by mail.

1 cup hulled barley
1 pound sugar
$1/2$ cup hops
$1/3$ ounce baker's yeast
water

Bring a gallon of water to boil in a large pot. Add the barley, sugar, and hops. Cover and simmer for $1/2$ hour. Remove from the heat, pour into a clean crock, cool a little, and add the baker's yeast. Cover and let ferment at room temperature for 4 days. Sterilize some bottles and boil the corks. Fill the bottles with beer and tie down the corks. I sometimes use mason jars with screwtop lids because corks of the right size can be hard to find—and because I prefer to drink from a wide-mouth container instead of a bottle.

Tepache

This fermented drink is about halfway between a beer and a punch. The Mexicans consider it a festive drink, vended commercially at fairs and fiestas, and I do, too. Tepache is made in many Mexican homes; in addition to being a refreshing drink, it is also used like wine in cooking. If you decide to make a batch, use unchlorinated drinking water. I make it with water from a deep well, but good spring water or bottled water will do. A high natural-mineral content doesn't seem to matter, but it's best to avoid highly chlorinated water, which may impede the fermentation.

1 large pineapple
4 cups brown sugar, firmly packed
2 cups barley
14 allspice berries
unchlorinated drinking water

Twist off the leafy head of the pineapple. Cut the pineapple into chunks, peeling and all, and either crush (saving the juice) or grind the pieces with a food mill (again saving the juice). Put the pulp in a crock or suitable nonmetallic container. Cover with 3 quarts of good water, adding the allspice berries. Stir with a wooden spoon or paddle—never metal. Cover the crock with a clean cloth and let stand for 2 full days.

To proceed, heat 1 quart of fresh water in a large pot. Add the barley and simmer until the grains swell and burst. Stir in the sugar and add the mix to the pineapple crock. Cover and let stand for 2 days, or until the mixture ferments. (The exact times depend on the temperature, but 2 days will usually be about right—longer in cold weather.) Strain the mixture through a clean fine-mesh cloth or several layers of cheesecloth. Strain it again. You'll have about 3 quarts of tepache.

Tepache is usually served from a punch bowl, poured over a large block of ice. Ice cubes can be used, but they melt quickly and may reduce the drink too drastically. For home use (where you may not want to use a whole block of ice) try shaking the tepache with ice in a cocktail shaker, then pouring the tepache off the ice into a suitable glass. It seems best coming off ice instead of being chilled in the refrigerator.

To the ladies I never serve tepache in a glass over ice cubes. Instead I use freshly cracked hard ice.

Nutritional Highlights

Although barley sustained many peoples for many centuries, its unique nutritional advantages are only recently being appreciated. Barley, unlike wheat, is a good source of both soluble and insoluble fiber. Thus, barley may help lower the absorption of dietary cholesterol and fat. It may also help improve blood glucose and lipid levels, which is especially important for diabetics. Although the facts are not conclusive (at least not to me), it is clear that barley is a very healthy and versatile grain—and a tasty one, too.

12

Millet

Mrs. Mumphard believed that everyone
should eat "millies" once a day.

—Bert Greene

illet is perhaps the world's oldest cultivated grain, and it still grows wild today. Although used mostly as bird seed in the Western World, millet is a major source of food in parts of Africa and Asia, partly because it thrives in hot, arid environments and has a short growing season, requiring only 65 days from planting to harvest.

In America, millet has only one cultural toehold: the Gullah settlements on the lowlands of coastal Georgia and South Carolina, and on the barrier islands. These are people of African descent who brought millet from their homeland and remained rather isolated (until recently) from the influence of the great American wheat belt. These days, the only new interest in millet is mainly among the health-food set and is sadly lacking in most standard American family cookbooks. One of the best selections of millet recipes can be found in Bert Greene's *The Grains Cookbook*. In New York City during the 1950s, Greene was influenced by a black cleaning woman, Lavinia Mumphard, of Gullah descent. She often cooked with millet, Greene says, which she referred to as "millies."

We can find millet as an ingredient in various recipes around the world. It is used in *uji*, an African gruel, and in both *chapatti* and *roti*, important breads in

India. Other recipes appear in areas where Africa and India have a marked influence, as in the Caribbean. For example, ground millet is an ingredient in a Christmas dish called *jug jug* in Barbados, where millet is called "guinea corn."

These days, millet is becoming more widely available in several forms, and it is being used in food products destined mostly for the health-food market. Culinarily speaking, we shouldn't overlook the subtle but distinct nutlike flavor of this ancient grain.

The Whole Seed

Millet stalks grow tall, sometimes reaching 15 feet. The seed heads at the top can be up to 14 inches long. The tiny seeds are covered with very hard, colored hulls. (The color depends on the variety, but some seed heads are quite striking in appearance.) The hulls are indigestible to humans, and must be removed before consumption. For this reason, it is best to avoid buying unhulled millet sold in feed stores and pet markets. Fortunately, hulling does not remove the germ of the grain, leaving almost all of the nutrients intact.

Hulled Millet

When hulled, millet seeds are yellow and quite small—no larger than bird shot—but the size depends on the variety. Pearl millet seeds are the largest, and, possibly for that reason, they are the ones commonly used for food. In general, hulled millet keeps well, especially if stored in an airtight container in the refrigerator. Once it is ground into flour, however, it quickly becomes rancid. So, buy hulled millet in bulk and use it for cereals and side dishes, or grind it as needed for flour. Hulled millet seeds, uncooked, can be added to baked goods, much like sesame seeds. They add a definite crunch to muffins. Hulled millet seeds can also be sprouted and used in salads, breads, and green juice.

Basic Boiled Millet

Cooking hulled millet is a little tricky, and subtle differences in technique will yield textures ranging from a sticky mass to rather fluffy, separate grains. For boiling like rice, use 1 part millet to 2 or 3 parts water (or stock). Bring the water to a boil, cover, reduce the heat, and simmer for 20 to 30 minutes. Using less water and cooking for a shorter time will yield a cereal with distinct grains; using more water and a longer cooking time will yield a mush or porridge. Soaking the millet overnight in water will decrease the cooking time by about 10 minutes.

Boiled Toasted Millet

As indicated above, hulled millet can be simply boiled in water, perhaps with a touch of salt, for 20 to 30 minutes. It has more flavor, however, if it is first browned and then cooked in chicken stock.

1 cup hulled millet
2^1/2 cups chicken stock
salt and freshly ground black pepper (optional)

Bring the stock to a boil in a saucepan. While waiting for the boil, heat a cast-iron skillet. Add the millet and cook on medium high heat for 4 or 5 minutes, or until golden brown, stirring as you go with a wooden spoon. The millet should pop slightly as it browns. Add the millet to the boiling stock. Salt to taste. Reduce the heat, cover, and simmer for 20 to 25 minutes, or until all the stock has been absorbed. Remove the saucepan from the heat, but let stand, covered, for 5 to 10 minutes. Sprinkle with pepper and fluff with a fork before serving. Fluffy millet can be used in salads, rice pilaf, soups, stuffings, and so on. Also, I like it as a side dish, topped with a little butter, soy sauce, or Thai fish sauce.

Hunza Steamed Millet

The Hunza people, noted for long life and healthy living in the remote foothills of the Himalayas, use millet in their daily diet, according to *Hunza Health Secrets*, by Renée Taylor, from which this recipe has been adapted.

1 cup hulled millet
water

Soak the grain overnight. When you are ready to cook, heat some water in the bottom of a double boiler. When the water comes to a rolling boil, add the millet to the top boiler. Steam for about 30 minutes, until the millet is tender. Fluff with a fork and serve like rice.

Millet Porridge and Polenta

Whole millet makes a nice breakfast porridge, served hot. When chilled the mush also makes a good polenta.

1 cup millet
3^1/2 cups water
salt to taste

Bring the water to a boil in a saucepan. Add salt and the millet. Bring to a new boil, lower the heat, and cook for 30 to 40 minutes, stirring from time to time with a wooden spoon, until the mush is thick. Serve as a breakfast cereal, topped with cream and syrup or honey.

If you want to make polenta, pack the mush into a mold. Chill in the refrigerator. Slice and serve like polenta, or fry like scrapple.

Note: In North Africa, a similar porridge or mush, made with coarsely ground millet meal, is called *tuo zaafi.*

Millet Soufflé

Here's a a tasty side-dish recipe adapted here from Raymond Sokolov's *With the Grain.* I use untoasted millet for this one.

$1/2$ **cup millet**
$1/2$ **cup grated Parmesan cheese (divided)**
$2/3$ **cup milk**
3 large chicken eggs, separated
salt and pepper to taste
water

Soak the millet overnight in 1 cup of water. When you are ready to cook, pre-heat the oven to 375°F. Place the millet and its water into the top of a dou-ble boiler. Bring a little water to boil in the bottom part of the double boiler. Steam the millet for 20 minutes. Mix the milk into the millet, then stir in the egg yolks, milk, and $1/4$ cup of grated cheese. Beat the egg whites until they hold peaks, then fold them into the millet mush. Pour the mixture into a soufflé dish, sprinkle with the rest of the cheese, set in a pan of steaming hot water, and bake in the center of the oven for 30 minutes, or until the soufflé sets and is nicely browned.

Kijangbap

In Korea, rice sometimes runs short during the long summer before the har-vest. In this traditional dish, millet is added to conserve the rice. It also makes an interesting and tasty variation in its own right, especially if the millet is toasted. The Korean short-grain rice (glutinous and sweet) goes nicely with millet.

$1 1/2$ **cups short-grain rice**
$2/3$ **cup millet**
water

Wash the rice in a large bowl, covering it with water and swishing it around with your hands. When the water becomes milky, pour it off and add fresh water. Repeat until the water remains clear. Soak the rice for 2 to 3 hours. Strain it and let dry for 1 hour. While waiting, place the millet in a cast-iron skillet and heat for 3 minutes, or until it is toasted brown, shaking the skillet as you go. Put the rice and toasted millet into a saucepan. Add 3 cups of water and bring to a boil on high heat. Stir briefly, cover, reduce the heat to very low, and cook for 20 minutes. Do not peek or remove the lid. Turn the heat to high for 30 seconds. Remove the saucepan from the heat and leave it, still covered, for 10 minutes. Serve as you would a pilaf.

Note: Koreans sometimes use barley instead of millet in this recipe. Also try a combination of $1/3$ cup millet and $1/3$ cup barley. I like to pour a little Asian sesame oil over the rice and millet, but I don't know whether Koreans would approve.

Millet Flour

Although millet flour is sold in specialized markets, it doesn't keep well and goes rather rancid and bitter in time. The best bet is to purchase whole millet (hulled) and grind your own at home as needed. Remember that the husk on millet is not easily digested and should be removed. The millet sold at feed stores has not been husked and should not be used. I recommend buying hulled millet in bulk from a reputable grain dealer and storing it in the refrigerator or freezer until needed. Then grind only as much flour as you need for the recipe at hand. The seeds are small, making the grain relatively easy to grind in most kitchen mills.

Millet flour is quite starchy and is very low in gluten. For risen breads, mix it with high gluten wheat flour only in small amounts—certainly no more than 25 percent.

A. D.'s Gullah Bread

I like to consider this one a Gullah creation, combining African millet with New World cornmeal. In any case, it's very tasty.

1 cup white whole kernel cornmeal
$1/2$ cup millet flour
2 cups milk
6 chicken eggs, separated
$1/4$ cup water
2 tablespoons bacon drippings or vegetable oil
$3/4$ teaspoon fine sea salt

Preheat the oven to 325°F and grease a 10-inch cast-iron skillet (one that has an ovenproof handle) or a suitable baking pan. Beat the egg whites until stiff; set aside. Mix the cornmeal and milk in a saucepan. Cook over low heat until the mixture thickens, stirring as you go with a wooden spoon. Cool to luke-warm. In a separate container, blend the egg yolks, water, oil, and salt. Add the millet flour and stir the mixture into the cornmeal. Fold in the egg whites. Turn the mixture into the skillet. Bake in the center of the oven for 40 to 45 minutes, or until done. Cut into wedges. Serve hot, preferably with fresh butter.

Sikkimese Pancakes

Millet grows well in the foothills of the Himalayas, and its flour is a stable in the cookery. These pancakes, or soft flatbread, are traditionally eaten with poultry or meat curries.

1 1/2 cups millet flour
1 cup water (more or less)
1 tablespoon cooking oil
salt to taste

Mix the flour with enough water (about 1 cup), together with some salt to taste, to form a pancake batter. Heat the oil in a skillet. Ladle about 1/4 to 1/3 cup batter into the skillet. Cook for a few minutes and turn, cooking until done like pancakes. Serve hot or warm.

Arrowhead Millet Muffins

Here's a recipe with millet flour as the main ingredient, and not just a filler to wheat flour. I have adapted the recipe from a brochure published by Arrowhead Mills, a major grain wholesaler. The original calls for orange flavoring. For this I have substituted a little fresh orange zest.

1 1/2 cups millet flour
1/2 cup soybean flour
1/4 cup brown-rice syrup or honey
1 cup orange juice or water
1/4 cup vegetable oil
1 tablespoon baking powder
1/2 teaspoon salt
1/4 teaspoon orange flavoring or orange zest

Preheat the oven to 375°F and grease two 6-hole muffin pans or a large pan with 12 holes. Mix the dry ingredients in a large bowl. Mix all the liquids separately and pour into the dry mixture, stirring thoroughly. Spoon the batter into 12 muffin holes. Put the pans into the center of the oven. Bake for 15 to 20 minutes, or until done.

Rabari

Here's a slightly fermented gruel from India, where millet flour is sometimes called *bajari da daliya*. I prefer to make the dish with lightly toasted millet, freshly ground. The ground cumin is available in supermarkets, but it's much better to buy whole cumin seeds and crush a few as needed with your mortar and pestle.

1 cup yogurt plus more for serving
2 tablespoons millet flour
1/2 cup water
salt to taste
ground cumin to taste

Heat the water in a pan and add the millet flour and 1 cup yogurt, along with a little salt. Stirring as you go with a wooden spoon, simmer over very low heat for 10 minutes, taking pains to keep the yogurt from separating. When the gruel thickens a little, set it aside, cover, and leave at room temperature for about 24 hours, until it ferments slightly. Serve cold in bowls with yogurt, sprinkling with ground cumin to taste.

Roti

Here's a great flatbread from Ceylon, where it is usually made without the benefit of measuring cups, and where, according to Charmaine Solomon in *Far Eastern Cookbook*, "Spoon measures would be looked upon as an affection."

2 cups roti or millet flour
1 cup water
1/2 cup freshly grated or desiccated coconut
1 teaspoon salt
butter or margarine

Mix the millet flour, coconut, and salt. Stir in just enough water to form a stiff dough (about 1 cup). Knead the dough until it does not stick to the sides of the bowl. Cover and rest for 30 minutes. Shape the dough into balls about

1 1/2 inch in diameter. Pat these down to circles about 4 inches in diameter. Grease a griddle or cast-iron skillet with butter or oil, heat, and cook for a few minutes on each side. Serve hot with curries.

Note: Very similar flatbreads are made in India and Africa from millet flour. Sometimes "roti" flours are marketed in health food stores. What makes this version Ceylonese is the coconut. In Ceylon, according to Ms. Solomon, roti is also made with rice flour.

Nutritional Highlights

Millet is almost 15 percent protein—richer than rice, corn, or oats—and it is higher in fiber than other commonly used grains. It is especially high in iron, magnesium, phosphorus, and potassium. Hulled millet is very easy to digest, and it is used as baby food in Africa. It is low in gluten, making it one of the least allergenic of grains.

One word of caution. Millet contains goitrogenic stuff that may contribute to goiter in some countries where it is an important part of the diet. Most of this stuff is contained in the hull, however, and is usually removed before the grain is marketed for human consumption. In any case, this is not an important consideration for people who enjoy a reasonably balanced diet; but it could become important to people who raise their own millet and use it unhulled. In addition to being goitrogenic, the hulls are quite indigestible, as previously indicated.

13

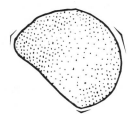

Tef

A mountain plant of Abyssinia, cultivated everywhere there. . . .

—*Sturtevant's Edible Plants of the World*

I n his book *The Frugal Gourmet on Our Immigrant Ancestors*, Jeff Smith gives us a complicated, highly spiced recipe for raw beef. It calls for a number of ingredients, including Berber sauce and a spiced butter, which in turn require more stuff. All together, you need 35 ingredients or measures thereof in addition to the raw beef. That's hardly frugal—unless you're preparing raw meat for the queen of Sheba. Ordinary Abyssinian maids probably got by with less garnish, I dare presume.

At the same time, Smith suggests eating the raw beef with an interesting desert flatbread called *injera*, traditionally made with a slightly fermented sponge of tef flour. In most cases, the meat and other food was simply piled onto individual rounds of injera, and the whole thing was eaten. Of course, the bread soaks up the good juices. It's a sensible custom—rather like eating the plate and dishrag—especially practical for nomadic peoples. Tef (an ancient milletlike grain) and tef flour is still available, even in America, but the recipe that Smith chooses to share with us calls for all-purpose white wheat flour (Gold Medal, he claims, works best) fizzed up with club soda.

The *Africa News Cookbook* also sets forth a recipe using wheat flour and club soda. Still another book specifies flour, whole wheat flour, and cornmeal. A recent vegan-magazine recipe calls for 2 cups tef flour, 2 cups whole wheat flour, and 4 cups white flour, along with a cup of sourdough starter. Still another recipe, getting closer now, calls for ⅔ tef flour and ⅓ wheat flour, helped along with a little yeast.

The real injera, however, requires no yeast, as the grain has a natural propensity for fermentation, and the old-time injera bread is made only with tef flour, water, salt, and a little oil on a griddle, as reflected by the recipe below. Add club soda at your culinary peril. Be warned, however, that real injera may not be for everyone. One nineteenth-century English traveler wrote, "Fancy yourself chewing a piece of sour sponge and you will have a good idea of what is considered the best bread in Abyssinia." In response to this, *The Lost Crops of Africa* points out that people are not as closed-minded these days and that injera is winning kudos in affluent nations. "Perhaps the most intriguing of all the world's staples, injera is a bread like no other other. Moist, chewy, and almost elastic, it has a unique look and feel." Club soda? Tsk tsk. Let's at least try to cook the real thing.

In any case, the ancient grain is currently available whole, as a flour, and as a processed pasta. There are several varieties of tef (sometimes spelled teff or t'ef), all bright-green grasses. The straw is used for making adobe in Ethiopia, and in some places it is cultivated and cut as hay.

⨒ The Grain ⨒

Tef is a tiny, tiny grain—1 $\frac{1}{150}$th the size of a normal wheat berry. In fact, the word *tef* means "lost," in Amharic. Drop a cupful on the floor and you'll know why. Several varieties are cultivated, yielding white or ivory, brown, and red berries. The white kind has a sweet chestnutlike flavor, while the others are a little more earthy. These days, however, tef is rather hard to find, and the Western buyer must take whatever is available.

Regardless of color, the grain can be stored in a cool, dry place for several months, or longer in the refrigerator. The whole grains are sometimes used in muffins and other baked goods.

Tef Porridge

Having a sweet molasses flavor and aroma, tef makes a nice breakfast cereal. It is a little sticky, and goes best with a touch of heavy cream.

1 cup tef grain
3 cups water
1 teaspoon salt

Heat the water to a boil. Stir in the tef and bring to a new boil. Reduce the heat and simmer, uncovered, for 15 minutes, or until the grains are chewy.

Serve as a cereal with a little cream, or as a side dish for a meal. It goes nicely with highly spiced fare.

Fried Tef Polenta

When cooked, tef grains tend to stick together, which makes it a natural choice for making polenta, fried mush, and perhaps scrapple of various kinds.

2 cups tef
6 cups beef stock
cooking oil
flour
salt

Bring the beef stock to a boil, then add the tef and a little salt to taste. Simmer for 20 minutes. Pour into a loaf pan and let cool until firm, preferably overnight. Slice thinly, dust with flour, and fry in hot oil. Serve with a little honey and perhaps a few strips of crisply cooked bacon.

The Flour

If used sparingly—no more than 20 percent—tef flour can be mixed with wheat to make risen breads. But be sure to try the native bread below with pure tef, naturally fermented, without yeast.

Injera

Essentially, this is a sourdough flatbread with a rather spongy texture, moist and chewy, ideal for soaking up the juices of the meal. There are many versions, but this one requires no packaged yeast, baking powder, or club soda. It's the real stuff. If properly made from freshly grown tef flour, it will stay soft and spongy for 3 days. When made with other wheat grains, it becomes hard after only one day.

1 1/4 cups tef flour
4 cups lukewarm water
vegetable oil
sea salt, finely ground

Mix the tef flour and water in a wooden bowl, cover with a cloth, and let stand at room temperature (or a little warmer) for 3 or 4 days, until the mixture bubbles and has a sour taste and fermented aroma. It should be the consistency of pancake batter; if not, add a little more flour or a little more water as needed. Stir in the sea salt to taste. Heat an 8- or 9-inch skillet or griddle and grease with vegetable oil. Dip out ¼ cup of batter and pour it in a stream, working from the edge in toward the center, forming a spiral in the skillet. Quickly tilt the skillet back and forth, causing the batter to spread out thinly. Cook for a minute or two, until bubbles form and the batter can be lifted around the edges. Quickly turn the batter with a spatula and cook the other side for a minute or so. Remove the injera round, letting it cool, and proceed with the rest of the batch. Ideally, the rounds should be thinner than a lumberjack's pancake but thicker than a French crepe. Serve the injera as a finger bread, or use it (as the Ethiopians do) as an edible plate to hold a curry or other spicy dish.

Note: This injera is not an easy bread to make. If it fails to ferment properly from the wild yeast in your area, try again, or perhaps dissolve 1 tablespoon of active dry yeast and 1 teaspoon honey into ¼ cup of the lukewarm water and allow it to work until frothy. Then mix and proceed as directed above.

Tef Pancakes

Here's a recipe that I have adapted from the Marskal Tef Company, which says the pancakes are so rich and satisfying that they can be eaten without a topping. It's true, but I'll take a little syrup or a touch of honey on mine.

2 cups tef flour
2½ cups apple juice
2 tablespoons vegetable oil
1 tablespoon vanilla
1 tablespoon baking powder
1 tablespoon arrowroot
½ teaspoon sea salt, finely ground

In a large bowl mix the tef flour, baking powder, arrowroot, and sea salt. Stir in the apple juice, vegetable oil, and vanilla. Heat a griddle, lightly brushed with oil. Drop ¼ cup or so of the batter and cook until done on the bottom. Turn and cook until done. Stack the pancakes. Serve hot with or without butter and a little syrup or honey.

≈ Nutritional Highlights ≈

Tef is a good source of protein, iron, and B vitamins. It is said to have 17 times more calcium than wheat. Because the tef grain is so small, it leads all grains in its percentage of germ and bran, making it an excellent source of fiber.

14

Sorghum, Fonio, and Other Third Millennium Grains

Already sorghum is a booming new food crop in Central America.

—*Lost Crops of Africa*

As the world's population grows, we the people need to rid ourselves of false assumptions about the indigenous grains of Africa and other parts of the world. Some of these grains thrive in areas unsuited to wheat or corn—and they may taste even better, earlier judgments notwithstanding. Here are a few remarks to consider, taken mostly from a book called *Lost Crops of Africa: Vol. 1, Grains*, published by the American Academy of Sciences. Actually most of these crops—and there are dozens—have not been forgotten in their native lands. They have simply been neglected and put down by European colonists.

⋙ Fonio ⋙

This ancient grain has been cultivated for thousands of years in West Africa, but it has been largely neglected in important places. As *Lost Crops of Africa* points out, "Part of the reason for this neglect is that the plant has been misunderstood by scientists and other decision makers. In English, it has usually been referred to as 'hungry rice,' a misleading term originated by the Europeans who knew little of the crop or the lives of those who used it. Unbeknownst to these outsiders, the locals were harvesting fonio not because they were hungry, but because they liked the taste." In short, fonio was, and is, held in high esteem as table fare and was, and is, much preferred to rice.

Fonio has recently been billed as one of the world's best-tasting cereals, and it is used to make porridge and couscous, ground into flour for breadstuff, popped as a snack, and brewed for beer, *tchapalo*, said to be famous in northern Togo. Called *acha* in some areas, fonio grows on poor soil. In short, it could well provide more food for the world's poor people—and a culinary treat for the rich. It may be difficult to find even in health-food stores, but these days the Internet opens international markets. I'll be looking for it. Meanwhile, I'm taking a closer look at the ordinary crabgrass growing in my yard. It's a close relative of fonio and has actually been cultivated for grain since ancient times.

⋙ Sorghum ⋙

A lot of sorghum has been raised in North America. In the past, one variety or another has been used for syrup and chewing, for broom straw, for animal feed, and, these days, for experimental fuels to run our cars and trucks. But it is not popular as a grain for human consumption and never has been, except possibly for the syrup. Most "whole grains" books don't even mention sorghum—with a notable exception being *The New Book of Whole Grains*, by Marlene Anne Bumgarner. The grain or its flour is not often marketed at the retail level in North America, and readers may have trouble finding it. Yet, I have seen thousands of acres of it growing in our fields, used mostly as cattle feed, and it is not impossible to find. A Texas firm called Jower is marketing sorghum flour—under the trade name "Jower."

Why bother? Because the grain is just too important to ignore, and some varieties thrive under conditions that do not produce ample wheat and corn and rice. As the world's population doubles again, sorghum may help feed whole populations, and already does play an important role in India as well as Africa.

So, watch for sorghum to show up in more and more retail grain markets in the future. For now, try feed stores, farmers (some of whom may call it milo), and seed outlets. Also try those listed in the Sources section, and remember that markets do change, slowly.

Sorghum Chapati

This Indian flatbread, made on a griddle or in a skillet, should be rather light, full of air bubbles, and yet pliable. Although the ingredients are simple, making chapati correctly requires some thought.

3 cups whole sorghum flour
1 cup lukewarm water
1 tablespoon melted butter or ghee, or margarine
1¹/₂ teaspoons salt
boiled egg (optional)

Save out about ¹/₂ cup of the flour for use when rolling the dough. Place the rest in a mixing bowl. Stir in the salt and cut in the melted butter. Add the water all at once, then mix until you have a dough. Knead for at least 10 minutes—or up to 20 minutes if you want a lighter bread. Shape the dough into a ball, cover it with plastic wrap, and let it rest at room temperature for at least 1 hour and as long as 12 hours (the longer the lighter, up to a point). Shape the dough into balls about the size of golf balls. Keep the balls covered with a damp cloth. After dusting the bread board lightly with some of the reserved flour, roll each ball out to a circle of 4 to 6 inches. Heat the griddle or skillet to medium high, just so; if it isn't hot enough, the chapati won't puff—if too hot, it will burn. Going one at a time, place a chapati on the griddle for about 1 minute. Turn and cook the other side. While cooking, carefully press around the inside edge of the chapati with a hot pad or a slice of boiled egg; this will help seal the chapati, holding in the bubbles and making it light. Stack the chapatis as you cook them and cover with a towel until served. Serve warm with butter and curry dishes.

⬥ Other Grains and Grasses ⬥

At one time the Sahara was a green land, and over 60 surviving species of grass are still used there as sources of food. In fact, *kreb*, perhaps the most famous food of the area, is a mix of a dozen or more wild grains, the exact mix depending on what is available from region to region, season to season. Whether or not any of these wild grasses will ever be cultivated, it is important that the natural grasslands be preserved.

In addition to the wild grasses, several other grains are cultivated in Africa. The ancient grains *tef* and *Kamut*, available in North America, are covered in chapters 13 and 6 respectively. The food grains include several species of African rice, the rare wheat known as emmer, Ethiopian oats, and others. So, anyone interested in culinary adventure would do well to explore Africa in more culinary detail—and with an open mind.

Other parts of the world also hold culinary treasures, and only recently have we been introduced to quinoa and amaranth, long after the New World gold has been exploited. What treasures grow in the foothills of the Himalayan rim? Or in Australia? The aborigines didn't have wheat until the white man came—but they ate breadstuff of some sort. For that matter, there is much exploring to be done in our own country, as I hope will be made clear in the Wild Grist chapter (chapter 20). Further, on our own farmlands in the Midwest, Texas, and elsewhere we have thousands of acres of sorghum and millet and soybeans and other good foods that are used to feed cattle and are made into tofu and such packaged products. Sadly, even our wheat farmers buy their bread at the supermarket these days.

PART FOUR

Other Breadstuff

Buckwheat and chickpeas really are hard fruit kernels, not true grains. Beans and peas aren't grains either, but they are widely available in different varieties and are quite versatile, especially when ground into meal or flour. Seeds, nuts, and edible wild grist—which can be delicious as well as highly nutritious—round out this rather diverse and somewhat adventurous section.

15

Buckwheat

With its deep, toasted, grassy-earthy flavor,
buckwheat is not a timid grain.

—*Waves of Grain*

Buckwheat farming has never been intense in North America, and culinarily it is associated mostly with flapjacks. In recent years, however, buckwheat production is on the rise, owing in large part to the health food market. The crop is raised mostly in the Northeast and Midwest, with the hot spot being the area around Penn Yan, New York. Also, an annual buckwheat festival is held in West Virginia. Because buckwheat is a hearty plant and requires no chemicals in the field or processing plant, it is a good choice for organic farming. Consequently, its use will probably continue to increase in the future.

Worldwide, buckwheat is a staple only in central Asia (where it probably originated), eastern Europe (especially Russia), and isolated parts of the globe. In both Japan and Korea, however, the popular soba noodles are made primarily of buckwheat flour, although they might also contain wheat or even yam flour.

Buckwheat is sometimes planted as a cover crop. That is, it is planted off-season to keep weeds from taking over, then it is plowed under as a green manure. Bees love the stalk's flowers, and buckwheat honey is sold commercially. It's a dark, heavy honey. In England, I have read, buckwheat is grown mostly as a grazing crop for sheep, or to feed pheasants.

～ Buckwheat Groats ～

Buckwheat is really a fruit seed, not a grain. The seeds are oddly triangular in shape and have a thick, hard hull. The hull, which makes up about 20 percent of the bulk, must be removed before the seed is usable as a grain or in breadstuff. The whole seed, however, can be sprouted and eaten like bean or wheat sprouts.

When the hull is cracked, a cream-colored kernel is revealed. These are called groats or white groats. The whole white groat can be used in various recipes or ground into a flour, or perhaps cracked into grits and marketed as cream of buckwheat. To cook this stuff, follow the directions on the package. Usually, however, cracked buckwheat is toasted and called kasha (see page 208). If used without toasting, the groats are often called whole white buckwheat, and the term is useful. (By comparison, whole kasha has a toasted color.) White buckwheat has a more delicate flavor than kasha, and can be used as rice or pasta.

White Buckwheat Groats

Cooked whole groats can be used in various recipes, or fluffed and used as a pilaf. Here's a basic recipe.

1 cup hulled buckwheat
2 cups water or chicken broth
salt to taste

Bring the water to a rolling boil. Add the buckwheat and salt to taste. Bring to a new boil, reduce the heat, cover, and simmer for about 12 minutes. Do not overcook, unless you need a porridge. The cooked white buckwheat can be used in other recipes, or eaten as a mild pilaf.

Note, however, that kasha has more flavor. Note also that many people recommend coating buckwheat groats with egg or egg white before cooking. Whole white groats, however, do not require the egg coating. When cooking kasha, the egg coating helps prevent the groats from turning to mush.

Buckwheat Sausage

Buckwheat sausage of one sort or another is made in Russia and several other parts of Europe. Sometimes the sausage is made with the aid of blood, and sometimes with liver, trotters, or snouts, along with various other ingredients. I have added a little beef broth to the recipe below, adapted here from my book *Sausage*, just in case the buckwheat turns out a little on the dry side.

6 pounds fresh pork butt
4 pounds cooked buckwheat groats
3 tablespoons salt
2 tablespoons black pepper
1 teaspoon ground marjoram
beef broth, as needed
hog casings

Cook the buckwheat in water and set aside to cool. Cut the pork into chunks suitable for stuffing, spread it over your work surface, and sprinkle evenly with the salt, pepper, and marjoram. Grind with a ¼- to ⅜-inch plate. Mix in 4 pounds of the cooked buckwheat and some beef broth if needed. Stuff into hog casings. Cook by simmering the links in broth or by baking.

Groats and Mushrooms

Regular button mushrooms from the supermarket can be used in this recipe, but I find that dried mushrooms are hard to beat—and morels are my favorite, closely followed by dried wild chanterelles.

1 cup white buckwheat groats
10 dried morels
2 cups chicken stock
3 tablespoons melted butter or margarine
salt to taste
pepper to taste

Wash the mushrooms and soak them in water for several hours; drain, cut into thin strips, and sauté for a few minutes in the butter. Set aside. Heat the chicken stock and have ready on the boil. Place the groats in a pot along with some salt. Pour in the boiling chicken stock. Add the sautéed mushrooms. Cover and simmer for 40 minutes, or until the groats are done. Add a little more chicken stock or water if needed. Add more salt and freshly ground black pepper to taste.

Variation: Also try this recipe with kasha instead of white groats.

 Kasha

Hulled buckwheat is often toasted to bring out the flavor, which also darkens the grain. Called kasha, toasted groats are available commercially in whole, coarse, medium, and fine grades. For most recipes, medium will do and may be the only grade available in many retail outlets.

Kasha can be used in many recipes, such as the Middle Eastern tabbouli, that call for bulgur or cracked wheat. Here are my suggestions.

Basic Kasha

Following the Russian culinary lead, it has become more or less traditional to treat roasted buckwheat groats, or kasha, with an egg wash before boiling in water or stock. As pointed out above, the egg coating keeps the groats from becoming mush.

1 cup medium-grain kasha
2 cups chicken stock
2 tablespoons butter or margarine
1 chicken egg, beaten
salt and freshly ground black pepper to taste

Bring the chicken stock to boil in a pot, along with the butter, salt, and pepper. While heating the chicken stock, mix the kasha and egg in a small bowl, stirring about thoroughly to coat every grain. Heat a heavy nonstick skillet over medium-high heat. Add the kasha and egg mixture. Cook for 2 or 3 minutes, stirring constantly with a wooden spatula, breaking the mixture apart. The idea is to cook the egg on the surface and keep the groats separate. When the stock is boiling, add the egg-coated kasha. Cover the pot and turn the heat to low. After cooking for 10 minutes, remove the cover and check the kasha. The groats should be tender. All the liquid should be absorbed; if it isn't, cook for a few more minutes. Fluff the kasha with a fork and serve hot or warm.

Kasha Pilaf

Try a bed of this pilaf instead of rice with shish kebobs, or use as a side dish to a main meal.

1 recipe cooked kasha (see above recipe)
$1/2$ cup chopped mushrooms
$1/2$ cup chopped onion
$1/4$ cup chopped green onion tops
$1/4$ cup chopped red bell pepper

$1/4$ cup chopped toasted pecans
2 tablespoons butter or margarine
chopped fresh parsley
salt and pepper to taste

Cook the kasha by the previous recipe and set aside. Melt the butter in a skillet, then sauté the onion, mushrooms, green onion tops, and red bell pepper for 5 or 6 minutes. Stir the sautéed onion mixture, along with some salt and pepper, into the cooked kasha. Transfer it to a serving bowl, fluffing it nicely with a fork, and sprinkle with chopped parsley.

Dolma

Stuffed grape leaves are popular in the Middle East and recipes abound in cookbooks. These are often served as *mezze*, or hors d'oeuvres. Meat dolma are usually made with a rice or bulgur along with ground lamb and various seasonings. Kasha also works, as used in this recipe. The grape leaves can be fresh or pickled in a brine, either canned or sold from a barrel. The directions below are for canned grape leaves, but use fresh if you have them. I have used wild grape leaves, but some of these are too small for stuffing. Fresh leaves should be softened by inserting them a few at a time into boiling water until they are limp. It's best to grind your own lamb (or mutton, if you can find it), using shoulder or other good meat, if you have a sausage mill. I also use fresh lean pork, especially when I grind a batch for making sausages. I have also ground several pounds of meat especially for stuffing grape leaves (or fig leaves). Stuffed uncooked dolmas can be frozen until needed.

1 pound ground lamb or mutton
1 cup medium-grain kasha
$2^{1}/2$ cups chicken broth
1 jar grape leaves in brine (about 50 leaves)
1 cup chopped tomato
several thin tomato slices
1 cup chopped onion
4 cloves garlic, minced
$1/2$ cup freshly squeezed lemon juice
$1/4$ cup minced fresh parsley
$1/4$ cup minced fresh celery leaves (optional)
1 chicken egg, lightly whisked
3 tablespoons olive oil
1 teaspoon crushed dried mint leaves
$1/2$ teaspoon coriander

$^1/_2$ teaspoon ground cinnamon
salt
water

Place the grape leaves in a pot of boiling hot water, stirring them to separate the leaves. Soak for 20 minutes. Drain. Soak in cold water for 20 minutes. Drain. Soak. Drain well. Heat the olive oil in a large skillet. Sauté the ground lamb, onion, and garlic until the meat loses its pinkness. In a bowl, toss the kasha in the whisked egg, coating the groats. Add the kasha to the skillet, along with all the herbs and spices, 1 cup of the chicken broth, chopped tomato, and $^1/_4$ cup of the lemon juice. Toss and stir to mix the stuffing thoroughly. Preheat the oven to 325°F. Grease a 7- by 11-inch baking dish, then line the bottom with the thin tomato slices. Place a grape leaf on a flat surface, shiny side down. Trim off the stem. Spoon 1 or 2 tablespoons of the stuffing to the stem end (the amount of stuffing used will be limited by the size of the leaf). Fold the sides of the leaf over the stuffing, then roll it. Arrange the dolmas in the pan over the tomato slices as you go, letting them touch each other in the dish. Form two layers. Mix the rest of the broth and the lemon juice, then pour it over the dolmas. Cover the dolmas with aluminum foil, then weight the top with an ovenproof dish of suitable size; this will keep the dolmas from unwinding. Bake in the center of the oven for 1 hour. Turn off the heat and let the dolmas coast for 30 minutes. Remove the dolmas and place in a serving dish. Serve hot.

Note: These can also be cooked in a large skillet, weighted with a plate, covered, and simmered over very low heat for 2 hours or longer. Add a little water from time to time, if needed. For more flavor, insert garlic cloves here and there among the dolmas as they cook.

Kasha Varnishkas

This traditional Jewish dish originated in northern Europe and is commonly eaten by the Russian Jews. Usually served with beef or other meat, it is made with buckwheat groats or kasha mixed with bow-tie pasta. The ratio of kasha to pasta isn't exact and varies from recipe to recipe, cook to cook, time to time.

1 cup medium-grain kasha
1 to 2 cups precooked bow-tie pasta, al dente
1 cup chopped onion
2 cups chicken stock
2 tablespoons butter or margarine
1 tablespoon olive oil or melted chicken fat

1 large chicken egg
salt and pepper to taste

Heat the olive oil in a skillet or saucepan on high heat. Sauté the onion for about 10 minutes, stirring often, or until browned. Set aside. Whisk the egg in a bowl and stir in the kasha, coating all the groats evenly. Heat a pot on high heat. Add the kasha, stirring constantly for 5 to 10 minutes, until the egg has set and the grains are lightly toasted. Add the chicken stock, and salt and pepper to taste. Turn the heat to low and simmer until all the broth has been absorbed, about 12 minutes. Mix in the butter, sautéed onion, and pasta. Serve warm with the meat course.

Buckwheat Flour

Available commercially, buckwheat flour comes in two varieties: light and dark. The dark kind contains more (but not all) of the hull, which gives the flour a more pungent flavor and more fiber than the light. If you grind your own, you can use either whole groats or hulled groats, or perhaps a combination if you want to control the darkness. Either light or dark stores well, but both should be kept in an airtight glass container, preferably in the refrigerator.

Blini

The small Russian pancakes called blini are traditionally made with buckwheat flour. These days, white wheat flour is probably more commonly used, or perhaps half-and-half. But try a batch of the real stuff; then, if you are so inclined, substitute half home-ground wheat flour or white flour. Traditionally, blini are served with caviar or smoked salmon, or with syrup or jam along with plenty of good butter.

1 1/2 cups buckwheat flour
1 cup milk
4 large chicken eggs, separated
1/2 cup melted butter or margarine
1/2 package dry yeast (1/4-ounce size)
1 teaspoon sugar
1/2 teaspoon salt

Heat the milk to smoking, but do not boil it. Cool to lukewarm and put in a bowl. Stir in the yeast. Beat the egg yolks until they thicken, then stir into the yeast milk, along with the buckwheat flour, sugar, salt, and 3 tablespoons of the butter. Put the bowl in a pan of warm water, cover with a towel, and let the batter rise until it doubles in volume, which will take 1 1/2 to 2 hours. Beat the egg whites until they are stiff, then fold them into the batter. Brush a griddle or cast-iron skillet with melted butter and heat it on high. Drop 1 tablespoon of batter onto the griddle, cook until golden brown, brush the top (uncooked side) lightly with melted butter, and turn. Cook the rest of the batch, several at a time. Serve with sour cream, melted butter, and caviar, or with sour cream, melted butter, and smoked salmon. I also like them with fig preserves, and, of course, they can be stuffed with ground meat and onions—then fried in butter.

If this recipe seems to overwork the butter, remember that blini was once a festive treat during the week-long festival called *Maslyannitza*—or butter week—preceding Lent.

Easy Blini

Here's a rather simple version of blini adapted from *Russian Cookbook*, by Kira Petrovskaya.

2 cups buckwheat flour
1 1/2 cups lukewarm milk
1/4 cup sour cream
2 tablespoons melted butter or margarine plus more for the skillet
2 chicken eggs, lightly whisked
2 teaspoons baking powder
2 teaspoons sugar
1/2 teaspoon salt

Mix the flour, baking powder, sugar, and salt. Sift three times. Mix the whisked egg, sour cream, and butter; stir in the warm milk. Add the flour mixture and mix well. Heat a little butter in a cast-iron skillet or griddle. Drop the batter in by the teaspoonful. The batter should spread out to a diameter of no more than 2 inches. Cook several at a time, depending on the size of your skillet, but do not overcrowd. Turn once as each side browns—only a minute or two. Add a little butter to the skillet after each batch, applying it with a brush or a feather (as the Russian peasants do).

To serve, top each blini with 1 tablespoon of sour cream, then top off with 1 teaspoon of caviar (preferably black, but red will do) or a slice of smoked salmon. You can also serve the blini with butter and jam. Kiri Petrovskaya says she likes them with just sour cream. I agree, and I also suggest a simple homemade yogurt cheese.

Serves 4 to 6 Americans or 2 Russians.

Buckwheat Pancakes with Blueberries

Here's a popular American breakfast. It is often served with maple syrup, but I really like a good thick sugar-cane syrup—or honey. Use fresh blueberries. If these aren't available, try frozen berries or reconstituted dried berries. Any good honey will do, but I have to vote for my local tupelo honey—Ulee's Gold—that is the theme of the Tupelo Festival here in Wewahitchka, Florida.

2 cups buckwheat flour
3 cups milk
1 cup blueberries
1/4 cup melted butter or margarine
1 tablespoon honey
1 teaspoon baking soda
1 teaspoon salt
1/2 teaspoon baking powder
syrup or honey of your choice (topping)
pats of butter

Mix the buckwheat flour, salt, baking soda, and baking powder in a suitable bowl. Separately, in a large bowl, mix the milk, honey, and melted butter. Beat in the dry mix, working it until you have a smooth batter. Stir in the blueberries. Grease a griddle or large skillet. Over medium heat, ladle a blob of batter, shooting for a pancake about 3 inches in diameter. Cook until the pancake forms bubbles. Turn and cook the reverse side for a minute or two. Cook another one, and another, and so on until the batter is used up. Stack the pancakes on plates, adding a pat of butter between each one, and serve with syrup or honey, perhaps along with Canadian bacon.

Buckwheat Date-Nut Bread

I tested this bread by a recipe I found in a brochure published by Kenyon Corn Meal Company, but I took the liberty of adding one of my favorite ingredients—chopped dates.

2 cups buckwheat flour
1/2 cup graham flour (sifted whole wheat)
1/2 cup white cornmeal
1 1/2 cups milk
2/3 cup molasses
1/2 cup chopped nuts
1/2 cup chopped dates

1 tablespoon baking soda
1 tablespoon baking powder

Mix the flours, cornmeal, baking soda, and baking powder and sift. Stir in the milk, molasses, nuts, and dates. Spread the mixture evenly into a well-greased baking pan; let stand for 20 minutes. While waiting, preheat the oven to 350°F. Bake in the center of the oven for 40 to 45 minutes. Eat hot or cold, sliced. I like it spread with butter and a little honey.

Cheju Island Batter

Buckwheat is popular on Korea's Cheju Island, where it is used in breadstuff and as a fritter batter. The batter is somewhat sticky, making it useful for coating onion rings and other vegetables for frying.

1 cup buckwheat flour
1 chicken egg, beaten
$1/2$ cup water
$1/2$ teaspoon salt
$1/8$ teaspoon baking powder

Mix all the ingredients in a suitable bowl, adding enough water for a medium-thick consistency. Use as a dipping batter for deep-frying seafood, strips of meat, and vegetables.

Nutritional Highlights

Buckwheat is a very good source of protein and soluble fiber, and is said to control glucose levels better than other carbohydrates do. It is also rich in lysine, which is missing in corn and some other grains. It is gluten-free.

16

Chickpeas

They are used in Spain a great deal,
being an essential ingredient in many soups.

—*Larousse Gastronomique*

The chickpea isn't really a grain. It's not a pea, either. Some peoples of Spanish descent call it the garbanzo bean, but, no, it's not a bean. It does, however, grow two kernels in a pod. Whatever it is, the chickpea has a rather large, roundish kernel that has a delightful crunch, even after long cooking. The chickpea is almost always a yellowish cream color, but black is also available.

The chickpea is an old food, going back to the hanging gardens of Babylon, ancient Egypt, and prehistoric times. Over the ages the chickpea became a food for the poor man and was more or less neglected in more prosperous regions of the world. This, finally, is changing.

⚜ Whole Chickpeas ⚜

I love whole chickpeas as a snack and as an ingredient in salads and other dishes. Canned chickpeas can be used in most recipes, but it's really easy to cook your own using the recipe for Nahit, below, perhaps omitting the pepper. I consider a little salt necessary.

At one time, chickpeas tended to have a tough outer skin, which required that they be soaked for a long time in a solution of baking soda and water. Even then the outer skin had to be removed by hand. Improved varieties have all but eliminated the tough skin, so that most modern chickpeas do not have to be skinned. But quality does vary and the old tough-skinned chickpeas may still be raised in some remote areas of the globe.

Most of the packaged chickpeas available in modern markets are all pretty much the same, and all have a long shelf life. Bulk chickpeas, however, show quite a bit of variation. Some have to be cooked a little longer than others.

Barley notwithstanding, chickpeas are perhaps the perfect ingredient for soups and stews because they withstand long, slow cooking, and their somewhat large size provides a substantial crunch. I use them often in soups cooked in a Crock-Pot. Overnight soaking is not necessary if the soup is simmered for a long while. Chickpeas are especially popular in soups of Spanish origin, such as those used in parts of the West Indies; in most such recipes they are listed as garbanzo beans.

In any case, here is a variety of recipes for using this interesting groat for flavor, texture, and nutrition in noshing foods as well as soups and stews.

Nahit

Sufficiently boiled chickpeas have a texture that somehow reminds me of boiled green peanuts, except that chickpeas have more crunch. Since I have eaten boiled chickpeas, well salted, as noshing fare for some years, I was pleased to learn that the Jewish people nosh on them during Purim.

16 ounces dry chickpeas
water
1 teaspoon salt plus more to taste
pepper to taste

Wash the chickpeas well, cover with water, and soak overnight. Using the same water, bring the peas to a boil. Add 1 teaspoon of salt and a little more water if needed. Lower the heat, cover tightly, and simmer for 2 hours, or until the chickpeas are tender. Drain the peas in a colander and shake them over low heat until they are very dry. Add more salt to taste, along with a little black pepper. Serve cold as a snack.

Roasted Chickpeas

Here's an easy finger food, eaten like peanuts, or perhaps tossed in a salad. Use freshly cooked chickpeas, or canned.

2 cups cooked chickpeas, drained
1/4 cup olive oil
2 or 3 cloves garlic, minced
salt to taste

Rinse and drain the chickpeas. Preheat the oven to 350°F. Toss the drained chickpeas in the olive oil, adding the garlic and salt. Spread the chickpeas on a large, shallow baking pan. Bake in the center of the oven for 30 minutes, or until golden, stirring from time to time. Serve warm or at room temperature.

Note: Sometimes, I admit, I omit the fresh garlic and sprinkle the chickpeas with garlic salt or even with lemon-pepper seasoning.

Channa

Here's a noshing-fare recipe from Trinidad. Although this is cayenne country all right, the recipe may be heavily influenced by the Indian population. In any case, use either canned or home-cooked chickpeas.

2 cups cooked chickpeas
salt to taste
cayenne pepper to taste

Preheat the broiler. Drain the chickpeas, but do not completely dry them. Spread the chickpeas over a shallow pan, sprinkle them with salt and cayenne, and broil them about 4 inches from the heat for 3 or 4 minutes, or until they are golden brown. Serve channa warm with cold drinks.

Note: The real stuff will be on the hot side, but you may want to hold back on the cayenne on your first batch. Or, why not sprinkle half the batch heavily and the other half lightly?

Chickpea Salad

This easy salad from Morocco is one of my favorites. I often keep it in the refrigerator (made without the parsley) as noshing fare.

2 cups dry chickpeas
1/3 cup extra virgin olive oil
1/4 cup minced fresh parsley
juice of 1 lemon
1 teaspoon salt

Soak the chickpeas overnight in water. Boil for about an hour, or until tender, and drain. Mix all the ingredients together in a bowl suitable for serving. Chill until needed.

Australian Chickpea Salad

This unusual salad from Australia can be made with canned chickpeas, or, better, you may soak and boil a couple of cups until tender.

2 cups cooked chickpeas
1 carrot, peeled and julienned
3 tablespoons extra virgin olive oil
juice of 1 lemon
lettuce leaves
1 teaspoon freshly chopped mint
1 teaspoon paprika
sea salt and freshly ground pepper to taste

Drain the chickpeas and dry with a cloth or paper towel. Toast the chickpeas in a skillet over medium heat for about 10 minutes, shaking them to avoid scorching. In another skillet or small saucepan, sauté the carrot in 2 tablespoons of olive oil. Remove from the heat and set aside. In a small bowl, mix a dressing with 1 tablespoon olive oil, the lemon juice, mint, salt, and pepper. Lay a bed of lettuce leaves in a salad bowl. Pile the chickpeas and carrot on top. Sprinkle with the dressing and a little paprika.

A. D.'s Chickpea Stir-fry

In Mexico, a chickpea vegetable dish calls for chorizo sausages, skinned and chopped, cooked in a skillet along with onion, pimiento, and garlic. I cook a similar dish using sliced pork "country" sausage, smoked and on the hot side. It's very good and easy. The pork sausage that I use has about 25 percent fat. If a lean sausage is used, the stir-fry may need a little more olive oil from time to time.

1 cup cooked or canned chickpeas, drained
$1/2$ pound smoked pork sausage
1 large onion, sliced lengthwise and separated
1 large red bell pepper, cut into strips lengthwise
1 cup sliced mushrooms
3 cloves garlic, minced

1 tablespoon olive oil
salt and freshly ground black pepper to taste

Cut the sausage into wheels about ¼ inch thick. Heat a little olive oil in a skillet, preferably cast-iron, and sauté the sausage wheels for a few minutes, until done and lightly browned on both sides. Remove the sausage, setting aside. Sauté the chickpeas until lightly browned, stirring as you go; remove and set aside. Sauté the onion and garlic until the onion starts to brown. Add the bell pepper and mushrooms. Cook for a couple of minutes, then add the cooked sausage and chickpeas, along with some salt and freshly ground pepper to taste. Serve hot as a side dish.

Note: I can make a complete meal of this dish, served along with some crusty flatbread and sliced tomato or heart of palm with a little homemade mayonnaise. Or, yes, with pasta.

Trotter Soup

Calf's feet are often used for this soup in the Middle East, but these are not readily available in American markets. Trotters (pig's feet) are available in our supermarkets and meat shops, usually nicely scraped, split, and ready to cook. The real prize, however, might well be camel's foot, which is large and soft for walking in the sand. Think about it.

2 trotters, split
1 cup chickpeas
¼ cup olive oil
2 hard-boiled chicken eggs, sliced (garnish)
1 teaspoon turmeric
salt to taste
red pepper flakes to taste
water

Boil a pot of water and add the trotters. Bring to a new boil and let stand for a few minutes; drain and dry them, discarding the water. Heat the oil in a stove-top Dutch oven or other suitable pot. Brown the trotters, turning several times, until lightly browned. Add about 2 quarts of water, along with the chickpeas, turmeric, salt, and red pepper flakes. Cover and simmer for 3 or 4 hours, until the meat is ready to fall off the bone. Add more water from time to time if needed. Remove and bone the trotters, putting the meat back into the pot. Or, if your guests are not squeamish, serve them with the soup. Serve hot in bowls, garnished with sliced egg.

Note: A thicker version of this dish can be served on the plate instead of in a bowl. Also, note that many soups and stews from South America, Mexico, and the West Indies also serve trotters in soups and stews. Sheep's feet are also eaten, and bear paws are considered gourmet fare in China and Russia.

Garbanzo Bean Soup

This filling soup is popular in the Tampa Bay area, where Cubans provided the labor for the cigar industry years ago. It's very, very good. To cook it, you'll need a large pot—preferably a cast-iron stove-top Dutch oven. The recipe has been adapted here from my book *Sausage*.

1 pound chorizo sausages
2 pounds smoked ham hocks
1 pound dry garbanzo beans
4 large onions, chopped
8 cloves garlic, chopped
4 medium potatoes, diced
1/2 green bell pepper, chopped
1/2 red bell pepper, chopped
1 small cabbage, shredded
salt and freshly ground black pepper to taste
3 bay leaves
1/2 teaspoon saffron
water

Put the ham hocks and garbanzo beans into the pot, along with the bay leaves. Cover with water, bring to a boil, reduce the heat, and simmer 1 1/2 hours, or until tender, adding more water (boiling hot) from time to time if needed. Add the sausage, potatoes, onions, garlic, bell peppers, cabbage, saffron, and salt and pepper to taste. Increase the heat until the soup boils, then lower the heat, cover, and simmer until the potatoes are done. Water may be needed all along, but remember that the soup should be quite thick. Serve hot along with plenty of crusty Cuban bread. I sometimes make a whole meal of this soup.

Ionian Isle Soup

Most of the chickpea soup recipes that I have seen call for sausage, pig's feet, or some such animal ingredient. Here's one, from the Greek island of Corfu, that is suitable for vegans.

1 pound chickpeas
1 medium potato
$^1/_4$ cup olive oil
1 head of garlic
juice of 2 small lemons
1 teaspoon minced rosemary
salt and freshly ground black pepper to taste
flour
water

Soak the chickpeas overnight, drain, and rinse. Place the chickpeas in a large pot and cover well with water. Bring to a boil. Add the olive oil, garlic, rosemary, salt and pepper to taste. Reduce the heat and cover the pot. Add enough grated potato to thicken the soup. Simmer until the chickpeas are tender, adding more water if needed. Stir the flour into the lemon juice, then add the paste to the soup just before serving, stirring well.

Pureed Chickpeas

Cooked chickpeas are easy to puree in a blender or food processor, or even with a mortar and pestle. They can be used to thicken soups and stews, or used in salads. Two of the major uses of this form of chickpea are in a tahini "salad," or dip, and in meatless burgers.

Hummus

This puree, used as a dip or condiment, is available commercially—but homemade (using freshly squeezed lemon juice) is easy and better. The tahini in the recipe is available in ethnic-food shops of Middle Eastern or Asian bent, or it can be made at home (see chapter 18.)

1 cup dried chickpeas
$^1/_2$ cup tahini
juice of 2 large lemons
3 cloves garlic, minced
salt to taste
water

Rinse and drain the chickpeas. Place them in a suitable container, cover with water by at least 4 inches and soak overnight. Drain, place in a pot, cover with 2 inches of water, and simmer for $1^1/_2$ hours, or until the beans are tender.

(Stir from time to time and add a little more water if needed.) Drain the chickpeas, saving a little of the pot liquid, and place in a food processor or blender. (They can also be mashed by hand with a mortar and pestle, or pushed through a sieve.) Puree until smooth, gradually adding the lemon juice, tahini, salt, and minced garlic as you go. Add a little of the pot liquid if needed to achieve a creamy mix.

Note: Hummus can be used as an ingredient in meat or vegetable dishes, but it is more often served as a dip—but seldom plain. It is poured into a serving dish, spread out just so with a spoon, drizzled with a little olive oil, dusted with paprika (sometimes with a little cayenne), sprinkled with minced parsley, studded with whole cooked chickpeas on top, and served with a warm Arab bread (pita) or crackers, and olives or sliced cucumbers.

Falafel

According to the recent edition of *Joy of Cooking*, falafel, a sort of vegetable burger patty made with chickpeas, is a popular street food in New York City and in the Middle East. *A Book of Middle Eastern Food* gives a different version, *ta'amia*, made with dried fava beans, said to be an Egyptian national dish with strong Coptic ties; but the book notes that the Israelis have adopted the dish, using chickpeas instead of fava beans. As street food, falafel is often served with pita or some such Arab bread and with various condiments. The patties can also be served for lunch along with salad and a suitable bread and maybe a sauce. There are a number of recipes, and a commercial quick-mix is packaged and marketed in some ethnic-food shops. The real stuff is made from soaked chickpeas (or fava beans), mixed with onion and spices, pounded into a paste, shaped into patties, and fried like a burger. The modern practitioner may want to zap the mix in a food processor instead of pounding it.

1 1/2 cups dry chickpeas
1/2 cup minced fresh parsley
1/2 cup chopped onion
2 large cloves garlic, minced
1 teaspoon freshly ground cumin
1 teaspoon ground coriander
1 teaspoon salt
3/4 teaspoon cayenne pepper
1/2 teaspoon baking powder
olive oil
flour (if needed)

Place the chickpeas in a nonmetallic container, add enough water to cover by at least 2 inches, and place in a cool place for 24 hours. Rinse them and place them in a food processor. Add the other ingredients, except for the oil, and process into a coarse puree. Let the paste sit for an hour. Rig for deep frying. With wet hands, shape the paste into balls about 1 1/2 inches in diameter. Flatten the balls into patties and fry in deep oil until golden brown. (Try a test patty first; if it tends to fall apart, stir a little flour into the mixture.) Serve hot with sliced cold tomatoes or tossed salad, along with a flatbread and hummus.

Note: If you want falafel burgers, make larger patties. Place a fried patty in a pita-bread pocket, along with shredded lettuce, sliced tomato, and tahini sauce (or perhaps a little mayonnaise).

Split Chickpeas

A small skinless chickpea is split and sold in Indian markets, to be used more or less like split peas. The following recipe is typical.

Chana Dhal with Rice

The chickpea is important in Indian cuisine, and the small split variety is sometimes used instead of split peas or red lentils in dhals. If the chickpeas are pureed (as in this recipe), the dhal is said to be soupy, to be eaten with rice. If used whole, the dhal is said to be dry, to be eaten with bread. In either case, dhal is often the main source of protein in the Indian meal.

1 cup small split chickpeas
1 medium onion, sliced
1 medium tomato, diced
2 jalapeño peppers, seeded and chopped
2 tablespoons chopped fresh cilantro
2 cloves garlic
1 teaspoon minced fresh gingerroot
1 teaspoon salt
1/2 teaspoon ground turmeric
long-grain rice (cooked separately)
fried onion slices (cooked separately)
3 cups water

Soak the chickpeas overnight in water. Rinse and put them into a pot along with 2 cups of water. Bring to a boil, adding the onion, garlic, ginger, and turmeric. Reduce the heat and simmer for 30 minutes. Puree in a food mill, or mash by hand if necessary. Stir in 1 cup of water and the salt. Simmer for about 20 minutes, until the mixture thickens to the consistency of soup. Add the jalapeño, tomato, and cilantro. Serve with rice and fried onion slices. Feeds 4.

Chickpea Flour

Chickpeas grind down to a fine flour. It is available at health-food stores and other outlets, and it can be ground at home from off-the-shelf supermarket chickpeas, usually available in the ethnic-food section and sometimes under the name "garbanzo beans." The flour should be stored in an airtight container under refrigeration. I have ground chickpeas with a small mortar and pestle, which is a slow go. The rather large berries grind easier in hand-cranked or small electric mills if they are first split or otherwise crushed. Home-ground chickpea flour usually requires sifting.

The flour can be used in breadstuff, or as a thickener in soups and stews. More and more it is being used for dusting meats before deep frying.

Chickpea Polenta

There is pretty good evidence that the famous Italian cornmeal polenta was once made with chickpeas, chestnuts, and perhaps even acorns. Chickpeas were certainly eaten by the ancient Romans, and Cicero is said to have had a wart on his nose as large as a chickpea.

> 2 cups chickpea flour
> 5 cups water
> 1/2 cup minced onion
> 2 tablespoons butter
> 1 cup freshly grated Parmesan cheese
> 1 teaspoon salt
> 1/2 teaspoon black pepper
> olive oil

Heat the butter in a skillet and brown the onion. Bring the water to a boil. Add the browned onion, salt, and black pepper. Gradually—but vigorously—stir in the chickpea flour, adding it in a small stream. The idea is to prevent lumps from forming. Cook, stirring constantly, until the mixture thickens. Stir in the Parmesan. Pour the mixture into a greased bread pan. Cover and chill. Before serving, slice the polenta (about 1/4 inch thick) and brown in olive oil. Serve hot or warm.

Tohu

Here's a surprise from Burma, adapted here from *The Burmese Kitchen*, by Copeland Marks. It is similar to tofu, and can be used in pretty much the same ways. In Upper Burma, tohu is cut into 2-inch fingers and fried—twice, in a wok. First, 1 cup of oil is heated and the tohu pieces fried 3 minutes, until golden in color. The pieces are removed and cooled. Then they are fried again for another 3 minutes, until crisp, and served as an appetizer. Try this. Here's how to make the tohu.

> 3 cups chickpea flour
> 15 cups water
> 1 teaspoon salt
> 1 teaspoon peanut oil
> 1/4 teaspoon ground turmeric

Mix the chickpea flour and water with a whisk. Set aside for 12 hours at room temperature. Strain about 4 cups of the mixture through a thin cotton cloth. Scrape the residue from the sides of the cloth and discard it. Repeat until all of the mixture has been strained. Let the liquid settle for 3 hours. With a ladle, carefully remove and discard 6 cups of liquid from the top without stirring up the bottom. Select another large pan and rub the bottom with the peanut oil. Pour in most (saving 1 cup or so) of the liquid remaining in the first pot, adding the salt and turmeric. Set aside the sludge remaining in the first pot; it will be used later as a thickening agent. Bring the liquid to a boil, reduce the heat to medium, and cook for 30 minutes, stirring as you go with a wooden spoon. Add the sludge and cook for another 10 minutes, still stirring, until the mixture thickens. Remove the pan from the heat. Line a loaf pan, about 12 inches long, 4 inches wide, and 3 inches deep, with a clean cloth. Pour in the thickened liquid and allow to cool, uncovered, overnight. Slice as needed and use like tofu, or fry by the directions set forth above.

Chickpea Fish

With roots as Lenten fare in the Ethiopian Coptic church, these treats made with chickpea flour are usually eaten with soups or as a snack or appetizer. Be warned that this recipe calls for lots of cayenne, so cut back on the measure if you don't care for hot stuff.

> 2 cups chickpea flour
> 1/2 cup minced onion

$^{1}/_{3}$ cup peanut oil plus more for frying
$^{1}/_{4}$ cup cayenne pepper
1 teaspoon ground ginger
$^{1}/_{2}$ teaspoon cinnamon
$^{1}/_{2}$ teaspoon salt
$^{1}/_{4}$ teaspoon ground cloves
water

In a cast-iron pot, cook the onion on low heat until slightly browned. Add about $^{1}/_{3}$ cup of water and $^{1}/_{3}$ cup peanut oil. Simmer for 5 minutes. Mix the cayenne, ground ginger, cinnamon, salt, and ground cloves; stir the mixture into the pot. Bring to a boil, reduce the heat, and simmer for 10 minutes or so. Keep it very hot; later you'll need it boiling. While waiting, mix the chickpea flour and about $^{1}/_{2}$ cup of water, making a dough stiff enough to form into a ball. More water may be needed, added only a little at a time. On a floured surface, roll the dough out to $^{1}/_{4}$ inch thickness. Cut the dough into fish shapes with a cookie cutter or knife, decorating with eye, mouth line, fins, herringbone scales, and so on. Fry the fish in hot oil (at about 325°F) until they are crisp and brown, turning several times as you go. With a slotted spoon, drain the fish one at a time and add them to the boiling pot liquid. Try not to break the fish. Simmer for 5 minutes, then lift each fish out with a slotted spoon and drain on paper towels. Serve with the pot liquid dished up as a dipping sauce.

Chickpea Chapati

Chickpeas are popular in parts of India, and the flour made from them is called "gram flour." It is sometimes used along with wheat flour, as in this recipe for chapati, the national flatbread. I have adapted the recipe from *Bread*, by Gail Duff. Ms. Duff's recipe uses part plain cake flour, which is what I also recommend. The recipe also calls for ghee, or clarified butter, which can be purchased in Indian markets. If you grow your own cilantro, use some of the root along with the leaves. Any kind of chili pepper will work, but it's best to remove the seeds and inner pith. Try a fresh jalapeño if readily available.

1 cup chickpea flour
1$^{1}/_{2}$ cups cake flour
1 cup ice-cold water
2 tablespoons ghee or margarine
1 small to medium onion, minced

1 small green chili, seeded and minced
1 tablespoon minced fresh cilantro
salt to taste

Mix the chickpea flour, cake flour, and salt in a bowl. Stir in the onion, chili, and cilantro. Make a well in the center of the flour and very gradually pour in enough of the water to make a soft dough. (You may have a little water left.) Divide the dough into 10 more or less equal balls. Using a floured board, roll each ball out to a diameter of 6 or 7 inches, like corn tortillas. These tend to form air holes, so be careful. Heat a cast-iron griddle or skillet over medium heat and lightly grease it with ghee or margarine. Have ready a warm dish and a clean, dry cloth. Using a thin spatula, place one of the rounds on the griddle. Cook until a bubble or two forms. Turn and cook the other side for a minute or two, until cooked through. Turn again and cook a few seconds on the first side, then place the chapati on the heated dish and cover with the cloth. Cook the rest of the batch one at a time, staking them as you go.

Nutritional Highlights

Waverley Root, foods scholar, has pointed out that the chickpea "provides a maximum of nourishment for a minimum of expenditure, whether it be in the form of money or labor. . . ." They are low in fat and high in fiber, containing lots of potassium, calcium, iron, and vitamin A.

17

Beans and Peas

*Hopp'n' John fetch de luck fur conuh able fur
wu'k eb'ry day ub de New Yeah.*

—*Gullah Cooking with Maum Chrish'*

Most of the world's cultures have made good use of beans and peas, and various species are indigenous to the Americas, Africa, Europe, and Asia. Dried beans are especially useful because they store well.

Usually, dried beans are soaked in water overnight, then cooked in water until done. I confess that I usually bypass the soaking process, preferring to merely cook them longer. Most cookbook writers will take issue with this. In any case, beans are being used more and more in salads, often with several colors adding to the whole.

Some well-known varieties include the azuki, a small red bean of the Orient; the anasazi, a red and white speckled bean from the Southwest; the black turtle, popular in Mexico and Latin America; the pinto, the staple for the western cowboy; the lima bean; the kidney bean; the fava of the Old World; and so on, including some very tasty and interesting heirloom varieties that are making their appearance but have not yet gained supermarket availability.

A few of the more important beans are discussed below. Chickpeas are not peas or beans and are covered in a separate chapter (16), partly because they offer so much to the modern cook and have been grossly neglected in American cookery.

❧ Soybeans ❧

I have read that soybeans contain about 38 percent protein, higher than that contained in any other legume, and that is why they are used as a meat substitute for vegans and people in need. In my opinion, however, there is no satisfactory substitute for meat in man's diet, and I think soybeans are quite tasty when considered in their own right.

Unfortunately, I have discovered the culinary joys of soybeans only in recent years, although I have been fond of soy sauce for a long time, considering it a great culinary discovery. During my early days, I was raised on a farm that produced many tons of soybeans—and we never even considered eating them! What a pity. They are good fresh (green), and can be eaten raw or cooked like garden peas.

Dried soybeans are also good in soups and stews, and they can be ground into meal, which is available commercially. The beans are even roasted and used as noshing fare in some parts of the world (as in the following recipe) and "soy nuts" are available from health-food stores and other outlets. Sometimes soybeans are called soya or soja.

Pebok Si Hlaw

Here's a recipe for noshing fare as enjoyed in Upper Burma, according to *The Burmese Kitchen*, by Copeland Marks. Don't be alarmed by the large amount of salt listed in the recipe. It doesn't stick to the soybeans and can be used later for cooking other recipes, although it turns to a tan color.

1 pound soybeans
2 cups kosher salt
water (room temperature)

Rinse and drain the beans. Cover with new water and soak for 15 minutes. Drain briefly in a colander, then put the wet beans into a container, cover with a clean cloth, and let sit overnight. When you are ready to proceed, heat the salt in a cast-iron skillet. Add the soybeans (which should still be moist) and cook over medium-high heat, stirring as you go with a wooden spoon, for 10 to 15 minutes, until the beans are dry and crisp. When pinched between thumb and finger, Marks advises, the bean should crack and crumble. Put the beans into a metal sieve and sift out the salt. Cool the beans and store in a jar, tightly covered. I use mason jars sealed with a vacuum-pack system.

Soybean Crisps

For this interesting recipe I am in debt to *The Family Whole Grain Baking Book*, by Beatrice Trum Hunter. The recipe calls for date sugar, which is available in Asian and Middle Eastern markets. Substitute a light brown sugar if you must.

1 cup toasted soybean flour
1 cup oat flour
2 cups date sugar
3 tablespoons vegetable cooking oil
3 tablespoons water

Preheat the oven to 300°F and grease some cookie sheets. Mix the soybean flour, date sugar, oil, and water. Blend in enough oat flour to make a drop dough, about 1 cup. Drop the dough by the spoonful onto the cookie sheets. (Each drop should flatten out, cookie-shaped, but should not run too much.) Bake for 8 to 10 minutes, until brown. Using a thin spatula, remove the crisps from the cookie sheets while still hot. These measures will make 5 or 6 dozen crisps, depending on how you drop them.

Lentils

For ages lentils were considered food for peasants in Europe, and they have never been popular in America. The Middle East and Asia seem to be the modern strongholds, and perhaps Africa. They are gaining ground, however, and will continue to do so as long as the trend toward whole grains and beans continues. For one thing, they cook much quicker than other beans and, being thin-skinned, they require no soaking. Since they cook in only 20 minutes or so, they are perfect for cooking along with rice.

There are several sorts, all members of the pea family, but the common lentils sold in supermarkets are green lentils and brown lentils. The small black beluga lentils are harder to find, but they have a more attractive appearance when served on their own, or perhaps mixed with white rice. Also, there is some confusion about what's what, with names like Indian lentils and Egyptian lentils and red lentils being found in some sources but not in others.

Lentil flour is available, but may be difficult to find. In any case, it's easy to purchase common lentils off the bean rack at the supermarket and grind your own flour, if you've got a grain mill. There are not many American recipes for lentil flour, but here is a surprise from the Far East.

Mohinga

In the *Far Eastern Cookbook,* by Charmaine Solomon, this interesting fish soup is billed as the national dish of Burma. It calls for quite a bit of lentil flour, called *besan,* and a strong shrimp paste called *ngapi* or *blachan,* which can be purchased in some Asian markets. (I will allow a little anchovy paste in my version of the recipe.)

The real stuff also requires a surprise: the inner pith from the tender upper part of a banana tree. If you don't have a suitable banana tree at hand, substitute canned bamboo shoots or (better) heart of palm, sold in some supermarkets. (This is the heart of a palm tree, called swamp cabbage here in Florida. It is canned in Brazil and Central America.) The recipe also calls for coconut milk, which can be made at home from a fresh coconut or purchased canned, available these days even in some supermarkets. (But avoid the sweetened piña colada creams sold in whiskey stores.) The fish fillets used in the recipe should be white and mild, such as cod or flounder, and boneless.

I like mohinga for a main meal, but in Burma, Ms. Solomon says, it is popular as a snack and is sold in roadside stalls and by vendors who peddle it on carts from house to house. So, be sure to try this one if you are tired of American chowder and French soup.

4 fish fillets (about $1/4$ pound each)
1 pound egg noodles
4 cups thin coconut milk
2 cups thick coconut milk or coconut cream
$1/2$ pound banana stalk, heart of palm, or bamboo shoots
$1/4$ cup lentil flour
$1/4$ cup peanut oil
2 tablespoons Asian sesame oil
2 tablespoons lemon juice
4 medium onions, peeled and sliced
4 cloves garlic, peeled and minced
2 fresh hot chili peppers, seeded and minced (or to taste)
1 teaspoon Asian shrimp paste (*ngapi* or *blachan*)
salt to taste
water

Cook the egg noodles, following the directions on the package, drain, and set aside. While the noodles cook, heat the peanut and sesame oils in a suitable pot, preferably a cast-iron stove-top Dutch oven. Sauté the onions, garlic, and chili peppers for 5 or 6 minutes, stirring with a wooden spoon. Add the thin coconut milk, fish fillets, banana stalk, and a little salt. Bring to a boil, cover tightly, lower the heat, and simmer (do not boil vigorously) for 15 minutes.

Stir the shrimp paste into a little water, then add it to the pot. Cover and simmer for 5 minutes. Stir in the lemon juice and thick coconut milk. Put the soup and egg noodles on the table in separate serving bowls. Add a serving of noodles to each eating bowl (preferably deep bowls) and ladle the soup on top. Both the noodles and the soup should be quite hot.

I like this soup with a crusty French bread or hardtack, but it is customary to offer an assortment of vegetable accompaniments, such as sliced onions, roasted chickpeas, and chopped cilantro (also called coriander).

Note: In *The Burmese Kitchen*, Copeland Marks gives another version of mohinga, which, like chicken soup, has many recipes. His calls for toasted rice, semolina, roasted peanuts ground to a meal, and chickpea paste. He also adds that catfish are popular these days in mohinga.

Lentil Fry Bread

Here's a variation of *falafel*, a fry bread made in both India and Africa from ground lentils or beans. I use lentils here, but feel free to mix in other beans, chickpeas, or black-eyed peas. Also try making the flour from lentils or beans that have been toasted lightly.

2 cups lentil flour plus more for dusting
1 medium to large onion, chopped
1 large chicken egg, beaten
1/2 teaspoon ground red chili pepper or cayenne
salt to taste
water
peanut oil

In a bowl mix the flour, egg, onion, salt, and red pepper with enough water to make a dough just stiff enough to form balls about 2 inches in diameter. Shape the balls and dust them with lentil flour. Heat about 2 inches of peanut oil in a stove-top Dutch oven to 375°F. Fry the balls until nicely browned, drain, and serve hot.

New World Beans

All of the beans of the haricot family are native to the Americas, where they were an important part of the Indian diet and have been dated as far back as 7000 B.C. All of these beans can be ground into flour and used for making breads and gruels, and to thicken gravies and soups. Some of these are too large for easy grinding in some mills, in which case they must be cracked before grinding. I reduce them to grits in a hand mill, then grind them in an electric mill on a fine setting. The resulting flour should perhaps be sifted, but I seldom go that far.

Most of the conventional recipes call for the whole bean, not the flour, meal, or grits. A number of these call for a mixture of beans and rice, as in the Cuban dish called Christians and Moors (see page 134), made with shiny black beans. The famous Red Beans and Rice of Louisiana is covered below, along with New England Baked Beans. Hoppin' John is covered under the Black-Eyed Peas heading (see page 236). In recent years, beans have become a part of most chili recipes. I'll have to go on record as being against cooking the meat and beans in the same pot. Beans can be cooked separately and added to the chili in individual bowls, if anyone should want them, along with chopped onions, sour cream, and so on.

Red Beans and Rice

Traditionally, this dish is made with smoked sausage and attempts to leave out this ingredient are culinarily subversive. In Louisiana, Red Beans and Rice is often cooked on Monday, the day for washing, and, at one time, the water from the rice was used to starch the clothes before they were ironed. But the dish is good any day of the week, if properly made. I like it on a cold day during winter. The recipe below has been adapted here from my book *Sausage*.

2 pounds smoked sausage (in casings)
2 pounds smoked ham hocks
1 pound dry red beans
4 large onions, chopped
6 cloves garlic, minced
water
salt and pepper to taste
rice (cooked separately)

Rinse the beans, put them into a suitable pot (preferably a cast-iron Dutch oven), bring to a boil, and cook for 5 minutes. Then turn off the heat and let the beans sit for at least an hour. Pour the water off the beans. Add three quarts of fresh water to the beans, then add the onions, garlic, and ham hocks. Bring to a boil, reduce heat, cover tightly, and simmer for an hour, or until the beans are tender. Remove the ham hocks and pull off the lean meat, which is put back into the pot. Cut the sausage into 3-inch lengths and add them to the pot. Add a little salt and pepper to taste. Simmer for 30 minutes, stirring from time to time and adding a little more water if needed. Serve the dish in bowls over rice. Feeds 7 or 8.

New England Baked Beans

Beans were raised by the Northeastern Indians and, along with corn, formed a big part of the early American colonial diet. Although there are hundreds of variations on baked-bean dishes, often called Boston baked beans, here is one that I highly recommend. Most of the Boston recipes seem to call for molasses, which was shipped up from Jamaica for making rum. This recipe from New Hampshire, reworked here from my book *Cast-Iron Cooking*, calls for maple syrup and may be closer to Yankee country cooking. I modified the procedure somewhat to make use of a modern oven with thermostat.

1 quart dry beans (try navy beans)
$1/2$ pound slab salt pork
$1/2$ cup maple syrup
1 medium onion
$1/2$ tablespoon salt
$1/2$ teaspoon powdered mustard
water

Put the beans into a nonmetallic container and cover with water. Cover the container and soak them overnight. Drain the beans and put them into a cast-iron pot. Cover with water, bring to boil, and simmer for an hour. Drain the beans. Preheat the oven to 250°F and put on some water to boil. Chop the onion and put it into the bottom of a cast-iron pot of suitable size. Add the beans to the pot. Mix the maple syrup, mustard, and salt, then spread this mixture over the beans. Put the slab of pork on top of the beans so that the rind is up. Cover the beans and pork with boiling water. Bake at 250°F for 8 hours. Add a little water from time to time.

Black-eyed Peas

Also called cowpeas, this Old World legume was brought to America from Africa. It is usually marketed in dried form (available in the beans section of supermarkets) although home gardeners should know that this pea is much better (at least to me) when shelled green and simmered until tender, along with a smoked ham hock or two. In Africa, the black-eyed peas were traditionally used in many ways, and were often ground into a meal for breadstuff. Nutritionally, they are rich in potassium and fiber.

Hoppin' John

Black-eyed peas are traditionally eaten on New Year's Day, and are said to bring good luck for the rest of the year. But "good luck" may be open to discussion. According to *Gullah Cooking with Maum Chrish'*, eating the dish on New Year's Day will make you healthy and able to work every day of the year. Moreover, the dried peas are soaked on New Year's Eve, which is when they "take up" the luck.

1 cup dried black-eyed peas
1 cup rice
1 cup cooked smoked pork, diced (hopefully from the ham bone)
1 ham bone (leftover from a baked cured ham)
1 medium onion, diced
salt to taste
4 cups water plus more for soaking

Put the black-eyed peas in a nonmetallic container. Cover with plenty of water, allowing for expansion. Soak overnight. The next day, drain the beans and put them into a pot with 4 cups water. Add the ham bone. Cook until the peas are done. Drain the peas, saving the pot liquor. Pull any meat off the ham bone and chop enough to measure out 1 cup, saving the rest. If there is no meat on the bone, use any cooked pork, preferably smoked. Put the peas, rice, onion, salt, and chopped pork into a pot, along with 4 cups of pot liquor from the peas and ham bone. Bring to a boil, cover tightly, reduce the heat, and simmer for 20 minutes. Remove the cover and simmer until all the water has been absorbed or evaporated. Serve hot with crackling bread and chilled scallions, if available.

A. D.'s West African Fried Fish

Just as the slave trade brought cowpeas to America, it took chili peppers to West Africa, where they are now an important part of the cuisine. Under several similar names that all mean "pepper-pepper," piri-piri sauce is a standard condiment over much of Africa. It is usually made by steeping hot red chili peppers in olive oil and vinegar, with a little salt. For a reasonable substitute, mix some Tabasco sauce, Louisiana hot sauce (made with red cayenne peppers), or some such fiery red chili sauce with a little olive oil.

catfish or walleye fillets (any mild white fish will do)
cowpea meal
piri-piri sauce (see above text)

salt
peanut oil for deep frying

Brush or lightly rub each fillet on both sides with piri-piri sauce. Stack the fillets and set them aside in a cool place for 30 minutes or so. Rig for deep frying at 375°F. Sprinkle each fillet lightly with salt, roll in the pea meal, shake off the excess, and fry a few pieces at a time in peanut oil until nicely browned. Drain and serve hot.

Mung Beans and Sprouts

These small beans are important in Asia. They are known primarily as a source of bean sprouts, used in stir-fries, soups, and salads, but the unsprouted beans and meal are also used. Being small, they are relatively easy to grind, and I recommend that they be purchased in bulk, stored, and used as needed, either whole or ground.

Other beans can also be sprouted, but some beans don't respond as successfully as others, and a few, such as pintos, literally stink during the process. I use a little clear-plastic sprouting system, in which I can stack the trays and grow several "crops" simultaneously. This makes experimentation very easy, and, of course, these days home cooks are making sprouting wheat and other grains. I suspect that this form of gardening, although ages old, is in its infancy in America.

Bean Mixes

A number of commercial dried bean mixes are available, and it's easy for the cook to mix his own. Soup mixes are especially popular, and a variety of beans give a salad different crunches and color. Mixing beans with beans for grinding into meal doesn't make much sense, aesthetically speaking, but experimentation won't hurt a thing. See also chapter 21, Ezekiel Mixes.

Nutritional Highlights

Dried beans and peas are loaded with vitamins and minerals, including calcium, potassium, and iron. They are low in fat and high in soluble fiber. Bean sprouts are also high in vitamin C. See also the soybean section on page 230.

18

Seeds

The first cultivated crop in the Southwest was probably sunflower.

—Field Guide to North American Edible Wild Plants

O f the thousands of edible wild and domestic seeds known regionally to mankind, a few are available these days in our supermarkets or other ready outlets. Many of these are used as a garnish or decoration for pastry and breads, and some, like nuts, make convenient snacks. Others, such as anise, are used for flavorings and spice. Some seeds even provide color to food, such as the annatto of Mayan cookery. A few perfectly edible seeds, such as those from cantaloupe, are usually thrown out as trash these days, and many more cultivated seeds are raised and marketed by the ton as bird feed. As our cookery becomes even more eclectic, however, we see strange new seeds popping up here and there in our cookbooks. Nigella, for example.

Melon and Squash Seeds

The seeds of watermelon, cantaloupe, squash, and cucumber are edible and often consumed in Mexican and Latin American countries. Actually, the seeds can be eaten fresh (from ripe melons) or dried and ground, often used to thicken soups and stews. Also, the seeds are sometimes mixed together, as in the next two recipes.

4-Seed Orgeat

An ancient European drink, orgeat was originally made with barley. The French started making it with almonds, as it is still made in some lands (see the almond listings in chapter 19, Nuts.) The Spanish brought the almond version to the New World, which was short of almonds but strong on seeds from squash. Today, the drink is made in rural Mexico and Central America with a variety of melonlike seeds, as reflected in this recipe. Note that the exact measure of any one seed isn't very important, as long as the total is 2 cups.

1/2 cup dried squash seeds
1/2 cup dried watermelon seeds
1/2 cup dried cucumber seeds
1/2 cup dried cantaloupe seeds
1 quart water
1/2 cup sugar
1 tablespoon freshly ground cinnamon
peeling of 1 kumquat
orange flower water

Wash all the seeds and grind them in the husks or shells. Stir the ground seeds into the water, adding the sugar, cinnamon, kumquat peel, and orange flower water. Let stand for several hours in a crock or large glass jar, stirring with a wooden spoon. Strain the liquid through a cloth and squeeze the milk from the pulp. Refrigerate. Serve in glasses over cracked ice.

4-Seed Sherbet

Here's a surprise from Central America, where all sorts of melon seeds are ground and used in orgeat and similar fare. Often the seed flour is combined with ground almonds, reflecting the Spanish influence in the New World.

2/3 cup almonds
1/4 cup cantaloupe seeds
1/4 cup watermelon seeds
1/4 cup cucumber seeds

¹/₄ cup squash seeds
1 quart water
²/₃ cup sugar
zest of 1 lemon

Grind the almonds and all the seeds without removing the shells or skins. Mix the resulting flour and stir into the water. (I use a fruit jar tightly capped so that I can shake it from time to time.) Let stand for an hour. Strain the liquid through a cloth and into a clean jar. When it strains down to a drip, squeeze the milky juice out of the nut and seed pulp. To the liquid add the sugar and lemon zest. Shake well and let stand for 1 hour. Shake again and freeze in a mold. Serve frozen.

Variations: Add a little vanilla (another Central American native), and use any combination of dried melon seeds, adding up to 1 cup. Fresh melon seeds can also be used.

Sunflower Seeds

Sunflower plants, native to North America, are now being farmed on a commercial basis in many parts of the world—especially Russia. Except in early cultures, the seeds have been used primarily as a source of oil. In recent years they have been popular as noshing fare. Wild sunflower seeds are also edible, and were much used by the American Indians, who toasted and ground the seeds (whole) with mortar and pestle into meal. The Indians also cultivated the sunflower, from Canada to Peru, and considered it a major source of food. The meal was used in breadstuff, mixed with water to make a drink, or mixed with bone marrow for a high-energy snack.

Modern sunflower hybrids have enormous heads and can be grown in the home garden, yielding seeds for bird feed and human consumption. The heads are easy to harvest. The whole seeds can be ground very coarsely in a mill, then put into water; the hulls will float to the top (and can be roasted and used as a coffee substitute) and the meats will settle to the bottom. The meats can then be dried and ground into a meal, a suitable substitute for part of the flour in recipes for muffins and breads. To make sunflower oil, grind the nut meats into grits and put them into vigorously boiling water. Boil for a while, then cool and skim the oil off the top.

For those who don't garden, sunflower seeds are widely available in supermarkets (in small packs) or in bulk from seed dealers, bird-food outlets, and health-food stores. The seeds are available either whole or hulled, ready for grinding into meal or for use as a nut.

Sunflower Seed Cakes

Here's an easy recipe adapted from *The Art of American Indian Cooking*, by Yeffe Kimball and Jean Anderson.

3 cups hulled sunflower seeds
3 cups water
1/2 cup cooking oil (preferably sunflower oil)
6 tablespoons fine white cornmeal
salt to taste

Bring the water to a boil in a large saucepan. Add the sunflower seeds and salt. Cover tightly and simmer for 1 hour on very low heat, stirring from time to time. Puree the mixture in a blender, or using a mortar and pestle if you must. Mix in the cornmeal, a little at a time, until you have a stiff dough (about 6 tablespoons). Add more salt if needed. Shape the dough into cakes about 3 inches wide. Heat the oil in a heavy skillet until it spits back at you. Brown the cakes 2 or 3 at a time on both sides, turning once. Drain on a brown bag. Add more cooking oil, if needed.

Sunflower Kisses

These delightful sweets are easy to make and are especially good if made with a real unrefined brown sugar (as compared with supermarket brown sugar, which is usually made by adding molasses to refined white sugar). You might also try date sugar or palm sugar.

1 cup sunflower-seed meal
1 cup brown sugar
5 chicken-egg whites
1 teaspoon finely grated lemon zest

Preheat the oven to 300°F and lightly sprinkle some cookie sheets with flour. Beat the egg whites until they begin to stiffen. Gradually add the brown sugar, beating as you go, until the whites are very stiff. Mix in the sunflower-seed meal and lemon zest. Drop onto the cookie sheets by the teaspoonful. Bake in the center of the oven for 15 to 20 minutes. It's best to allow the kisses to cool a little on the cookie sheets before removing them.

⁓ Sesame Seeds ⁓

The cultivation of sesame for its seed probably started in eastern Africa, later spreading to other tropical and temperate regions of the earth. Usually, these days, the seeds are raised primarily for their oil, and sesame was in fact one of the first seeds cultivated especially for oil production. In America, sesame oil was at first used mostly in shortenings and margarine, but these days we see it marketed under its own name as a cooking oil and salad oil. (The Asian sesame oil, made from parched seeds, is primarily a flavoring agent, but sesame oil has been used for a long time as a frying medium in Japan.)

In Sicily and other areas, sesame seeds have been used for many years to scatter on the top of breads, and in confectionery. The Africans used the seeds in soups and puddings long before they were known to the Western world. The Hindus parched the seeds and ground them into a meal called *rehshee*. In the Middle East, the seeds are ground into a paste called tahini (see recipe below), which seems to be gaining in popularity these days. Also, in Greece the seeds have been popular in sweets for many years.

Sesame seeds are available in bulk and in small packages. The meal, or flour, of sesame may be difficult to find, but it's easy to grind your own in a home mill. In the future (I predict) we will find sesame "cake" used in more and more products. This is the part left after expressing the oil. This by-product is very high in protein—with most of the fat removed.

Tahini

This paste, not unlike peanut butter, is a popular appetizer in parts of the Middle East. Often it is used as an ingredient in salads and other recipes. Tahini is marketed in outlets that specialize in Greek and Middle Eastern fare, and it is fast becoming available in general health-food stores and upscale supermarkets. It's easy to make it at home if you've got sesame seeds and a grain mill. It can be made with toasted seeds only, or perhaps half-and-half, as suggested in my recipe.

1 cup ground sesame seeds
1 cup ground toasted sesame seeds
sesame cooking oil
salt to taste

Put the ground seeds in a blender, along with a little salt. Pour in a little sesame oil, blending as you go, until you have a smooth paste. Put the paste into a jar, seal, and refrigerate until needed. I usually try to eat it within a week or so, but it really has a long storage life. After several days of storage, however, oil will start to accumulate on top of the tahini, just as it will on creamy homemade peanut butter. So, stir the paste before using it.

Tahini can be eaten as is with pita bread or crackers, but it is best when used as an ingredient in some other hors d'oeuvres, such as hummus (see recipe on page 222).

Tahini Sauce with Yogurt Cheese

There are hundreds of sauces made with tahini. Many of these contain lemon juice and are used over fish or vegetables. Here is one of my favorites. To make the yogurt cheese, drain plain yogurt overnight in a strainer lined with a cloth, elevated to drain away the whey; I make this often, using the strainer from an old coffeemaker, lined with a paper filter.

1 cup tahini
1 cup yogurt cheese (see above)
$1/4$ cup lemon juice
$1/4$ cup grapefruit juice
$1/2$ cup cold water
1 teaspoon crushed garlic
$1/2$ teaspoon fine sea salt

Make the tahini (see previous recipe). Place it into a food processor. Blend in the garlic, lemon juice, and grapefruit juice until well mixed. Add the water and salt; blend until the mixture is smooth. Mix in the yogurt cheese. Serve with boiled or steamed vegetables.

Variation: Omit the yogurt, add a little olive oil, and serve the sauce over grilled fish.

Tahini Salad with Parsley

Often tahini is mixed with lemon juice and other ingredients to make a salad, served in a bowl, garnished with boiled egg, and eaten with pita bread. I like it on crackers.

$1/2$ cup tahini
$1/2$ cup lemon juice
$1/3$ cup minced fresh parsley
2 cloves garlic
salt to taste

cold water
boiled eggs, sliced (garnish)

Crush the garlic in a large bowl and add a little lemon juice. Mix in the tahini (see above recipe) and a touch of salt. Beat in the lemon juice. Add the parsley and enough cold water to make a smooth cream (this can be accomplished more easily in an electric blender). Taste. Add more lemon or salt, if needed. Serve in a dipping bowl, garnished with sliced boiled eggs, along with pita or crackers.

Pastélli

Here's an old Greek recipe from the Ionian islands, where it is something of a treat for children and poor folk on festive occasions. It is sometimes sold in health-food stores. Traditionally, the candy is prepared on a marble slab, but any hard, smooth surface will do.

¾ pound sesame seeds
½ pound honey
1 teaspoon orange zest

Heat the sesame seeds in a skillet, shaking as you go, until they are lightly toasted. Heat the honey in a saucepan until it begins to boil. Add the orange zest and toasted sesame seeds. Boil until a teaspoon of the mixture forms a ball when it is dropped into a glass of cold water. Carefully pour the mixture onto a smooth surface and shape into a square about ½ inch thick. Cut into bars about 3 inches long and 1 inch wide, making about 50 pieces. Store until needed. To prevent sticking, separate each piece or layer with wax paper or plastic film. For long storage, wrap each piece.

Charleston Benne Wafers

I found this recipe, and its title, in Marion Cunningham's revised edition of *The Fannie Farmer Cookbook*, and I suspect it goes back to the Gullah culture of the Carolina and Georgia lowlands and barrier islands. In any case, it is known that the slaves of this area brought sesame seeds from Africa. "Benne," by the way, is simply another name for sesame seeds.

1 cup light brown sugar
½ cup sesame seeds, lightly toasted
3 tablespoons all-purpose flour
1 large chicken egg, beaten

1 tablespoon butter or margarine
1 teaspoon vanilla
salt to taste

Preheat the oven to 350°F. Grease some cookie sheets with butter and sprinkle lightly with flour. Toast the sesame seeds in a cast-iron skillet, shaking as you go, until light brown. Combine the sesame seeds with the rest of the ingredients in a bowl, mixing thoroughly. Drop the mix by the teaspoonful onto the cookie sheets, leaving about 2 inches of spread space between each drop. Bake for 4 to 6 minutes, until lightly brown. To prevent sticking, remove the wafers from the cookie sheets while they are still warm.

Note: In keeping with my Gullah theory for this recipe, I sometimes cook it with home-ground millet flour, another traditional Gullah food brought over from Africa.

Sesame-Honey Spread

Here's a snack that is being marketed in health-food outlets. It's easy enough to make your own, using either a blender or a mill of some sort.

1 cup sesame seeds
2 tablespoons honey
1/4 cup water
salt to taste

Toast the seeds in a skillet, shaking as you go, until they are lightly browned. Cool. Grind the seeds into a fine meal or flour. Bring the water to a boil. In a serving bowl, mix the sesame meal, honey, water, and a little salt. Mix well. Cover and refrigerate until needed. Serve on toast or bread.

Variation: Mix in a little peanut butter and more honey.

Fish Sesame

Although my favorite fried-fish recipes call for only a light dusting with fine white whole-kernel cornmeal, I like to cook this one every now and then for a change. Children are especially fond of it. I use a mild fish, such as black bass or grouper or walleye. The exact measures aren't critical for the recipe, but I like to serve at least 1/2 pound of fish per person.

fish fillets
sesame seeds

flour
chicken egg, beaten
peanut oil for deep frying
salt

Rig for deep frying at 375°F. When the oil is hot, dust the fillets lightly with salt and flour, roll in the egg, roll in the sesame seeds, shake off the excess, and drop carefully (using tongs) into the hot oil. Cook a few pieces at a time until nicely brown. Drain thoroughly on brown paper. (Draining fried foods, always a very important step, helps keep the crust crispy.) Serve hot.

Flaxseed

Flax might well have been first cultivated as a food. In time, it became more important for fiber production—especially for linen cloth—and for linseed oil. A number of varieties were developed, usually to produce a better seed or fiber. The seed varieties have a short stem with many seed-head branches; the fiber varieties, a longer stem with fewer seed heads. Most of the cultivated flax is harvested mechanically these days with a huge combine, but in some undeveloped areas small plots are still gathered by hand. The home gardener can raise and gather a few plants for seed and flour simply by cutting and drying the seed heads. When thoroughly dry, the seed heads are thrust into a paper bag and thrashed about.

Flaxseed has been found in the ruins of the Stone Age lake dwellings in Switzerland, and the fiber was used by the ancient Egyptians for wrapping mummies. Pliny, the Roman historian, mentioned flaxseed being used as human food, and, I understand, the roasted seeds are used as food even today in Ethiopia. In Bombay, the unripe seed heads or bolls are eaten. (Home gardeners may want to try a boll, perhaps sautéed in butter or steamed.) At the end of the twentieth century, American health-food advocates point out that flaxseed is a good source of soluble fiber, that it lowers the bad cholesterol and elevates the good.

Usually, flaxseed is added as a minor ingredient to long recipes. The flour or meal can also be used as an ingredient in breads and cereals. Flaxseed flour may be difficult to find, but the seeds are sold in small packages and in bulk. (One outfit markets bulk seeds in 5-pound bags for only $6.50, which seems to me a good bargain in the modern health-food market.) For making bread, try using 1 tablespoon flaxseed flour per cup of wheat flour.

One supporter recommends using flaxseed, along with ground seeds and nuts, to thicken drinks, and I have seen several orgeat recipes that call for a small amount of flax meal.

Mustard Seed

Mustard seed and mustard powder are widely available in spice markets, and the seeds are sold in bulk, available in white, brown, and black varieties.

Prepared Mustard

It's easy to make your own mustard paste if you have a good grain mill or blender, especially if you prefer the brown mustards. Here's my recipe.

1 cup ground mustard seeds (brown, if available)
1 cup wheat flour
1 cup water
grated horseradish (optional)

Heat the flour in a cast-iron skillet, shaking as you go, until it is nicely browned. In a serving container, mix the flour, ground mustard seeds, and enough water to make a paste. Add some grated horseradish, to taste, if you want a hot mustard. Better yet, make two batches, one hot and one mild.

Note: you might also grind $1/2$ cup of mustard seeds to make powder for your spice rack.

Poppy Seed

Generally considered a sprinkle for baked goods in North America, poppy seeds play a more important role in some cultures. In Asia Minor, the heads of poppy plants are eaten when green; they have a hot taste, and are considered a delicacy. Of the several varieties of poppy, some are used primarily as a source of vegetable oil, sometimes considered a rival to olive oil. The Iranians, I understand, often sprinkle poppy seeds over rice. The seeds are also used in soups and stews, especially in Russia and northern Europe, where vast fields of poppy plants are cultivated for food. In old Vienna, a dish of noodles with poppy seeds was a festive Jewish dish for Purim. According to *Larousse Gastronomique*, the leaves of poppy are also eaten like spinach, although they are slightly narcotic.

Poppy grows wild in North America, and, for some reason, it seems to be especially plentiful along railroad beds. One day I'm going to pick some and dry the heads for seed. Meanwhile, poppy seeds can be purchased in small packages in supermarkets, and in bulk from seed and grain suppliers.

Kutia

Here's an old Polish dish that has become a traditional Christmas Eve dessert. I enjoy it throughout the year, and especially in the late spring when the new crop of tupelo honey becomes available in my neck of the woods.

2 cups poppy seeds
1^1/2 cups wheat berries
^{1}/4 cup heavy cream
6 cups water
honey

Soak the wheat berries overnight in 6 cups of water in a nonmetallic container. The next day, place the berries and the soaking water into a pot, cover, and simmer for about an hour, or until the berries are tender. Add a little more water if needed. Drain the berries and cool. In a suitable bowl, beat the cream and poppy seeds into the berries. Sweeten with honey to taste. Chill. Serve cold.

Poppy-Seed Treats

Here's an unusual treat adapted from *The Family Whole Grain Baking Book*, by Beatrice Trum Hunter.

2 pounds poppy seeds
2 cups ground hazelnuts
2 cups honey
^{1}/2 cup maple sugar

Grease and flour two 8- by 8- inch pans, 2 inches deep. Mix the honey, sugar, and poppy seeds in a saucepan. Cook on low heat for about 30 minutes, stirring from time to time, until the mixture thickens. Stir in the ground hazelnuts, mixing well. Turn the mixture into the pans, spread evenly, and refrigerate until it sets. Cut into 1-inch squares. Wrap each piece in wax paper. Refrigerate until needed.

19

Nuts

*Caucasians like to spend cold winter evenings around
a fireplace, roasting chestnuts and telling old tales.*

—*Cooking from the Caucasus*

Being packed with vitamins, minerals, and protein, nuts helped feed mankind long before agriculture was developed. Nuts are also quite high in oils and monounsaturated and polyunsaturated fats. Most nuts, however, are low in fiber and starch, with the exceptions including chestnuts and brazil nuts.

The modern world's most popular nuts are discussed under the headings below, but many more varieties are highly esteemed regionally around the world. Also, some other nuts are covered in chapter 20, Wild Grist.

Generally, nuts mature in the fall of the year and are available in the shell at that time in roadside stands and in supermarkets. Some are available year-round, often salted and toasted. Dry raw nuts in the shell, as well as shelled nuts, are best stored in an airtight container in a cool place. Put some emphasis on cool. Of course, nuts in the shell keep better than shelled. Nuts also keep nicely in the freezer—two years or even longer. Since nuts are low in moisture, they can be refrozen without damage.

BLANCHING NUTS

Some nuts, such as almonds, have an outer shell and a skin (sometimes bitter) that covers the meat. This skin can be removed, if it is prudent to do so, by pouring boiling water over the nuts or by immersing them in boiling water for a minute or less. When the nuts cool, the skins are easy to rub off. Note that peanuts, hazelnuts, and pistachios can be skinned by first toasting them in an oven at about 350°F for 10 minutes or so. When they cool, the skins are easily rubbed off. English walnuts and pecans do not require blanching.

CRACKING AND SHELLING NUTS

Unfortunately, nutcrackers don't work equally well for all kinds of nuts. Cracking the nut is easy, as a rule, but the trick is to crack it in such a way that the whole kernel or a large part of it comes out easily. For pecans, it's best to use a lever-operated longitudinal cracker. Generally, a hammer and a hard surface are about as good as any cracker, especially if the hard surface has an indentation to hold the nut in place.

GRINDING AND CHOPPING NUTS

Most nuts can be chopped in a food mill of some sort, and some can be reduced to fine flour. Some nuts are high in oil, however, and will clog up some mills, especially stone mills. The meal of some nuts is available commercially.

English Walnuts

The walnuts discussed under this heading are what Americans call English walnuts—which the English call Persian walnuts. They can be found growing wild from Europe to the Himalayas. The walnut was once an important part of European cuisine, especially French. In times of famine, the European peasants even ground walnut shells together with acorns to make their daily bread. Today the nut's stronghold is probably in the Caucasus and eastward into Iran. In America, the English walnut has never been much more than noshing fare, although it is now cultivated in California and elsewhere. (The American black walnut, discussed on page 253, is a much stronger-tasting nut.) Generally, the English walnut is comparatively easy to crack and shell, and the meats also grind easily. The recipes below lean toward walnut meals, and those who are fans of roasted chestnuts also may want to roast walnuts. So, pick up a large bag of unshelled nuts and try the following.

Roasted Walnuts

Preheat the oven to 425°F. Place some unshelled walnuts in a shallow pan. Roast in the center of the oven for 15 minutes. Serve warm, in the shell. I also like these roasted in hot ashes in camp or on the hearth in the den.

Austrian Walnut Cake

Here's a tasty surprise from *The New Book of Whole Grains*, by Marlene Anne Bumgarner, who said it took her a long time to believe that there was no flour in the cake. "In Europe," she says, "this cake is often topped with a coffee cream." I like it after dinner on a cold evening along with Irish coffee—or on a hot evening along with a Black Russian.

2$^{1}/_4$ cups cracked walnut meats
6 large chicken eggs, separated
1$^{3}/_4$ cups sugar

Preheat the oven to 350°F and grease a springform cake pan. Grind the nuts into a flour. Separate the eggs. Mix the sugar and egg yolks, then beat until foamy. Mix in the walnut flour. Beat the egg whites until quite stiff, then fold them into the walnut mixture. Pour the batter into the greased springform pan. Bake in the center of the oven for 45 mintues—without peeking or opening the oven. After 45 minutes, gently remove the cake from the oven and let sit for 10 minutes before removing from the pan. Serve warm or cold. Also try the next recipe, an even easier dessert made without flour or springform cake pan.

Walnut Coffee Dessert

Note that this tasty confection needs no cooking.

1 cup ground walnuts
1 cup ground dates (pitted)
$^{1}/_2$ tablespoon brandy
whipped cream

With mortar and pestle, pound the walnuts and dates together, helped along by the brandy. Spread the mixture to a thickness of $^{1}/_2$ inch. Cut into diamond shapes. Serve with a little whipped cream atop each piece, along with a cup of steaming freshly brewed coffee.

Azerbaijani Pheasant Stew

In the past, great bird hunting was available to the sporting men in the Caucasus area, and from the Caspian Sea across the plains or steppes to the Far East falconers took pheasants and great bustards and bitterns and other good birds in large numbers. Nomadic cooking on the steppes was probably on the primitive side—that is, sticking a bird onto the tip of a sword and roasting it over a campfire—but around the Caspian grew a variety of fruits and vegetables and nuts, allowing a great cuisine to develop. Here is a recipe from that heritage.

In addition to lots of walnuts, this recipe calls for pomegranate juice, an ingredient that may be difficult to locate in some areas. As it happens, five pomegranate trees grew on the farm where I was born, and once I wrote a poem about them bursting open in autumn and laughing with rows of bright red teeth. It's an image that I had tucked away for posterity, and I was rather shocked to learn that a Turkish poet had beat me to the punch line a millennium or so ago.

Anyhow, after you obtain a couple of large ripe pomegranates simply peel the fruit, shell out the translucent red seeds, and discard the bitter pith. Then press the juice from the seeds. (Be warned that pomegranate juice will stain your shirt.) If you can't find any fresh pomegranates, you may be able to purchase some juice in ethnic grocery outlets that specialize in Middle Eastern fare. You can also buy concentrated pomegranate syrup, which I allow in reduced proportions, although it has honey or sugar in it.

2 pheasants
1 medium onion, minced
1/4 cup butter or margarine
2 cups chicken or pheasant broth
2 cups walnuts
1 cup fresh pomegranate juice (see text above)
juice of 2 lemons
salt and pepper to taste
1/2 teaspoon cinnamon

Grind the walnuts coarsely in a meat grinder or zap them in a food processor. Pluck the birds and cut them into pieces—breast halves, drumsticks, thighs, and bony parts. Wash, drain, and sprinkle with salt and pepper. In a heavy skillet, heat the butter. Sauté the pheasant pieces on both sides until lightly browned. Drain the pieces on a brown bag. Next, sauté the minced onion for 3 or 4 minutes. Then stir in the ground walnuts. Add the chicken broth, pomegranate juice, lemon juice, cinnamon, and a little salt and pepper. Bring the mixture to a boil, stirring as you go. Reduce the heat, simmer, and stir for 10 minutes. Add the pheasant pieces to the skillet, making sure that all of them are coated with sauce, cover, and simmer on very low heat for 40 minutes or longer, until the pheasant is tender. Move the pieces about and turn them over from time to time. Serve hot over fluffy rice.

Fesenjan

Although the recipe above is for pheasant, a similar dish made with duck, walnuts, and pomegranate juice is said to be one of the national dishes of Iran, where it is called *fesenjan*. So, if you want to eat Iranian instead of Azerbaijani, use mallard instead of pheasant. Season with a pinch or two of cardamom and sprinkle additional ground walnuts atop the dish before serving it forth. Eat *fesenjan* with a crusty rice. (See chapter 10, Rice.)

Black Walnuts

These nuts have a strong flavor and are not for everybody. It's best to use them sparingly, perhaps as a topping for ice creams or in candy. As pointed out in chapter 20, Wild Grist, black walnuts grow wild in several areas, usually in the foothills of the Ozarks and Appalachians. They are also used as yard trees, and I was fortunate enough to grow up in a household with two such trees. One of my older sisters gathered these in November and picked out enough meats to give as Christmas gifts, packing them in old-time "fruit jars" with a glass top and dressed with ribbon and bow. It was a tedious process, for the nuts were very difficult to extract from the hulls. Part of the game, of course, was in getting out a big piece of meat. I don't think we ever succeeded in extracting a whole nut half. My reward for helping her was a batch of divinity fudge, made according to the recipe below.

These days black walnuts are available packaged, but they are expensive. In any case, it's best to store the nuts in the refrigerator or freezer. I don't recommend grinding these into meal or flour, although the grits make an excellent topping.

Sister's Black Walnut Divinity

This recipe can also be made with chopped pecans, in which case each piece is topped with a pecan half. My favorite, however, is made with bits and pieces of black walnut.

¾ cup black walnut pieces
3 cups sugar
¾ cup white corn syrup (Karo, we called it)
3 large chicken-egg whites
1 teaspoon vanilla extract
½ cup water

Heat the water to boiling in a saucepan. Stir in the sugar and syrup, bringing to a new boil. Reduce the heat and cook to 238°F on a candy thermometer. Quickly remove the pan from the heat and allow to cool. While waiting, beat the egg whites in a bowl until they are stiff. Pour half of the sugar mixture into the egg whites, stirring as you go with a wooden spoon. Place the mixture back onto the stove and heat to 290°F, again using the candy thermometer. Quickly remove from the heat and stir in the rest of the sugar mixture. Stir in the nuts and vanilla. Stir constantly until the mixture thickens. Drop a teaspoonful onto waxed paper. If it holds its shape and doesn't flatten out, proceed to drop the rest. Cool and enjoy.

Pecans

I was born and raised on a farm on the outskirts of a small town and we had several pecan trees, including a paper shell that produced the best nuts I've ever eaten. In recent years I more or less retired to several acres in another small town, and I purchased the property partly because of its 14 large pecan trees, some ancient and draped with Spanish moss. But I'll have to admit that grinding pecans into meal didn't occur to me until I saw pecan meal advertised in a catalog of nuts and other noshing fare from Sunnyland Farms! I might add that this commercial product isn't produced by actually grinding the meal. Instead, it is the smallest of the bits and pieces left from shelling and grading the pecans mechanically (a complicated process). Also be warned that grinding pecans at home may clog up some mills.

All pecans are oily and should be stored in a sealed container at low temperature. Pecan meal is even harder to keep fresh and should be frozen unless it will be used right away. In addition to meal and whole nut halves, pecans are also marketed in bits and pieces.

I don't want to get started on recipes for pecan pies or praline variations. Space is limited in a book like this, and anything I say on either subject would surely stir up either the Texans or the Cajuns—probably both. Anyone interested in pecans and pecan cookery should take a look at a slim volume called *The Pecan Tree*, by Jane Manaster.

There are even opinions on roasted pecans. A Georgia recipe calls for a little vegetable oil and Worcestershire sauce. A Texas recipe for "barbecued" pecans calls for ketchup, butter, Worcestershire, hot sauce, and salt, and another for spiced pecans calls for egg-white coating, cinnamon, cloves, nutmeg, sugar, and salt, if you can believe all that. In any case, here are a few of my favorites.

A. D.'s Toasted Pecan Halves

Use whole pecan halves for this recipe, saving the bits and pieces for another purpose, if you shell out your own. Omit the salt from this recipe at your culinary peril.

1 cup pecan halves
2 tablespoons fresh butter or margarine
salt to taste

Melt a little butter in a cast-iron skillet on medium-high heat. Add the pecan halves and cook, stirring as you go with a wooden spoon, until the pecans start to brown. Remove from the heat, sprinkle with a little salt, and allow to cool down slowly in the cast-iron skillet. Drain on a brown bag and serve as noshing fare. Be warned that pecans burn easily, so watch what you are doing and trust your nose.

Note: I also use olive oil in this recipe.

Parched Pecans

Similar in result to the recipe above, this recipe is cooked on a shallow baking pan in the oven.

1/2 pound pecan halves
1/4 cup melted butter or margarine
salt to taste

Preheat the oven to 250°F. Place the pecan halves, without overlapping, on the bottom of a shallow baking pan or shallow cookie sheet. Pour on the melted butter. Sprinkle with salt. Put into the center of the oven and cook for 20 minutes, stirring every 5 minutes. Cook for a few more minutes, stirring every 2 minutes, until nicely browned. (Do not overcook; remember that pecans scorch easily.) Remove the pan from the oven. Cool and eat on the spot or store in a tightly closed container until needed.

Dates Stuffed with Pecans

Instead of trying my luck in roadside eating houses or fast-food joints, I will sometimes eat from wayside supermarkets. All I need for lunch is a package of dried pitted dates and a jar of mixed nuts, both of which ride well and require no refrigeration or special wrapping. Invariably, however, I will eat off the pecans first. It therefore makes sense to combine pecans and dates.

dried dates
large pecan halves, roasted

Using a sharp knife cut a slit in each date lengthwise, cutting all the way to the pit. Work the pit out. Insert a pecan half in the cavity and close the date around it. Eat out of hand.

Pecan Log

Here's a recipe for using up pecan bits and pieces. If you have to chop whole halves, so be it.

chopped pecans
1 cup cream
1½ cups light brown sugar
¾ cup cane syrup
3 tablespoons butter or margarine
corn syrup (Karo)

Cook the butter, cane syrup, brown sugar, and cream in a saucepan, covered, for 5 mintues. Remove the cover and cook until the mixture starts to form a soft ball. Cool for about 15 minutes. Roll the mixure into a log about 3 inches long. Pour the corn syrup into a smooth saucer (or small plate), and sprinkle the nut bits in another smooth saucer. Roll the log in corn syrup, then roll it in the pecan pieces. Cut into slices for serving, or simply break in half for two.

Pecan Muffins

Here's a recipe adapted from an old brochure published by Sunnyland Farms, which markets pecan meal.

1 cup pecan meal
1 cup white flour
1 cup whole milk
½ cup peanut oil
½ cup sugar

1 chicken egg
2 teaspoons baking powder

Preheat the oven to 400°F and grease some muffin tins. Mix all the ingredients in a small bowl. Pour or ladle into the tins, filling each cavity about 2/3 full. Bake in the center of the oven for about 25 minutes, or until done.

Chickpea Fry Bread with Pecans

Pecan meal can be used as a minor ingredient in hundreds of bread recipes. Here is one of my personal favorites, cooked with the aid of Asian sesame oil.

1 1/2 cups flour from toasted chickpeas
1/2 cup pecan meal
1/2 cup oat meal
1 medium onion, minced
1 tablespoon minced chives or green onion tops
1 teaspoon salt
Asian sesame oil
1 cup water

Mix the chickpea flour with the water in a large bowl. Mix all the rest of the ingredients except the sesame oil. Heat about 1/8 inch of sesame oil in a skillet. Shape the dough into patties and place into the hot oil using a spatula. Mash the patties with the spatula to flatten them. Fry on both sides, turning once, for a few mintues, or until done. Serve warm or cold. These are tasty—and quite filling.

Almonds

I read somewhere that almonds are the most widely known and the most widely cultivated nut trees. Maybe—except that they aren't really nuts. They are the stone from a fruit tree, similar to plums. They bloom earlier than most fruit trees and produce many white blossoms, which might well help account for part of their popularity in almond-producing climes, mostly round the Mediterranean and Asia Minor. In America, commercial almonds are grown mostly in California.

In any case, mankind has made very good use of almonds. They are available in several forms—whole, sliced, or slivered, blanched or not. (There is also a bitter almond but I have never run across one.) I like almonds for grinding because they are harder than most nuts and aren't as apt to turn to butter.

Almonds are often used in desserts and sweets, especially in Europe and the Middle East. Scandinavia also makes good use of almonds in such dishes as *oktka-ka*, a Swiss cheesecake, and *möndlusnúdar*, an Icelandic almond roll taken with coffee. Almonds are also used in a few famous entrées, such as trout almandine, and are often used as a garnish in green beans. Here are a few of my favorite almond recipes.

Muhallabia

Rice pudding is served in many parts of the world, but it is usually made from cooked whole grains and is usually considered rather mundane fare. Good, yes, but still mundane—sometimes made with leftover rice. In the Middle East, however, rice flour is sometimes used in puddings along with ground nuts, and the dish demands more respect. In fact, the recipe below, adapted from Claudia Roden's *A Book of Middle Eastern Food*, has been called the most regal and delicious of puddings.

3/4 cup ground almonds
1/4 cup rice flour
1 to 2 tablespoons cornstarch
5 cups milk
2/3 cup sugar
1/4 cup orange blossom water (or rose water)
chopped almonds and pistacho nuts
crystallized rose petals or violets (optional)

Mix the rice flour and cornstarch, adding just enough of the milk to make a paste. Pour the rest of the milk into a saucepan, add the sugar, and bring to a low boil. Using a wooden spoon, gradually stir in the rice flour and cornstarch paste. Simmer, stirring constantly, until the mixture thickens a little—you will feel a little resistance to the wooden spoon. Add the orange blossom water or rose water, stir in the ground almonds, and remove the pan from the heat. Cool for a few minutes, then pour the pudding into a glass serving bowl or perhaps individual serving dishes. Chill. Before serving, decorate the top with a pattern of chopped almonds and pistachios. Add a few crystallized rose petals to the pattern, or garnish along the rim.

Ancient Nut Sauce for Fish

Here's an old sauce calling for ground mustard seeds and ground nuts. The more modern tarator sauces (not to be confused with tartar sauce) are also made with ground walnuts, almonds, or pine nuts, along with various other ingredients.

1/2 cup ground almonds
ground mustard seeds
white vinegar or wine vinegar

Mix a little vinegar with the almonds, making a thin paste. Stir in some ground mustard seeds to taste, along with perhaps a little more vinegar. Serve with fried or baked fish.

Panellets de Piñons

These Catalonian cookies, made with the aid of sweet potatoes (sometimes incorrectly called yams) and ground almonds, are baked commercially in Barcelona and other hot spots, according to *The Catalan Country Kitchen*, by Marimar Torres, from which this recipe has been adapted. They are traditionally eaten on All Saints' Day. This recipe calls for pine nuts, but other nuts (usually chopped) can also be used for the coating.

3 cups blanched almonds
1 cup pine nuts
1 cup cooked sweet potato pulp (canned will also work)
2 cups sugar
3 chicken egg yolks (divided)
2 teaspoons finely grated lemon zest
1 teaspoon vanilla extract

Boil a sweet potato or two for about 30 minutes, or until tender. Peel and mash it, then measure out 1 cup of pulp. Combine it with 2 of the egg yolks and the rest of the ingredients except for the pine nuts. Mix well until you have a soft dough. Let the dough rest for 30 minutes. Preheat the oven to 350°F and grease a baking sheet. Shape the dough into golf-ball-sized pieces and coat them with pine nuts. Brush each ball lightly with egg yolk and place it on the cookie sheet, spacing them 1 inch apart. Bake in the center of the oven for 15 minutes. Enjoy.

❧ Peanuts ❧

Sometimes called ground peas, ground nuts, or goobers, peanuts are really legumes, not nuts. They probably originated in the Andes of South America, went to Africa during colonial days, and came back to Virginia. Today they are raised in several countries. Most of the harvest is done mechanically these days, but I can remember different times.

On the family farm of my upbringing we raised about 100 tons of peanuts each year. We ate raw peanuts, roasted peanuts, and boiled green peanuts (one of the world's great delicacies, now appreciated in parts of Southeast Asia and a few hot spots in the American South), and we also used them from time to time to make peanut brittle and other recipes. One of my uncles maintained that you could live on roasted peanuts and milk. I would add peanut butter and blackberry jelly sandwiches.

Still, one of the greatest culinary shocks of my life came back in the fourth grade, well over half a century ago. Our school received a large batch of peanut meal and other peanut products, all developed by Dr. George Washington Carver at Tuskegee Institute in Alabama to help promote the peanut for the benefit of area farmers. I liked the cookies and other goodies that my mother baked with the meal, but peanut meal never caught on and I have never seen it available commercially. But I still remember the event, and it helped shape my culinary curiosity at an early age.

Most of the peanuts sold today are either roasted or raw (usually in the shell), made into peanut butter, or expressed for their oil. Peanuts yield a very good cooking oil that has a high smoke point (allowing you to cook at high temperatures), has no strong flavor or odor (contrary to some culinary books), and does not readily absorb the taste or odor of whatever is cooked in it.

In my neck of the woods, green peanuts (almost mature but not dried out) are sometimes sold in supermarkets. These can be eaten fresh or boiled or simmered in the shell until tender (usually about 2 hours), using water that has been well salted (at least 1 tablespoon salt per quart of water). Remember that the nuts are still in the shell, so that not too much of the salt gets inside. In parts of the South, boiled peanuts are sold at roadside stands and sometimes at ball games, but all too often they use dried peanuts that have been soaked in water. This simply won't do. For best results, the peanut vines are pulled up (or plowed up) and the mature nuts are picked off, still green. (The immature nuts, called pops, have no meat and won't do for boiling.) The freshly dug nuts are washed and cooked immediately, or frozen in the shell until needed. Boiled peanuts are usually eaten cold, but they are much better when warm, still steaming from the boil. Some people put cajun spices into boiled peanuts, but I don't allow this practice at my house.

Parched or Roasted Peanuts

These, by my definition, are dry peanuts cooked in the shell. Usually they are put on a tray and baked in the oven until they are crunchy and have a wonderful aroma. Shelled peanuts can also be cooked in this manner. In either case, these are unsalted nuts. The shelled peanuts can be eaten out of hand. For use in recipes, they should be worked between the palms and winnowed to get rid of the skins.

Fried or Sautéed Peanuts

These are shelled dry peanuts that are cooked for a few minutes in a skillet in a little peanut oil. Stir often with a wooden spoon or shake the skillet to help prevent scorching. Sprinkle with salt, then drain on a brown bag. The same results can be achieved by baking the peanuts in a shallow baking pan with a little oil.

Peanut Butter

This recipe can be made in a blender, and can be either smooth or raw, depending on how good your blender is and how long you zap the nuts.

1 cup shelled dry peanuts
$1/2$ to $3/4$ tablespoon peanut oil
$1/4$ teaspoon salt

Preheat the oven to 350°F. Put the peanuts into a shallow pan and bake in the center of the oven for about 15 minutes. Cool a little and rub the nuts a few at a time between the palms to remove the husks. Winnow the nuts and place about half of them into the blender, along with the oil and salt. Blend until you like the consistency and chunkiness. Add a little more oil if needed.

This recipe can be repeated if you need a large batch. Most homemade peanut butter will accumulate a little oil on top and should be stirred before using.

Ugandan Peanut Sauce

Peanuts have become a part of the cuisine of Africa south of the Sahara. This sauce is from Uganda, adapted here from *The Hot Sauce Bible*, by Dave DeWitt and Chuck Evans, and was no doubt made from any of the several "ground nuts" that grew in that area before peanuts arrived from the New World. The peanut butter (see above recipe) can be either smooth or chunky. The sauce is used with fried fish or chicken (or guinea fowl).

1 cup peanut butter
$1/2$ pound dried fish
4 medium tomatoes, chopped
2 medium onions, chopped
2 teaspoons peanut oil
2 teaspoons cayenne powder
1 teaspoon curry powder
salt to taste
water

Soak the fish overnight in water. If convenient, change the water several times. Drain the fish, then bone and chop it. Heat the oil in a skillet. Sauté the onions for 5 minutes. Add the tomatoes and cook, uncovered, for anoher 5 minutes. Add $2^{1}/2$ cups of water, the fish, peanut butter, cayenne, curry, and salt to taste. (If you are using highly salted dried fish, additional salt may not be necessary.) Simmer uncovered on very low heat for 45 minutes, or until the sauce thickens to suit you.

Note: I usually omit the curry powder because I simply don't like the way the stuff smells. The best curries are not made with such a powder.

Sallie Hill's Peanut Brittle

Here's a recipe from Sallie Hill, a foods editor for the Southern Living section of the old *Progressive Farmer* magazine. This was later developed into the highly successful *Southern Living* magazine, where I was once an editor, of sorts.

2 cups raw peanuts
2 cups sugar
$3/4$ cup corn syrup
$1/4$ cup water
2 teaspoons baking soda
$1/8$ teaspoon salt

Cook the sugar, syrup, water, and salt in a pan until the sugar dissolves. Add the raw peanuts. Do not stir—but watch it carefully. Cook until the mix reaches the hard-crack stage (300°F on a candy thermometer), then remove it from the heat. Quickly stir in the baking soda; mix well, causing the candy to puff up. Pour on a greased surface (marble if available) and spread thin. The thinner the better. It will harden quickly and should not stick to the surface if it has been cooked enough. Break into pieces and store in a round tin.

Chestnuts

Chestnuts were once important to many of the world's peoples. In North America, the American chestnut grew over much of the country and was extensively eaten until a blight all but wiped out the species earlier this century. Today most of the market chestnuts are of the European or Asian sort.

In modern-day America, the chestnut is used mostly as noshing fare, usually roasted in the fall. It is also used in stuffings for goose or turkey and as a puree to accompany wild boar or other highly marinated game. The nut is also enjoyed in Europe and Asia, but perhaps the only place where it is a real part of the culture these days is on the island of Corsica. Reportedly, this dates back to the Middle Ages, when the farmers of the island switched from grains to chestnuts to avoid paying taxes to foreign invaders. In any case, before the potato was introduced from the New World, chestnuts were the basic food of many poor people in Europe. Oddly, chestnuts are considered vegetables in some quarters.

Freshly matured chestnuts are available commercially in the fall, especially around Thanksgiving and Christmas. These are usually cooked before they are eaten. Canned chestnuts are also available. Chestnut flour is not easy to find, but it is available by mail order. I buy it in 5-pound bags and store it in my freezer. It is a fine flour with a sweet smell and taste, and it makes a smooth, heavy dough.

Corsican Polenta

Chestnuts, as well as chickpeas, were probably used to make the early Italian polenta. Pretty much the same dish is made even today in Corsica and perhaps in rural Italian towns with plenty of chestnut trees.

1 1/2 cups chestnut flour
1 quart water
salt to taste

Boil the water in a pot, adding the salt. Take the pot off the heat and gradually but vigorously stir in the chestnut flour. Mix until all lumps are gone. Return the mixture to the heat and cook for about 15 minutes, stirring as you go with a large wooden spoon or spatula, until the mixture thickens. (Be warned that unattended, unstirred polenta will bubble with force, spitting all over your stove.) Pour the thickened mixture into a greased loaf pan. Chill overnight. The texture will be rather like a pudding or spoon bread; its taste, sweet but strong. I like it topped with whipped cream. This polenta can be unmolded and served as a loaf, but it is difficult to slice and fry, like corn mush.

Note: If you want it fried, take a tip from the French dish called *Croquettes de Marrons.* That is, cut the mixture (after it has been chilled) into small portions, sprinkle with flour, dip in beaten egg, and roll in bread crumbs. Deep-fry in clarified butter.

Peeled Chestnuts

There are several ways to peel chestnuts. My way is to cut a cross on the flat side of each nut. Place the slashed nuts in boiling water for 5 minutes. Remove the nuts and put them into a container of cold water. Shell and skin each nut. Use these in chestnut puree or other recipes.

Roasted Chestnuts

Cut a slit on the flat side of each nut. Preheat the oven to 450°F. Spread the nuts on a shallow baking sheet or ovenproof skillet. Cook for about 15 minutes, stirring a time or two, until the shells open and the nuts are easy to remove. Peel and serve these on the spot, while still warm.

Braised and Pureed Chestnuts

Shell and peel enough chestnuts to yield 1 pound. Heat a cup of beef broth in a saucepan. Add the chestnuts along with a little salt and pepper. Simmer for 20 minutes, then drain out the liquid. Heat the butter in a skillet on high heat. Add the drained chestnuts and shake the skillet constantly for a few minutes. Serve hot as a vegetable.

If you want a puree, put the braised chestnuts (while still very hot) into a blender along with a little heavy cream. Puree until you have the texture you like, adding more cream as needed.

The General's Chestnut Sauce

Here's a recipe adapted from one of my favorite books: *A General's Diary of Treasured Recipes,* by Brigadier General Frank Dorn.

1 cup minced chestnut meats
2 cups meat stock
3 tablespoons butter or margarine
3 tablespoons flour
1/4 cup sherry

1/4 cup finely chopped celery (with part of tops)
1 small to medium onion, finely chopped
2 tablespoons finely chopped parsley
2 bay leaves
salt to taste

In a skillet or suitable pan, heat the butter and sauté the onion for about 5 minutes. Stir in the flour with a wooden spoon, along with the meat stock, bay leaves, celery, and parsley. Simmer for 10 minutes, stirring as you go. Add the chestnuts, sherry, and salt, mixing thoroughly. Serve hot as a sauce for venison, beef, or poultry.

Bam Baap

Chestnuts are enjoyed in parts of Asia, as in this dish adapted from *The Korean Kitchen*, by Copeland Marks. The recipe calls for 6 large chestnuts, which, I understand, grow as large as small chicken eggs in Korea. I use a long-grain rice for the recipe. If brown or short-grain rice is used, increase the cooking times. I have also added a little salt to the list of ingredients.

2 cups rice
6 extra-large chestnuts (or 9 smaller ones)
3 1/2 cups water
salt to taste

Put the ingredients into a suitable pan. Bring to a boil, cover, and cook for 10 minutes, stirring a time or two. Reduce the heat and simmer for another 5 minutes, until all the water has been absorbed and the chestnuts have softened. Serve warm as a pilaf.

⋙ Pine Nuts ⋙

Pine nuts of one sort or another are eaten in Europe, Africa, and Asia, and are especially popular in the Middle East. Nuts of the piñon and other species of pine were once very important to some of the North American Indians and to settlers. Various pine nuts (usually gathered from the wild in different parts of the world) are available commercially, but the price is high these days. Usually, the nuts are used sparingly in breads, sweets, pilafs, and salads.

Two of my favorite recipes for pine nuts are set forth in chapter 20, Wild Grist. See also the recipe for *Panellets de Piñons* on page 259.

❧ Hazelnuts ❧

Several species of hazelnuts grow wild here and there around the world, including North America. Several other species are cultiveted and often marketed under the name "filbert." Some are called cobnuts (or cobs), Barcelona nuts, or Turkish nuts. In China they have been under cultivation for over 4,000 years. According to foods scholar Waverley Root, "The filbert was the second most widely eaten nut during the Stone Age, the first being the acorn. This does not mean that prehistoric man preferred acorns. Probably there were more of them." By whatever name, hazelnuts are simply divine and have a sweet taste.

Root also points out that the American Indians were making cakes of cornmeal and pounded filberts long before the Europeans arrived. So, grind a few and add them to your next batch of hoecake—or perhaps to your pound cake.

If you want to remove the skins from hazelnuts, it's best to toast them in the oven at 350°F for about 10 minutes, cool, and rub between the palms, winnowing as you go. These grind nicely in most grain mills, except for stone mills.

Fortunately, hazelnuts, in the shell or out, store much better than most other nuts. They will keep nicely in an airtight container even at room temperature, and will keep 2 years or longer in the refrigerator. So, purchase them in bulk and enjoy them all year. They will work in most recipes that call for nuts of any sort, and are at their best when lightly toasted.

❧ Cashews ❧

Cashews will grow on the lower tip of Florida, but for the most part they grow deeper in the tropics. They are native to Brazil, and are now raised in India and East Africa. Actually, the nut is the seed of a fruit or apple. The fruit is highly prized in Brazil and India but it doesn't store or ship well and must be eaten within a day of harvest.

In any case, the cashew is ideal for noshing fare or cocktail nuts, widely available in supermarkets. Roasted and salted, it is packaged alone or along with mixed nuts. In the latter case I go for them right after the pecans and brazil nuts have been picked out. The nut is usually marketed whole, and as such it makes a pleasing addition to salads and vegetable dishes. I especially like them in a chicken salad. Chopped cashews can be used in suitable recipes. The cashew is relatively soft and quite oily, however, and doesn't make meal easily. On the other hand, it is ideal for nut butter, which can be made in a blender or food processor. Try the following.

Cashew Honey Butter

I use commercially toasted and salted cashew nuts for this recipe, but bulk nuts will also work if they are lightly toasted before processing.

4 cups cashews
$1/4$ cup honey
peanut oil as needed
salt to taste

Put the nuts into a blender or food processor. Zap them in the pulse mode a few times. Add the honey, salt, and a little oil. Pulse a few more times. Test for consistency adding a little more oil as needed. Use immediately or refrigerate for longer storage.

Brazil Nuts

These large nuts grow in stately trees high in the rain forest, towering above the undergrowth. So far, the nut has resisted attempts to raise it elsewhere, and most of the nuts are harvested wild even today in Brazil, Peru, and other countries in the Amazon basin. The trees produce a large pod, the size of a coconut, with a hard husk. Inside the hard pod is a cluster of 12 to 20 nuts, each covered with its own hard shell! The nuts are marketed in the shell and shelled. It's best to buy either in bulk and store in the refrigerator.

I enjoy cracking brazil nuts on the hearth, with the aid of a hammer, but more often than not one does not get a whole nut—and sometimes the process results in a bruised finger, for it's hard to hold the nut and crack it too. That's part of the game. If whole nuts are important for the purpose at hand, however, forget the hearth and try placing the nuts in a pan of water. Bring to a boil and cook for 3 minutes. Drain and cover with cold water for 1 minute. Drain again. They will be easier to crack and the kernels will usually remain whole and easy to remove. They will still be crunchy, though, unless you boil them too long.

The size of brazil nuts is impressive, and the larger nuts bring higher prices. I usually buy them in bulk, shelled, and settle for a smaller variety harvested in Peru. While speaking of size, I might add that a much larger nut grows wild in the northernmost rain forests of South America. These are not marketed outside the area, however, because the harvest is intermittent and unreliable.

Brazil Nut Chips

Here's an unusual recipe adaped from an old book, *The Progressive Farmer's Southern Cookbook*.

1½ cups shelled brazil nuts, whole
2 tablespoons melted butter or margarine
1 teaspoon salt
water

Put the nuts into a pan, cover with water, and bring to a boil. Simmer for 2 or 3 minutes. Drain. Cut the nuts lengthwise into slices 1/8 inch thick. (This slicing is easier to accomplish with a slicing device, such as a French mandolin. A really good vegetable peeler might also work. In either case, watch your fingers.) Preheat the oven to 350°F and butter a shallow baking pan. Spread the slices on the bottom of the baking pan. Drizzle with the melted butter. Sprinkle with the salt. Bake in the center of the oven for 12 minutes, stirring a time or two. Be careful. These burn easily. Serve warm. These can be refrigerated for several weeks, then broiled as needed until hot and crisp.

Macadamia Nuts

These delicious nuts, relatively new to the Western world, are native to the rain forest of northern Australia, but their name doesn't come from a remote region. Instead, the nut was named for a Dr. John Macadam, who reportedly first discovered that the nuts are edible. The nut was taken to Hawaii, where it thrived in the volcanic soil on the hillsides. After much work at the University of Hawaii, improved varieties led to the nut being raised commercially. Ironically, attempts to raise the improved varieties back in Australia have been unsuccessful.

Today, shelled macadamia nuts are available whole, in halves, or in pieces. They are also available in the shell. The nuts are expensive, partly because of harvesting problems. Although the nuts grow in clusters like grapes, they don't all ripen at the same time.

Roasted Macadamia Nuts

Shell the nuts and rinse with hot water. Sprinkle salt over the nuts and let drain for 30 minutes. Preheat the oven to 350°F. Put the nuts into a shallow pan and bake in the center of the oven for 10 to 15 minutes. Reduce the heat to 250°F and bake for another 30 minutes or longer, turning them from time to time, until they reach a golden brown color. Cool and eat as a snack, or use as needed in nut recipes.

Macadamia Balls

Here's a finger-food recipe from Hawaii.

1 package cream cheese (8-ounce size)
1/4 cup chopped macadamia nuts
flaked coconut
cinnamon

Soften the cream cheese at room temperature. Mix in the nuts and a pinch or two of ground cinnamon. Chill the mixture in the refrigerator until shortly before serving time. Shape the mixture with your fingers into about 20 bite-sized balls. Roll each ball in coconut. Serve immediately with punch—or perhaps with a piña colada or two.

Macadamia Chocolate Chip Cookies

These are my favorite cookies. Although most good nuts will work in the recipe, macadamia halves are perfect.

1 cup all-purpose flour
6 ounces semisweet chocolate chips
1/2 cup macadamia nuts, lightly toasted
1/2 cup melted butter or margarine
1/2 cup regular sugar
1/4 cup dark brown sugar (packed measure)
1/4 cup butter or margarine, softened
1 large chicken egg
1 teaspoon vanilla extract
1/2 teaspoon salt
1/2 teaspoon baking soda

Preheat the oven to 375°F and line a large cookie sheet with aluminum foil. Mix together the flour, baking soda, and salt in a suitable bowl. Sift. In another bowl, beat together butter, sugar, and brown sugar; then beat in the egg and vanilla, working until smooth. Stir in the flour mixture, followed by the nuts and chocolate chips. Drop a teaspoonful at a time onto the cookie sheet, spacing the cookies 3 inches apart. When the pan is full, put it into the center of the oven and bake for 10 to 15 minutes, or until lightly browned. Ideally, each cookie should be crispy around the edges and soft in the middle. Slide the foil from the baking pan and set aside to cool. Then bake another panful. Repeat until all the batter has been used up. If you are in a hurry, bake more than one panful at a time. Eat what you can while the cookies are still warm, then store the rest between sheets of wax paper in a tin with a tight cover.

Pistachios

Sometimes called green almonds, these nuts have appealed to man's culinary fancy since ancient times, adding color as well as crunch to pilafs and other dishes—even sausages. They are especially eye-catching in desserts. Native to Persia and Asia Minor, the pistachio requires warm, arid conditions. Although they are raised commercially in California, the world's supply comes mostly from Iran and Turkey. The nuts grow in clusters on small deciduous trees.

Used sparingly more often than not, they are too expensive for grinding into meal. As noshing fare, they are eaten out of the shell.

20

Wild Grist

Nowadays, when people are again coming to appreciate the dark, wholesome breads of our ancestors, maybe the acorn will come back into its own.

—Euell Gibbons

A number of wild foods can be grist for the forager's mill, yielding meals, grits, and flour, as well as "coffee" grounds and spices. The listing below is far from being complete, and is intended as an appetizer. Identification is the big problem with wild foods, and, sadly, the guidebooks are not as helpful as the publishers like to think. Still, a good field guide is the best place to start.

Wild Amaranth

Edible amaranth of one sort or another grows wild over most of North America, free for the eating, and seed catalogs list garden varieties. The *Field Guide to North American Edible Wild Plants* discusses two kinds: *Amaranthus retroflexus*, also called pigweed and redroot (because its root is red), and *Amaranthus hybridus*, or green pigweed. Then the guide gets itself off the hook, saying that several other Amaranthus species are edible.

It is safe to say that one species or another is available to anyone in the United States (except possibly in Alaska) as well as in Mexico, Central America, and South America. Pigweed is in fact a nuisance weed in some areas. It is called pigweed because rural people once fed the hogs with it, and probably still do here and there. The leaves as well as the seeds of one species or another are eaten in India, China, Jamaica, and other parts of the world.

The wide availability of wild amaranth seeds is another good reason for investing in a kitchen grain mill. Try adding a little wild amaranth flour to your pancake mix, or perhaps cook the following muffin recipe.

Pigweed Muffins

If you can't find any wild pigweed seeds for this recipe, use commercial amaranth seeds or flour.

1 cup ground wild amaranth seeds
$1/2$ cup home-ground wheat flour
$1\,1/4$ cups milk
$1/4$ cup butter or margarine
3 tablespoons honey
2 chicken eggs, separated
2 teaspoons baking powder
$1/2$ teaspoon salt

Preheat the oven to 375°F and grease a muffin pan. Mix the ground amaranth seeds and wheat flour, along with the baking powder and salt. Combine the milk, egg yolks, butter or margarine, and honey; blend into the flour mixture. Beat the egg whites and fold into the batter. Spoon the batter into greased muffin tins and bake in the center of the oven for 20 minutes.

Note: Wild foods guru Euell Gibbons recommends roasting the seeds before grinding them. Remember that the leaves of amaranth plants are edible. The green leaves compare favorably with spinach, and even the dry leaves can be used in soups and stews.

Prickly Pear and Other Fruit Seeds

Various species of flat-stemmed prickly pear cacti grow in the East and the Southwest, and in Mexico and other parts of the world. All of these have edible pads, free for the picking, and some species are sold in some upscale supermarkets, under the name "nopale." The pads are delicious and I have cooked them for many years, having had good luck foraging along old railroad tracks. The pads have a slippery texture, like okra, that puts some people off. The fruits are also edible and are marketed as cactus pears and Indian figs in a dozen countries around the Mediterranean, Asia, and Australia. When gathered from the wild, both the pads and the figs have mean spines that must be removed before eating. Wear thick leather gloves. There are several ways to remove the spines. The Indians often burned them off, or at least blunted the tips, in hot coals. Sometimes one species or another of these plants grow in large clumps, making the fruits and pads available in great plenty. Anyone who has access to such good pickings should take a look at the recipes in *Uncommon Fruits and Vegetables*, an excellent book by Elizabeth Schneider.

Readers of this book should know that the fruits contain many hard, black seeds. The Indians dried these and ground them into a meal. I'm not going into detail about how they obtained the hard little seeds, but the modern practitioner may prefer to boil the fruits for jelly or syrup and strain out the seeds. They are best toasted lightly before grinding. Use the meal to thicken soups and gravies, or add it to pancake or bread mixes.

A few other fruits have edible seeds. Some of these, such as the wild persimmon, are quite large and very numerous. In fact, the Indians ground persimmon seeds into a meal, using it to thicken soups and stews and to make breads. Anyone who gathers wild persimmons might consider this. I have gathered half a gallon of seeds from under good trees, where the fruits had fallen to the ground.

Several other wild fruits have edible seeds or stones. The California laurel, for example, native to California and Oregon, bears an olivelike fruit—but only its seeds were eaten by the Indians of the region. Usually, the seeds were roasted and then ground into a meal for use in breadstuff.

Be warned, however, that not all fruit seeds are edible. The pits or stones of wild plum, for example, may contain hydrocyanic acid, the "cyanic" part of which scares me away. So, do your homework before grinding and eating just anything that looks like a seed or tasty drupe.

Acorns

Being widely available and easily recognized, acorns are perhaps the perfect food for novice foragers, a dependable staple for would-be survivalists, easy noshing fare for hikers, and a good first step for the back-to-nature set. There are some 58 species of oak in the Americas north of Mexico and more than 150 species south of the border, extending down into Central and South America. Worldwide, oaks comprise 500 species of trees and shrubs.

The acorns of the red oak group (which includes the black oaks) require two years to mature—and they are quite bitter. These bitter acorns can be used, however, after proper leaching in cold water. Be warned, however, that some acorns require long soaking and several changes of water.

The acorns of the white oak group are not as bitter as those of the red oak. Some of these can be eaten out of hand, like nuts. I am especially fond of the acorns from the live oak and the chestnut oak.

In any case, dry acorns can be hulled and ground into a flour for making breads or thickening stews. Here are a few recipes to try, mostly from American Indian cookery.

Choctaw Stick Bread

According to a French traveler of the 1700s, the Choctaw Indians sometimes made bread with acorn meal. First they pounded the acorns into a meal or flour, then placed this into a cane sieve on the bank of a stream. From time to time they threw water onto the meal, thereby leaching out the bitter tannin. Next, they worked the meal and a little water until they had a paste. Then they put the paste around a suitable stick and cooked it over an open fire.

The camper and the backpacker can use the same method today, thereby making bread without the aid of utensils. A little salt and sugar will improve the bread, however, at least to my taste. I also recommend the use of a little fine cornmeal or wheat flour, if you want to make a recipe of it. Note also that meal made from sweet acorns, such as live oak, do not require leaching. I have made this bread with live oak acorns freshly picked from low-hanging tree limbs.

Corn Husk Breads

The Indians made good use of corn husks (and green corn leaves) in their cookery. Tamales are, of course, made with the aid of corn husks, and other foods are wrapped in them. The corn husks add flavor to the bread and to the food. Either green or dried corn husks can be used. The latter should be soaked in hot water to soften them. Dry husks can be purchased today in supermarkets and Mexican-food stores. These are trimmed to a rectangular shape and are very convenient.

30 corn husks cut into rectangles
1 cup finely ground sweet acorn meal
1 cup finely ground white cornmeal
1/2 cup honey

salt to taste
water

Bring some water to boil in a large pot. Add the corn husks and simmer until they are pliable enough to make wrappers. Mix the acorn meal and cornmeal in a bowl of suitable size, then add enough boiling water, stirring as you go, to make a mushy dough or thick batter. Stir in the honey and a little salt. Remove the corn husks and drain them (retain the liquid) but do not dry them. Spread the corn husks and place about 2 tablespoons of the dough in the center. (The dough should spread a little but not quite as much as pancake batter.) Fold the long sides of the husk together, then make a fold on either end. Have ready some 1/4 inch strips of corn husks and tie the packets. Bring the liquid in the large pot to a new boil and drop the packets into it. Simmer the packets for 20 minutes, then remove. Cut the strings, open the husks, and enjoy.

Note: Be sure to taste the corn husk broth. If you like the flavor as much as I do, save it for making a soup. Incidentally, the Indians also used dried corn silks for flavoring soups and stews.

Steamed Black Bread Euell Gibbons

Here's one of my favorite recipes for acorn bread, adapted here from Euell Gibbon's *Stalking the Wild Asparagus.*

1 1/2 cups acorn meal
1/2 cup sweet acorn grits (coarsely ground acorns)
1 cup all-purpose white flour
1/2 cup sugar
1/2 cup dark molasses
1 1/2 cups sour milk
2 tablespoons salad oil
1 teaspoon baking soda
1 teaspoon salt

Mix the acorn meal, acorn grits, flour, sugar, salt, and baking soda. Add the molasses, milk, and oil. Wash some cheesecloth, wring it out, fold it to double the thickness, and put it over a round bowl. Put the batter onto the cloth, then bring the corners of the cloth together and tie. Suspend the bag over boiling water in a pot, cover, and steam for 4 hours, adding more water as needed. Serve the bread steaming hot. Gibbons says to serve the bread with baked beans, and I'll certainly go along with that. I also like it smeared with butter.

You can also cook this bread in a Crock-Pot. Put a trivet in the bottom (or rig a rack of some sort), put a little water into the pot, place the bag of dough onto the trivet, cover tightly, and cook on high for 5 hours.

Indian Venison Stew

The following basic recipe was widely used to stew venison all across North America. Of course, chestnuts, hickory nuts, and so on were also used in stews.

2 pounds cubed venison
spring water
1 cup sweet acorn meal
crushed juniper berries or hackberries (optional)
salt to taste

Put the cubed meat into a pot, cover it with water, and add the juniper berries. Simmer on very low heat—do not boil—for 6 or 7 hours, or until the meat is very tender. Stir and add a little water from time to time. About an hour before eating, stir in the acorn meal and a little salt. Add more water if needed. You should have a very thick, nourishing gravy to eat along with the meat. The juniper berries can be omitted, but remember that they are often used in game recipes and can sometimes be purchased in spice markets. Of course, you can also pick your own even in winter. Or you can substitute a few crushed hackberries or dried berries of the spice bush, or maybe allspice berries, which are another American ingredient.

Water Lotus Seeds

Called spatterdock, yellow water lily, pond lily, and water chinquapin, these plants produce a seed head that resembles a wasp's nest. One species or another grows in freshwater ponds and backwaters of North America, South America, India, Japan, and other countries. In China and Japan, the seeds as well as the large rootstocks are eaten. (Even the stem and the leaf, or pad, of the lotus can be boiled and eaten for food if it is harvested before the leaf has finished unfolding. In China, the leaves are also used to wrap pork and other meat prior to steaming it.) The American Indians ate the seeds either fresh or dried, or ground into a flour. They often parched the seeds on hot, flat rocks. They don't pop like popcorn, but they do swell up.

A giant lotus that grows in the backwaters of the Amazon has a pad large enough—up to 10 feet in diameter—to float a small child. The seeds were once an important grain for some of the natives.

I don't recommend that anyone harvest large numbers of lotus seeds indiscriminately—dried-flower arrangers do enough damage—but a few taken from large patches won't hurt a thing and will make some unusual eating. When mature and dry, the seeds have a hard shell. They should be cracked and hulled before grinding. Try a little of the flour mixed in with wheat flour in your favorite recipes.

Lotus seeds are sometimes available—at a high price—from Asian and gourmet-food dealers.

Wild Nuts

Edible wild nuts of one sort or another grow over much of the world, and wild nuts are sometimes harvested and sold at market, including Brazil nuts, pine nuts, and black walnuts. Most of the wild nuts can be eaten out of hand, used in recipes, or ground into a meal for use in breadstuff and as thickeners for soups and stews. Here is a short selection.

BEECHNUTS

Kin to the chestnuts and oaks, beech trees were very important to the Iroquois and other Indian tribes, who ate the nuts fresh or stored them for future use. They even ate the immature nuts as well as the young leaves in spring. The inner bark of the tree was also eaten in times of need. The early settlers also made good use of beechnuts. In addition to eating the nuts, they roasted and ground them for a coffee substitute and for use as a meal.

Beechnuts were also once an important food in Europe, where large stands grew, and might well have been a staple for early man. The nut contains 22 percent protein.

HICKORY NUTS AND PECANS

These delicious nuts make tasty nut breads and pies. They can also be ground into grits and meals. The hardest part, with hickory nuts, is getting them out of the shell.

Wild pecans, cousins of the hickory nut, are delicious. See the pecan recipes in chapter 19, Nuts.

Hickory Nut Honey Pie

Here's a hickory nut pie that makes all the work seem worthwhile. It's even better if you have dark wild honey.

1 cup hickory-nut meats
1 cup sugar
$1/2$ cup honey
$1/4$ cup butter or margarine
3 chicken eggs
1 teaspoon vanilla extract
unbaked pastry for 9-inch pie shell

Preheat the oven to 350°F. Melt the butter, then mix in the sugar, honey, and vanilla. Whisk the eggs lightly, then mix them into the honey butter. Stir in the hickory. Pour the mixture into a pastry-lined pie pan and bake for 40 to 45 minutes.

BUTTERNUTS AND WALNUTS

Several wild nuts of the *Juglans* clan are delicious and can be used to make meals and flours. Butternuts are closely related to the walnuts and bear nuts about 2 inches in diameter. The meats can be eaten raw or used in baked goods and confections, or ground into a meal for use in baking breads. Ground butternuts are also mixed with honey to form a spread for toast. According to *Earth Medicine—Earth Foods*, the Indians made a baby food by mixing butternut meal and pulverized venison in warm water. This mixture was used like milk.

Black walnuts also grow wild in some areas, and most of the commercial crop is gathered from the Ozarks and other places. I have known people who gathered wild black walnuts commercially. Although black walnuts can be ground into a meal, they are a little strong for breadstuff. But do try a few black walnut grits sprinkled over vanilla ice cream. See also chapter 19 and the recipe for my sister's divinity fudge (page 254).

Indian Milk

The American Indians didn't have domesticated cows, goats, or other milk-giving animals. For milk, they used nuts and seeds and, in the tropics, coconuts.

$1/2$ cup butternuts
1 cup water
1 tablespoon honey

Blend the ingredients with a mortar and pestle, or zap them in an electric blender or food processor. Use the mixture as a substitute for milk in recipes.

CHINQUAPINS

These wild nuts are cousins to the great American chestnut, which was virtually wiped out by a blight some years ago. Like chestnuts, chinquapins grow in burrs and also have a shell that must be removed before the meats are eaten. Small but tasty, chinquapins can be ground into a meal or flour. See also the chestnut section beginning on page 263.

HAZELNUTS

Both American and beaked hazelnuts grow wild. They make excellent eating and can be ground into meal. See also chapter 19.

PINE NUTS

Many of the 90 species of pine trees that grow mostly in the north temperate zone of the world have been important as a source of food—pine seeds or nuts—and some of these are available commercially even today. The commercial pine nuts (covered in chapter 19) are usually from tree species that produce rather large seeds and they are quite expensive these days.

In addition to the seeds, the bark and needles of pines have been used as food, especially in times of need. The American Indians sometimes ate the inner bark or pounded it into a flour for making breadstuff. The inner bark is full of sweet sap, especially in spring, and can be eaten fresh or dried for future use. The bark was an important source of food for some tribes, and the Mohawk name *Adirhon'dak*, means "tree eaters." The pine needles, a source of vitamin C, were also used to make tea. Even the ashes of pinewood were sometimes used in breads, along with ground seeds.

Out West, the Indians made good use of the seeds of the piñon, the ponderosa, and the digger pine. The Zuñi ate the nuts of the piñon pine raw or parched. When dried, they were sometimes ground into a meal, which was used for bread, sometimes mixed with cornmeal.

All of the pines have edible seeds, but they are difficult to get out of the cones. Usually, roasting the cones makes the seeds easier to remove, and gives them a better flavor. Grind a few pine nuts and mix the meal with ground sunflower seeds, as the Zuñi did. Mix with water until you have a mush, shape into thin hoecakes, and cook on a heated flat rock or cast-iron griddle.

Anyone interested in gathering, processing, and cooking pine nuts should read *The Piñon Pine*, published by The University of Nevada Press. A good selection of pine-nut recipes is also found in *The Rocky Mountain Wild Foods Cookbook*, but these are influenced more by Middle Eastern and European cookery than American. Good stuff, though.

Aztec Salad

Avocados have always been high on my list of salad ingredients, especially if I can beg or buy tree-ripened fruits—with blackened skins and nutty meat. Pine nuts fit right in. The pepper that I use is a rather mild, large Mexican pepper such as poblano, which can be used either green or red, depending on maturity. Substitute red bell pepper if necessary, or even strips of canned pimiento.

2 ripe avocados
1/2 cup pine nuts
1 medium to large tomato, chopped
juice of 1 large lemon or lime
3 scallions, chopped, with part of green tops
1 clove garlic, minced
1/2 teaspoon hot red pepper sauce (such as Tabasco)
salt and black pepper to taste
fresh parsley or cilantro (garnish)
fresh red pepper (garnish)

Roast the red pepper over a flame until it turns black all over. Wrap with foil and set aside for a few minutes to soften in its own steam. Peel and seed the pepper, then cut into thin strips. Set aside. Halve the avocados lengthwise and carefully remove the seed. Using a spoon, scoop out the meat, being careful not to tear the peel. Save the shells. Puree the meat, mixing in the lemon juice. Mix in the rest of the ingredients except for the red pepper strips and cilantro. Stuff the mixture into the four avocado shells. Garnish with red pepper strips and cilantro sprigs. Serve with wedges of fried corn tortillas.

Pine-Nut Pralines

I was a little surprised to learn from *The Only Texas Cookbook*, by Linda West Eckhart, that pralines are sometimes made from pine nuts in the panhandle of

Texas. Presumably, these were originally made from the nuts of the piñon and other panhandle species.

2 cups pine nuts
3 cups sugar
1 cup buttermilk
1/4 cup butter or margarine
1 teaspoon baking soda
1 teaspoon vanilla extract

Pour the buttermilk into a large pot and dissolve the baking soda in it. Stir in the sugar, cover, and put on the stove burner over medium heat. Cook to the soft-boiled stage (236°F on a candy thermometer) and promptly remove from the heat. Stir in the butter, nuts, and vanilla extract. Cool until you can hold the bottom of the pot. Beat the mixture with a wooden spoon until the mixture loses its gloss. Quickly drop heaping tablespoonfuls onto wax paper. Cool and enjoy.

Pine-Nut Flatbread

The Indians of the Southwest used the resin from piñon trees to make a non-stick surface on their griddle stones. These days a well-seasoned cast-iron skillet or flat griddle will do.

1 1/2 cups whole wheat flour
1/2 cup pine-nut meal
2 tablespoons shortening
2 tablespoons sugar
2 teaspoons baking powder
salt to taste
water

Mix all the dry ingredients and cut in the shortening. Slowly add enough water to make a dough. Knead for 5 minutes. Break off little pieces and roll out thin, about 1/8 inch thick, to make flatbread (or use a tortilla press, if you have one). Cook each cake on a skillet or griddle until golden brown, turning once. Serve warm or cold with homemade cactus-pear jam or jelly.

The Chufa and Other Nut Grass

A nut grass of the sedge family, the chufa has been eaten in Spain and other parts of Europe for ages. Also called rush nut, yellow nut grass, earth nut, and ground almond, it has even been cultivated for food. Its nutty tubers are eaten raw or cooked. When dried, the tubers can be ground into a flour, which is usually mixed half-and-half with wheat flour before making breads. If you want to harvest some to eat, look for it growing in a sandy soil, from which it's easier to pull with nuts still attached to the root.

Several other wild nut grasses can also be ground into flour.

Grass and Weed Seeds

A surprising number of grasses and weeds have edible seeds. Over 60 wild grasses were once eaten in Africa alone. In the past, some were eaten on a regular basis, and some, being difficult to harvest, were used in times of need. A few of these are covered below. See also the section on wild amaranth on page 271.

Purslane. It will surprise many people to learn that purslane is cultivated as a vegetable in some parts of the world, notably India and Iran. In the New World, it is sometimes marketed in Mexico. Although it grows profusely in the lower 48 states, it is usually considered a weed. The young leaves and flower heads are delicious as a potherb, and the stems make a good pickle. The seeds make a tolerable flour.

Lamb's Quarters. The leaves of this common plant make excellent greens, and the seeds can be dried and ground into a black flour.

Poverty Weed. In the Southwest, the Indians ground the seeds of poverty weed with mesquite, making a meal for bread. The young leaves can be eaten as a green. The roots are also edible, but they are not very tasty.

Plantin. The leaves make a good green. When dried and ground, the seeds make an excellent flour, which can be used for pancakes and flatbread.

Sour Dock. These plants grow to 5 feet in height and produce large seed heads, making the seeds easy to harvest—but they must then be hulled, winnowed, ground, and sifted. The flour can be mixed half-and-half with wheat flour for breads. The young leaves can be cooked and eaten as a green.

Reed Grass. These tall plants, often forming dense clumps, have large seed heads and edible tubers. The young shoots are also edible, used as a potherb. The seeds can be ground into a flour, but the plants do not always produce seeds.

Sunflower. About 60 species of wild sunflower produce edible seeds, and some varieties are cultivated on a large scale for their seeds. I have covered these in chapter 19. The American Indians ground the unshelled seeds into a meal and mixed it with bone marrow to form a nutritious dough.

To separate the nuts from the shells, run the whole seed through a hand mill on coarse setting. Put the mass into water, stirring about with the hand.

The hulls will float and the nuts will sink. Dry the nuts and grind them for meal, or use them as nuts. Roast the hulls and use them for making coffee.

Chia. This plant grows wild in California and parts of northern Mexico. The Indians used the seeds to make a highly nutritious "running paste," and the seeds, available in some garden-supply catalogs, have recently been touted as a wonder food. According to Sturtevant's Edible Plants of the World, "The seeds are collected, roasted, ground by the Indians, and used as a food by mixing with water and enough sugar to suit the taste. This mixture soon develops into a copious, mucilaginous mass several times the oiginal bulk. The taste for it is soon acquired, and it is then found very palatable and nutritious."

Tree Seeds and Beans

Often the small seeds from trees can be gathered, dried, and ground into grits or flour. I avoid many of these seeds, however, simply because I don't know whether or not they are poisonous. Mimosa seeds, for example, have been on my list for years, but I've never had the courage to eat them, although when I was a small boy I made my sister necklaces from them. The list below is far from being complete, but it may provide some interesting grist for the adventurous miller.

Maple. Surprisingly, the winged seeds of maple trees make excellent eating, and I once shelled out a "mess" of green seeds, cooking them like fresh peas. The seeds can also be dried and used like beans, or ground into a meal. It's best to gather the seeds, which grow two to the wing, before they are fully ripe. Dry them and store until needed. When fully dry, the seeds are easily winnowed from the wings.

Black Locust This American tree has very dense wood and it was at one time used for masts for sailing ships. I know from experience that the trees are very hard to fell. The black locust has an adventurous root system that makes it valuable for soil erosion control. The flowers and seeds are edible, and the latter were at one time highly esteemed by the Indians. Be warned, however, that the seeds have an acidic taste, which can be removed by boiling. (Also, note that some texts list these seeds as poisonous; others list the seeds as edible but warn of other parts being poisonous.) When boiled and dried, the beans can also be ground into meal.

Kentucky Coffee Bean. This tree produces pods of seeds. Dry and grind them into grits. Use like coffee. Be warned that the seeds should be quite dry before using them. The unripened seeds and the pulp surrounding them may be poisonous.

Spice Bush. These seeds were once dried, ground, and used as a spice. Several other berries were also used in this way. The Dakotas, for example, made a seasoning from dried hackberries.

Mesquite. Sadly, most Americans know mesquite only as a charcoal or packaged wood chip to flavor backyard cooking. At one time, however, mesquite was very important to the diet of the Indians of the Southwest. The Papagos, it has been said, ate so many mesquite beans that they were often called "bean people," and one American naturalist (E. L. Greene, who published during the late 1800s) said that meal from mesquite beans is perhaps the most "nutritious breadstuff in use among any people." More recently, mesquite has been called a "wonder food for the twenty-first century," and attempts are being made to make it available commercially. We'll see.

In addition to meal and porridge made from the seeds, the long seed pods (which resemble string beans) of mesquite also provide a sweet pulp, used by the Indians in various ways. The flowers also provide a nectar and honey. The sweet gum that appears on the bark of the mesquite can be chewed, or melted with water to make a syrup. Several drinks were made from the mesquite pods, including a beer.

Anyone who lives in the Southwest can gather mesquite beans, and I understand that mesquite meal is becoming available. In any case, if you've got a few beans, grind them and try a little of the meal in your muffin or pancake mix.

Wild Rice

Wild rice is harvested commercially, and cultivated "wild rice" is marketed in several states. It may surprise some people to learn that this marsh grass also grows wild in just about every state of the Union, and it is constantly being planted in ponds and marshes as duck feed. A similar wild rice grows in northern China, where it is not highly regarded as table fare. Another species of wild rice grows in Africa, and no doubt in other parts of the world; these may or may not be "true grains." Who knows the difference?

In any case, taking a little wild rice from suitable marshes for home consumption won't hurt a thing, up to a point. Restrained harvest might even help, since it will surely knock some seeds into the water, where they might sprout, instead of becoming bird feed. The Indian method of harvest is hard to beat. Using both hands, bend the stalks over the bow of a canoe with a stick and beat out the seeds with another stick. It can be eaten like commercial wild rice, or it can be ground into a flour. Try the flour in biscuits, half-and-half with wheat flour.

Here are a few recipes for wild rice, commercial or otherwise. Note that forged wild rice will quite likely be smaller than the commercial kind, and will contain mixed sizes. For that reason, the graded commercial kinds make the best pilaf.

Wild Rice Johnnycakes

Here's a recipe that I have adapted from *The Art of American Indian Cooking*, by Yeffe Kimball and Jean Anderson. It calls for bacon drippings, and I have allowed that ingredient in this version. Since the Indians didn't have pigs for bacon before the Europeans arrived, however, I suspect that the original might have been cooked with bear fat or sweet acorn oil. Also, the Indians weren't in the habit of adding salt to recipes, possibly because they ate so much salt-rich red meat.

1 cup wild rice
3 tablespoons white cornmeal
1 teaspoon salt
bacon drippings or vegetable shortening
3 cups water

Boil the rice in the water for 30 to 35 minutes, or until tender. Mix in the cornmeal a little at a time. Let cool and stir in the salt. Heat some bacon drippings in a skillet or other frying pan. Shape the mixture into cakes about 2½ inches in diameter, patting each cake out with your hands and placing it carefully into the skillet. Brown on both sides, turning once, and drain. Serve hot or cold.

Wild Rice Stuffing

Turkey stuffed with wild rice and corn bread is a traditional American Thanksgiving dinner. It's even better when prepared with a good country sausage.

⅔ cup wild rice
½ pound bulk pork sausage
3 cups chicken stock
2 cups crumbled corn bread
1 medium to large onion, chopped
8 ounces sliced mushrooms
3 ribs celery with green tops, chopped
6 cloves garlic, minced
1 cup diced apple
½ cup chopped pecans or walnuts
1 teaspoon dry sage
1 teaspoon dry oregano
salt to taste
freshly ground black pepper to taste

Bring the chicken stock to a boil in a large saucepan. Add the rice, bring to a new boil, reduce the heat, cover tightly, and simmer for 30 to 40 minutes, or until the rice is tender. Drain off the liquid. In a skillet, sauté the sausage until you draw grease. Add the onion, mushrooms, garlic, and celery; sauté until the onion is soft. Add to the rice. Mix in the crumbled corn bread, apple, nuts, sage, oregano, and salt and pepper to taste. This recipe will make enough stuffing for a small or medium bird, preferably wild or open range. If you have a big bird, double the measures.

Chicken Soup with Wild Rice

I like to cook this soup with a small barnyard chicken, but supermarket fare will do. It's best to use the whole bird, including the bones.

1 chicken, plucked, drawn, and disjointed
2 cups precooked wild rice
2 cups chopped onion
1 cup sliced carrot
1 cup sliced mushrooms
juice of 1 large lemon or lime
1/4 cup chopped fresh parsley or cilantro
1/2 tablespoon minced fresh thyme
3 bay leaves
salt and freshly ground black pepper to taste
water

Put the chicken pieces into a large pot, cover with water, add the bay leaves, bring to a boil, cover tightly, reduce the heat, and simmer for an hour or so, until the chicken is tender. Remove and bone the chicken pieces. Dice and reserve 2 cups of chicken meat, saving the rest for salad or sandwiches. Put the bones back into the pot liquid, cover, and simmer for an hour or two, adding more water if needed. Strain the stock, throwing out the bones and bay leaves. Cool the liquid and skim off the fat. Measure out 10 cups of stock, adding more water if needed to fill the measure. Put the stock into the pot, adding the onion, mushrooms, celery, carrot, parsley, thyme, salt, and pepper. Bring to a boil, cover, and simmer for 15 minutes. Add the diced chicken and simmer 5 minutes. Stir in the cooked wild rice and lemon juice. Serve hot with plenty of crusty bread.

Mixing and Grinding
Seeds and Grains

Mankind has always mixed various meals and flours, partly for convenience, partly to conserve one or more ingredient that was in short supply, and sometimes to mix nutritional properties, looking for the perfect food. In olden times, more often than not, the grains or seeds were mixed as gathered and then ground together in a primitive mill or with mortar and pestle. Modern practitioners with a kitchen grain mill can also mix the grains and seeds before grinding them.

21

Ezekiel Mixes

In recent years, we have added more and more ingredients to our recipes simply because we like to experiment—or because we (writers and TV chefs) feel the need, I suspect, to change a recipe a little. In any case, the ingredients for some of the mixes get I suspect longer and longer, as do our modern recipes.

The written recipe might have begun with Ezekiel., 4:9: "Take thou also unto thee wheat, and barley, and beans, and lentils, and millet, and vetches, and put them in one vessel, and make thee bread thereof. . . ." The word "vetches" is sometimes interpreted to mean "spelt," but I suspect that vetches may be exactly what old Ezekiel had in mind. In any case, the modern cook might want to add a little quinoa, and oats, and buckwheat. And soy bean flour, and ground chickpeas . . . and surely a little mesquite bean or other wild vetch. While I certainly don't object to such mixes, I think it's best to at least limit some recipes—especially those using meal or flour for bread—to one or two grains, simply to learn what tastes like what and which you prefer. Then, if you want to mix everything, have at it. I feel the same way about spices, and I believe that anyone who adds allspice to a list that already contains cloves and ginger and cinnamon is simply adding stuff by whim, not by whiff.

It's not unusual these days to see commercial mixes containing wheat, rye, millet, triticale, barley, spelt, beans of one sort or another, and lentils of one color or another. If you use these mixes for making breads, or if you concoct your own, remember that the operative grain for risen bread is still wheat. Of course, you can add wheat flour to a multigrain flour. One very good use of Ezekiel-type mixes is in beans and grains used for salads and soups, where the size and color of each contributes to the whole. Some of the supermarket bean mixes for soup contain 17 kinds. These are pretty in a jar as well as in a soup. If you create your own bean or soup mix, be sure to add some chickpeas for texture, shiny black beans for color, and humpbacked QK-77 groats for mystery and conversation.

Although I am not going deeply into multigrain breads in this chapter (having covered some in earlier chapters), I do feel obliged to set forth some notes on grain mixes.

Mixes for Granola and Muesli

There are thousands of recipes for granola and muesli mixes, and many are available commercially. If there is rhyme or reason to any of this, oats seems to be it. At this writing, I have in hand a gourmet-foods catalog that lists two dozen different granola mixes containing all manner of grains and seeds and nuts and dried fruits—and all contain oats in one shape or another, sometimes with both oat flakes and oat flour. The granola recipes below are for bars, and the muesli is for a cereal mix.

Granola Bars

These are usually eaten in bars as noshing fare, but they can also be crumbled and sprinkled over ice cream or fruit. The grain flakes, nuts, and fruits can be varied, but the rolled oats are necessary.

2 cups rolled oats
2 cups spelt or wheat flakes
2 cups barley flakes
1 cup slivered almonds
1/2 cup shredded dried coconut
1/2 cup dark seedless raisins
1/2 cup chopped dried dates
1/4 cup sesame seeds
1/4 cup brown sugar
1/2 cup honey
1/2 cup melted butter or margarine
1 tablespoon freshly crushed allspice berries
1 tablespoon vanilla extract
1/2 teaspoon salt
water, if needed

Preheat the oven to 300°F. In a large pan, mix the oats, barley, wheat, almonds, coconut, and sesame seeds. In a small bowl, mix the melted butter or margarine, honey, brown sugar, allspice, vanilla, and salt; pour this over the grains and mix evenly. If the mixture won't hold together at this point, boil some water and stir in. Spread the mixture evenly over two rimmed baking sheets or shallow pans. Bake in the center of the oven for 15 to 20 minutes, until the oats are golden brown. Remove from the oven, stir in the dates and raisins, and allow to cool to room temperature. The granola will become crisp as it cools. Cut into bars and store in an airtight container. It will keep for several days. For longer storage, put the container in the refrigerator or freezer.

Consider also the following nut granola.

Granola with Nuts

I am partial to this recipe—partly because I love nuts and have 14 pecan trees in my yard.

2 cups steel-cut oats
1 cup wheat germ
1 cup finely shredded coconut
1 cup chopped dates
1 cup chopped pecans
1/4 cup chopped slivered almonds
1/4 cup sunflower seeds
1/4 cup pine nuts
1/4 cup chopped cashew nuts
1/4 cup chopped English walnuts
1/2 cup butter or margarine
1/2 cup honey
1 tablespoon freshly ground allspice

Preheat the oven to 300°F. Mix together all the nuts, oats, coconut, and wheat germ; spread the mixture evenly over 4 cookie sheets. Heat the butter and blend in the honey, adding the allspice. Spread the honey butter evenly over the nut mixtures; stir until the nuts and oats are coated nicely. Bake for about 25 minutes, until golden brown. Take the cookie sheets from the oven and stir the dates into the granola, distributing evenly. Cool. Cut into bars, pack into airtight containers, and refrigerate until needed.

Muesli

I have mixed feelings about this stuff. The word is Swiss for "mush," and I think the original grain mix, developed by a Swiss physician as a nutritional aid, was soaked overnight in milk or yogurt; then, before serving in bowls, the mush was topped with chopped nuts and chopped dried fruit. I prefer to serve it like American cereals, with milk, a little brown sugar, nuts, and dried or fresh fruits. The nuts and fruits vary from recipe to recipe, and the mix below reflects my personal favorite. Many modern texts call for skim milk or nonfat yogurt, but I really want whole milk or, better, half-and-half. Sometimes I use tupelo honey instead of sugar. The rolled oats are mandatory.

3 cups rolled oats
1 cup chopped toasted pecans
$1/2$ cup sunflower seeds or pine nuts
$1/2$ cup wheat germ
$1/2$ cup dried currants
$1/2$ cup dried apple, chopped
$1/2$ cup dried dates, chopped
brown sugar or Mexican cone sugar
milk or half-and-half

Mix all the ingredients except the sugar and milk. Store in a suitable container with a tight lid until needed, but try to use the cereal within 10 days. Serve in bowls for breakfast, along with milk and sugar to taste.

22

Grinding Your Own

*I saw that I could easily raise my bushel or two of
rye and Indian corn, for the former will grow on the poorest
land, and the latter does not require the best, and grind
them in a hand-mill. . . .*

—Henry David Thoreau

A t one time during man's agricultural history, each family ground their own
grain with the aid of a crude quern mill, usually made of stone, or with mortar and pestle. The old ways started changing with the advent of large stone
mills, powered by wind or water or donkey. In Europe during the feudal age, the
landlords built large mills and ground the serfs' harvest of grain as a way of toll
or taxation. During this time, home-owned mills were actually illegal in some
parts of Europe.

In time, almost all of man's flours and meals were ground outside the household for one reason or another. In America, thousands of commercial mills, usually stone mills turned by waterpower, went into business along our streams and
provided a much-needed service as well as some excellent flours and meals. In
more recent years huge commercial millers pretty much replaced the community mills, and modern distribution and retail operations increased the need for
flours and meals with a long shelf life. With the aid of modern technology, millers
were able to produce a flour with almost indefinite shelf life. Thus, a few large

commercial millers started doing business from coast to coast, border to border. True whole grain fare became pretty much something of the past —except for pockets here and there in rural areas.

Earlier, but following the same trend, communal ovens proved of value to the housewife, who, until recent times, had no convenient electric or gas oven in the kitchen. Commercial bakeries thrived and started supplying our supermarkets. The result—a light, foamy bread made from white flour—changed our eating habits.

Thanks partly to the health-food movement, we are now experiencing a culinary renaissance in whole kernel flours and meals. Special markets have developed, and whole grain products are now becoming available even in our supermarkets. More and more small regional mills have started grinding, and we are seeing more small kitchen mills being developed for the home cook. I expect this trend to continue, for it opens up an exciting and healthy cookery for American families at a time when we are becoming more and more skeptical of market fare—which almost always contains chemical additives of one sort or another and almost none of the natural fiber and nutrients of the grain. In addition to the nutritional benefits, these handy portable mills yield the very freshest whole grain meals and flours available to the modern cook, just as coffee mills produce good fresh coffee and pepper mills produce great black pepper, both full of aroma and flavor.

Several brands and models of kitchen mills have come on the market in recent years. Check your local stores for availability, or consult the firms listed in the Sources section of this book. The Internet might also help those who are connected. Here's a quick overview of old and new gristmills, methods, and related equipment.

Mortar and Pestle. These old tools require lots of elbow grease, but they do a very good job for grinding small amounts of grain. Many primitive peoples still use large wooden mortars and wooden pestles or pounders. Typically, these are for stand-up two-handed pounding. Modern countertop mortar and pestle units are widely available, made either from marble, other stone, ceramics, or wood. I prefer the wood, except that they are a little harder to clean. And the larger the better, up to a point.

Primitive Roller Mills. These old devices usually had a saddle-shaped quern in which the grain was crushed with a stone roller, shaped like a rolling pin. Some of these were rather large, and the worker sat on one end of the quern. Variations were used in ancient Egypt and other places, and they are still used in some rural areas of Mexico.

Rotary Stone Mills. Large and small stone mills have been in use for a long time. Generally, a round flat stone with a hole in the center sits atop a similar bottom stone without the hole. Grain is poured into the hole of the top stone while it rotates on the stationary bottom stone, or while the bottom stone turns. The flour is ground between the two stones and filters out the edges or perimeter. Of course, the stones (or at least one of them) are tapered or fluted, or both, so that the grain feeds from the center outward, becoming finer and finer as it goes. These mills can be quite small, operated by hand, or they can be quite large. (Or in between. There are some neat production models on the market, suitable for small-scale regional milling for profit. See the Sources section at the end of this book.) The larger stone mills are powered by waterwheels, windmills, electric motors, gas-driven engines, or perhaps steam engines. In the past they were powered in some places by donkeys or mules. These are typically slow-grinding devices, which is an advantage because the process doesn't generate much heat. (High heat alters the oil in the germ of the grain and reduces the shelf life of the flour or meal.) Contrary to popular opinion, the type of power really doesn't make much difference, provided that the stones grind slowly. Consequently, the electric or gas engines must be geared down considerably.

Stone mills are ideal, albeit expensive these days, for grinding most hard grains, such as wheat and corn. Softer grains, seeds, and nuts, however, tend to produce too much oil, which can clog the pores of the stones and reduce their effectiveness.

Water Mills. These are simply stone mills that are driven by waterpower. Usually a dam is built, letting the discharge fall on a large bucket or paddle wheel. The wheel turns the gears, which turn the stones. The term "water ground" is so popular and is such a drawing card that many mills that actually run on gas or electrical power are operated at the site of a millpond or creek—and the meal or flour is sometimes billed as "water-ground" style. This term usually indicates a true whole grain product, presumably stone ground.

Auger-Fed Mills. These are designed like the old sausage mills, having a hand crank and an internal auger that feeds the grains into a grinding mechanism on the end. These are true grinders and have no cutting wheel like sausage mills. I have one, rather large, and find it quite useful for reducing large kernels such as corn or chickpeas down to grits, which can then be ground in a stone mill or small electric mill. Most of these auger-fed mills are made of plated cast-iron.

Small Electric Mills. These modern little mills are handy for grinding small amounts of grain. They simply sit on the counter and require no special mounting. Generally, they run at high speed, which is not a culinary plus, and normally use a steel burr mechanism to grind the grain. Some of these are expensive, some cheap. It's best to buy one that has interchangeable burrs or stones.

I own a small electric mill and would not want to do without it. Convenience is the key. In my opinion, it's better to reduce the grain to grits or even meal in a hand-cranked auger-fed mill than to finish the job in the electric mill or small hand-cranked stone mill. In fact, some of these newfangled electric mills will not even grind large kernels. But it's difficult to give advice here because we will no doubt see improved models as time goes on. The allure of whole grains is simply too great worldwide for manufacturers to ignore, and electric mills will always be in demand.

One criticism of electric mills is that they turn too fast, generating too much heat as the grain is ground. The heat tends to turn the oil in the germ rancid. In my opinion, this becomes more of a problem when storing a large batch of meal or flour. If you grind the meal or flour on an as-needed basis, the heat shouldn't be much of a problem. It also helps to grind the grain a little at a time. Grind it first on a coarse setting. Wait a while and then grind it again on a fine setting.

Anyone who is concerned about the temperature should get in touch with the manufacturers of electric mills before buying one. Some turn faster than others.

Roller Mills. Usually these are large high-speed mills for commercial flour or meal production.

Food Processors and Blenders. There are several modern electrically driven gadgets that chop food at a high speed, using a blade of some sort. These might do for making grits, meal, or even flour from some soft grains such as oats, but are not ideal for all hard grains such as corn or wheat. I don't recommend them for grinding grains, but some will do a good job with such eats as chunky peanut butter. There are, however, a number of types of these units, some of which are advertised as doing everything from juicing celery to grinding grain.

Sausage or Food Mills. Some books say that sausage mills can be used for some grinding purposes, but I don't recommend the practice partly because hard grains will dull the cutting edges, making the mill difficult to use for making good sausage meat.

Coffee Bean Mills. Coffee grinders can be used to make a coarse meal, but they are not ideal. They will grind relatively large berries, which can then be finished in another mill. For example, I once wanted to grind some soybeans into flour, but they were too large to work in my small electric mill. So, I cracked them in the coffee mill, then ran the grits through the electric mill, producing a fine flour.

Pepper or Spice Mills. Small pepper mills for table use can be used to grind a few tablespoons of flour or meal from some whole groats not much larger than a peppercorn. Larger grist, such as chickpeas, should be cracked in one way or another before grinding.

Nut and Seed Grinders. These are designed for grinding soft nuts and seeds. Actually, the technique involves cutting instead of grinding. In many grinding operations, the grist is mashed in the process, which tends to squeeze out the oil and gum up the works. Although these specialized grinders come in handy from time to time, they are not practical for general use.

Hand-Cranked Mills. These can be stone mills or steel burr mills, as discussed above. The point to be made here is that these units have to be mounted, and sometimes the clamp won't fit over a regular kitchen countertop. Those that mount with bolts are not practical for most kitchens, and those that mount with suction cups are simply not satisfactory.

Sifters and Sieves. The ordinary hand-cranked flour sifters help, but they don't go far enough. What's needed is an affordable set of sifters or sieves for home use. Such a set should ideally contain 4 units that nest together for storage. These would include: extra fine mesh for flour; fine mesh for white cornmeal; medium mesh for coarser meal (polenta); and coarse mesh for grits or cracked wheat. Surely such a set will become widely available for the growing number of grind-your-own practitioners, who as often as not have to rig their own sieves or sifters with various cloth weaves (as our ancestors did) or with screen wires of various mesh.

Gristmill recommendations? Much depends on the potential user's need and financial situation. Personally, I would dearly love to own an 8-inch stone mill that costs well over $1,000, but, being a man of modest means and limited need for flours and meals in quantity, I simply can't justify the outlay. I started out with a small electric mill that cost less than $100, and that would be my recommendation for most readers. Some of these accept only small grain, but they work well with wheat—and wheat is still the mainstay in breadstuff. Some of these inexpensive mills require no special mounting or setup, and are easy to clean.

Some purists will argue against the electric mill, saying that they grind the grain too fast and generate too much heat. I tend to agree, but I hold to my recommendation, based on need and time and circumstance. Most American cooks, many of whom work at other jobs, are simply not going to spend an hour or two turning a stone mill by hand.

Still, the well-made hand-cranked stone mill is the best way to go for those of us who have the time and the money and cherish the old ways. It's a sensuous pleasure to hand-grind wheat and other grains with good stones, somehow fulfilling and gratifying.

Sources

Several of the firms listed below sell grain mills by mail order, and there are a number of different models available, ranging in price from $50 to $1,500 and more. Shop around and consider your needs, as well as your budget, before buying. Whole grains and seeds can be purchased locally through health-food stores and in bulk from feed stores. Most feed stores that do not have what you want may be able to order it for you. Whole grains and seeds are also available by mail order, and through the Internet. Some seed companies can provide grains, but make sure that these have not been treated with pesticides.

Ackeny Lakes Wild Rice Co., P.O. Box 3667, Salem, OR 09302. Cultivated wild rice and blends, available packaged or in bulk.

Arrowhead Mills, P.O. Box 2059, Hereford, TX 79059. Organically grown whole grains, seeds, flours, grits, and mixes, available packaged or in bulk. This firm is primarily a wholesale source. Telephone: (806) 364-0730.

Birkett Mills, P.O. Box 440, Penn Yan, NY 14527. Buckwheat groats, flour, kasha, and mixes, along with wheat flours. Birkett also sells a mulch and even a pillow made of buckwheat hulls. Telephone: (315) 536-3391.

Brownville Mills, P.O. Box 145, Brownville, NE 68321. Grains, meals, flours, nuts, seeds, beans, and mixes, along with spices, health foods, dried fruits, trail snacks, and so on. Small packages and bulk.

Butte Creek Mill, P.O. Box 561, Eagle Point, OR 97524. Stone-ground flours and meals, whole grains and groats, mixes, bulgur, pastas, and so on. This old mill, listed on the National Register of Historic Places, is still turned by waterpower.

Chef's Catalog, 3215 Commercial Avenue, Northbrook, IL 60062. Grain mills and other equipment for home use. Telephone: (800) 338-3232.

Cooking.com, 2850 Ocean Park Boulevard, Suite 310, Santa Monica, CA 90405. Equipment, tools, foods. Telephone: (877) 999-2433. Website: www.cooking.com.

Cumberland General Store, 1 Highway 68, Crossville, TN 38555. Grain mills and old-time equipment for home, kitchen, and farm. An interesting catalog is available for $4, refundable with first order. Telephone: (800) 334-4640.

Dean and Deluca, 110 Greene Street, Suite 304, New York, NY 10012. Pozole, rice, beans, grains, and culinary treats such as caviar and truffles. Website: www.deananddeluca.com.

Delta Rehabilitation, Inc., 411 Bryn Mawr Island, Bradenton, FL 34207. Grain mills and bread machines.

Frieda's, Inc., P.O. Box 58488, Los Angeles, CA 90058. Quinoa, blue cornmeal, nuts, and other products of interest. Telephone: (714) 826-2561.

Garden Spot Distributors, 438 White Oak Road, New Holland, PA 17557. Organic and natural grains, seeds, beans, nuts, flours, mixes, and health foods.

Giusto's Specialty Foods, Inc., 241 E. Harris Avenue, South San Francisco, CA 94080. Amaranth and other grains. Telephone: (415) 873-6566.

Gray's Gristmill, P.O. Box 422, Adamsville, RI 02801. Rye and whole wheat flour, cornmeal, and various mixes. Jam, jelly, syrup, and a few gifts. Not a large product listing at present.

Gold Mine Natural Food Co., 7805 Arjons Drive, San Diego, CA 92126. Wheat berries, tef, and other grains and seeds, in small packages and in 50-pound bulk bags. At present they carry such hard-to-find items as lotus seeds and flour from mesquite beans. They also carry several grain mills, both stone and steel-burr types.

Indian Harvest, P.O. Box 428, Bemidji, MN 56619. Rice, wild rice, beans, pozole, and grains. An excellent mail-order source, offering such items as ancient kamut wheat, black barley, red rice, and purple posole, as well as many unusual and interesting mixes. Telephone: (800) 752-8588. Website: www.indianharvest.com.

Jaffe Bros., P.O. Box 636-Z, Valley Center, CA 92082. Grains, nuts, seeds, and other products of interest. Telephone: (619) 749-1133.

Jowar Foods, 113 Hickory Street, Hereford, TX 79045. Sorghum products, including whole grain, meal, and flour. Telephone: (806) 267-0820. Website: www.jowar.com.

Johnny's Selected Seeds, 1 Foss Hill Road, RR1 Box 2580, Albion, ME 04910. Garden, flower, and grain seeds, including buckwheat, wheat, amaranth, and so on. Grain and specialty seeds are available in packets, by the pound and by the bushel. Johnny's also markets seed sprouters and seeds suitable for making your own "bean sprouts," and an inexpensive burr mill, adjustable for grinding grits, meals, and flours as well as coffee. Telephone: (207) 437-4301. Website: www.johnnyseeds.com.

Kamut Association of North America, P.O. Box 691, Fort Benton, MT 59442. This association markets the ancient grain officially known as QK-77, along with flour, related literature, and other products made with QK-77. It's more common name is complicated by a registered trademark of Kamut International, Ltd. Telephone: (406) 622-5438.

Kenyon Corn Meal Co., 21 Glen Rock Road, P.O. Box 221, West Kingston, RI 02892. Cornmeals, flours, grains, mixes, and such New England delicacies as cranberry pancake syrup.

King Arthur Flour, P.O. Box 876, Norwich, VT 05055. Whole grains, flours, meals, mixes, baking ingredients, and equipment. Telephone: (800) 827-6836.

Lehman's Non-Electric Hardware and Appliances, P.O. Box 321, Kidron, OH 44636. Telephone: (330) 857-5757.

Lundberg Family Farms, P.O. Box 369, Richvale, CA 95974. Bulk rice (California-raised basmati, arborio, jasmine, and others), rice cakes, rice syrup, and mixes. Telephone: (916) 882-4551.

Magic Mill, 1515 South 400 West, Salt Lake City, UT 84115. Grain mills and bread-making supplies. Telephone: (800) 888-8587.

Maskal Teff, P.O. Box A, Caldwell, ID 83606. Tef grain and flour, primarily wholesale at present. Write for information.

Meadows Mills, Inc., P.O. Box 1288, North Wilkesboro, NC 28659. This company has been manufacturing stone gristmills since 1902, along with sifters, grits separators, and so on. They currently make several commercial models and an 8-inch mill billed as household or small-commercial. The firm also refurbishes other brands of stone mills. Telephone: (336) 838-2282. Website: www.meadowsmills.com.

Mountain Home Basics, P.O. Box 42, Clifton, CO 81520. Grain mills and other equipment for the kitchen. Telephone: (800) 572-9549.

New Hope Mills, Inc., RR 2, Box 269A, Moravia, NY 13119. Still using waterpowered equipment, this old mill has been grinding meals and flours for 170 years. They market bread flour, pastry flour, and various mixes.

Old Mill of Guilford, 1340 NC68 North, Oak Ridge, NC 27310. This old waterpowered gristmill, listed in the National Registry of Historic Places, has been doing business for over 200 years. They offer flours and mixes from wheat, oats, rye, buckwheat, and so on, along with cornmeal.

OurHouse.com, 2123 North Euclid, Princeton, IL 61356. Relatively inexpensive tools and equipment, such as flour sifters and mills. Hardware. Telephone (Toll-free number): (877)-202-2768. Website: www.ourhouse.com.

Purity Foods, 2871 West Jolly Road, Okemos, MI 48864. Spelt berries, flour, pasta, and other products, including books and booklets. Wholesale and retail.

R&R Mill, 48 West First North, P.O. Box 187, Smithfield, UT 84335. Grain mills, food grinders, and other equipment.

Redwood City Seed Company, P.O. Box 316, Redwood City, CA 94064. Seeds for gardeners and farmers, including tef, amaranth, durum wheat, and so on. Telephone: (415) 325-7333.

Southern Brown Rice, P.O. Box 185, Weiner, AR 72479. Brown rice in long, medium, and short grain; sold 1-, 2-, 5-, and 25-pound bags. Basmati and wild rice, and various blends, along with rice bran, rice flour, and rice cream. Gift baskets.

Vermont Country Store, P.O. Box 1108, Manchester Center, VT 05255. Whole grains, stone-ground meals, stone-ground flours, and mixes. General catalog available.

Walnut Acres, Penns Creek, PA 17862. Whole grains, flours, bran, meals, wild rice, and many mixes, along with baking essentials, gourmet foods, and noshing fare. They also market an electric kitchen mill for those who like to grind their own. Catalog available. Telephone: (800) 433-3998. Website: www.walnutacres.com.

Further Reading

This short selection of books is not intended to be a bibliography of the works consulted by the author while working on this book. Many of the best recipes have been adapted from books on ethnic cooking, such as the excellent *A Book of Middle Eastern Food*, by Claudia Rodin, and on regional American cooking. These books have been acknowledged in the text as appropriate.

Listed below are some books about grains, breads made from whole grains, and closely related topics. Some excellent bread-making books, however, are omitted because they deal almost exclusively with white flour. Also, some good general information is available in some of the large family cookbooks, such as *The Fannie Farmer Cookbook*.

Buff, Sheila. *Corn Cookery*. New York: Lyons & Burford, 1995.

Bumgarner, Marlene Anne. *The New Book of Whole Grains*. New York: St. Martin's Press, 1997.

David, Elizabeth. *English Bread and Yeast Cookery*. American ed. Newton Highlands, Mass: Biscuit Books, 1994.

Duff, Gail. *Bread: 150 Traditional Recipes from Around the World*. New York: Macmillan Publishing Company, 1993.

Greene, Bert. *The Grains Cookbook*. New York: Workman Publishing, 1988.

Grunes, Barbara, and Virginia Van Vynckt. *All-American Waves of Grain*. New York: Henry Holt and Company, 1997.

Hayes, Joanne Lamb, and Bonnie Tandy Leblang. *Grains*. New York: Harmony Books, 1995.

Hunter, Beatrice Trum. *The Family Whole Grain Baking Book*. New Canaan, Conn: Keats Publishing, Inc., 1972.

Lanner, Ronald M. *The Piñon Pine*. Reno: University of Nevada Press, 1981.

Manaster, Jane. *The Pecan Tree*. Austin: University of Texas Press, 1994.

Myers, Sarah E., and Mary Beth Lind. *Recipes from the Old Mill*. Intercourse Pa: Good Books, 1984.

Neal, Bill, and David Perry. *Good Old Grits Cookbook*. New York: Workman Publishing Company, 1991.

Orton, Mildred Ellen. *Cooking with Wholegrains*. New York: North Point Press, 1951.

Ruskin, F. R., ed. *Lost Crops of Africa*. Vol. 1, *Grains.*Washington, DC: National Academy Press, 1966.

Sokolov, Raymond. *With the Grain*. New York: Alfred A. Knopf, 1996.

Index